DISCOVERING THE TIDAL POTOMAC
A CRUISING GUIDE AND BOATING REFERENCE

by Captain Rick Rhodes

Text edited by Julie Wright
Artwork by Rolland Duncan
Printed by Automated Graphic Systems

Published 1998 by Heron Island Media
P.O. Box 45016
Washington, DC 20026
All rights reserved

1st Edition -- 1998

ISBN 0-9665866-0-3

TABLE OF CONTENTS

Chapters

BOOK ORGANIZATION

The first third of this guide addresses the area's rich heritage, tides, weather, navigational and boating skills, boating obstructions and concerns, and popular leisure activities found along the Potomac. Chapter 5 presents lists of marinas, restaurants, small boat ramps, fuel facilities, haul-out yards, and some groceries, hardware and lodging found along the Potomac.

The remainder and bulk of this guide, chapters 6-15, divides the Potomac into 10 regions. Chapter 6 starts in Washington and the subsequent chapters follow the flow of the river to the Chesapeake. Chapters 7-10 cover both the Virginia and Maryland shores. Further downriver, chapters 11 and 15 cover only the Virginia shore, while chapters 12-14 focus on the Maryland side.

Thirty-five **COLOR** NOAA chart excerpts accompany the latter sections of the guide. The location of marinas, restaurants, launch ramps, and other points of interests have been added to these color chart excerpts. The name of each river establishment is pasted right on the NOAA chart excerpt. I trust you will find this approach easier than constantly referring to an excerpt key located on a different page. Some NOAA chart excerpts are significantly enlarged (e.g., Colonial Beach, Cobb Island, and Aquia Creek) while other excerpts are slightly reduced (middle sections of the river). Each excerpt was expressly designed to fit on one page. Forty-three Global Positioning System (GPS) waypoints accompany this part of the book and are listed in appendix D. Also found in the appendices are thirty-one marina dock sketches (appendix B) and five locality street sketches (appendix C).

BACKGROUND

In the 1970s, during my Army years, I was introduced to boating on the Potomac while sailing 13-foot Sunfish out of the Fort Belvoir Marina. One fine sailor at Fort Belvoir, Lieutenant Colonel Charlie Porter, invited me out a few times aboard his Catalina 22-footer. Porter was a skilled sailor and won many races. Boating on the Potomac was infectious. Little did I know then, but the Potomac would become a large part of my life for the next 20 years.

I have been living aboard since 1985 and the Potomac has been my backyard. Since 1991, I've divided my live aboard time between two vessels -- a 33-foot sailboat (usually on the lower river) and a 28-foot powerboat (usually in Washington). During my time on the river in all parts of the 100-mile-long Potomac, I have harbored at 16 different marinas as a slipholder, and visited many more marinas as a transient. Life on the Potomac has been interrupted twice. In late 1994 and again in late 1995, two six month sailing trips aboard the 33-footer took me to Central America.

The purpose of my second trip was to research a *Cruising Guide on the Bay Islands of Honduras*. My heartfelt work on that Honduras Guide was completed after returning to the Potomac. But the guide's headway to the market has been prolonged and I didn't have custody of it. Stunned, I sought solace on the Potomac River. And once again, the Potomac inspired me. The Potomac beckoned me to learn more about it and to share my past and newly acquired insights in this guide.

CAUTIONARY NOTE

In researching and drafting this guide, I took extensive effort to ensure accuracy and provide you with the most up-to-date information. However, it is not possible to guarantee total accuracy. What I have described as a neglected establishment may have turned itself around by the time you visit the same place. Conversely, I may have visited and subsequently described a first-rate establishment that could have gone downhill. Nothing remains the same, and there is an element of subjectivity in writing any guide. Like most things in life, if you tackle the project with integrity, you cannot please everyone. Researching and writing this guide, I attempted to place the BOATER'S needs and interests at the forefront.

For inland navigation, official NOAA charts are the standard and are recommended. My reduced or enlarged NOAA chart excerpts do not contain all of the cautionary notes found on official NOAA charts. I posted "boater useful" locale "tags" atop these NOAA chart excerpts and made every attempt possible to avoid obscuring important NOAA chart detail (e.g., bridge clearances, etc.). But how can you place a marina or restaurant "tag" on a narrow neck of land without occluding some original detail? Some NOAA information could have become lost or blurred in the reproduction or photocopying processes. If an establishment "tag" is located on a narrow neck of land (e.g., Saint George Island or Harryhogan Point), the text should be closely followed. This guide is meant to be a supplement to official US government charts and publications. There is no substitute for prudent seamanship. This author-publisher disclaims any liability for loss or damage to persons or property that may occur as a result of interpreting any information in this book.

This guide is designed to edify you, provide you with more options, and enrich your days of boating on the Potomac. Should you find errors or omissions or have other constructive comments, I welcome hearing from you. If they are appropriate and I am able to substantiate them, I will make every attempt to include your suggestions in later editions. Presently I anticipate doing volunteer work overseas for a few of years and it may be difficult to communicate. Nonetheless, mail should eventually reach me addressed to:

Rick Rhodes
Heron Island Media
P.O. Box 45016
Washington, DC 20026

July 1998

viii

The Indians
The Colonists
Traditional Agriculture
Boating Chronicles
Domain
Watershed

THE INDIANS

Evidence suggests that Indian cultures were living in the Potomac area since as early as 1000 BC. The name "Potomac" in the Algonquin language roughly means "trading place," or perhaps a more literal translation "the river of trading people." Undoubtedly, the river conduit promoted native skills in trading the wide array of goods moving through the area. Later when the Native Americans traded with the "white man," the they were quite shrewd and well understood the economic principles of supply and demand. The Anacostia tribe cleverly cornered the fur market and another tribe cornered the copper market. The Indians generally drove hard bargains with the newcomers.

At the time of the colonists' arrival, about 30 different Indian tribes camped along the Potomac shores. Most in this group were the Piscataways. The Piscataways often allied with a larger confederation of tribes to the south, the Powhattans. The Powhattans and the Susquehannocks, large-built combative Indians to the north, were often at war with each other. Most Native Americans in this part of the East Coast spoke the Algonquin language.

By and large, in the earlier encounters, the Native Americans in this area were curious about, and generous to, the white man. The Native Americans of the Potomac introduced the white man to corn, potatoes, and tobacco. Native American words such as hominy, opossum and succotash entered the white man's vocabulary.

Sometimes the incidents that lead the white man to overreact and slaughter many innocent Indians were provoked, but many times it was simply a misunderstanding. After sporadic periods of much bloodletting on both sides, shaky treaties were usually established. Many Indians also succumbed to and died from the white man's diseases.

When Leonard Calvert arrived on the Potomac in 1634, the land was almost totally forested with many great trees suitable for ship masts. The white man cleared the forests partially for wood but mostly for tobacco, and the Native Americans were pushed out. The remaining Piscataways moved westward under the white man's pressure. Sadly, by the end of the 17th century, less than a 100 years after the white man arrived, almost all the Native Americans were gone from the tidal Potomac. At least, thankfully, we can still find many of their colorful names along the river -- Piscataway, Anacostia, Dogue, Mattawoman, Yeocomico, Nanjemoy, Conoy, Potopaco (corrupted to Port Tobacco), Arehokin (corrupted to Harry Hogan), and more.

THE COLONISTS

In 1607, Captain John Smith sailed into the Chesapeake and established the colony of Jamestown on the James River, a Chesapeake tributary south of the Potomac. Smith was a capable leader, seaman, and explorer. He bargained hard with the Native Americans and he earned the respect of many of them. During his Potomac sail he traded with the Native Americans for corn and furs, which were needed to keep Jamestown alive. He sailed as far as possible up the Potomac searching for that elusive Northwest Passage to the Pacific. Smith observed that the Indians seemed friendlier the farther away he traveled from Jamestown and the farther he traveled up the Potomac River. Smith was the first white man to chart the Potomac River and the Chesapeake Bay. After an unfortunate accident with gunpowder in 1609, he returned to England to treat his burns. After Smith's departure, Jamestown was in disarray. In 1614, when Smith crossed the Atlantic again, he explored New England.

After Smith's days on the Potomac, Captain Samuel Argall, Henry Spelman, and Henry Fleet continued trading with Potomac Indians for the supplies needed to sustain the Virginia colony. In 1613, Argall kidnaped Pocahontas, an Indian princess, near present-day Fairview Beach. In 1623, the unfortunate Spelman was killed by the Indians. Fleet was able to expand his Indian trade into a very profitable business. In doing so, he made enemies with many rival fur traders in Jamestown. When Leonard Calvert, with about 200 settlers, arrived on the Potomac in March 1634, Fleet was ready for a non-Jamestown ally. Fleet mentored the Marylanders living on the Potomac.

The Marylanders were intent on establishing a colony free of religious persecution. Although far from flawless, the Marylanders did establish a religiously tolerant society. Unlike other colonial settlements, no one in Maryland was ever put to death because of his or her religious beliefs. The Marylanders got along reasonably well with the Native Americans. The Indians taught the Marylanders how to hunt turkey and deer, to fish, and to oyster. Father Andrew White, a Jesuit priest and the spiritual leader of the colony, traveled extensively up and down the Potomac River and had much interaction with the Native Americans. Father White noted that the Marylanders progressed in six months as much as Jamestown had in six years. Captain Thomas Cornwallis and Mistress Margaret Brent expanded the realm of the Maryland colony. Both were close allies of the Calvert family and later became large landholders along the river west of Saint Marys City.

Not all Marylanders were pleased with the leadership of the Calverts. A few of the discontented forged out on their own and crossed the Potomac, establishing smaller settlements on Machodoc Creek and Nomini Creek on the Northern Neck of Virginia. From Jamestown, many disaffected and religiously persecuted also found their way to the isolated Northern Neck, which became a haven for the disenchanted. The lower Potomac was becoming the seedbed of leaders that our country would need during the American Revolution, a little more than a century ahead. Three of our nation's first five presidents came from the Northern Neck of Virginia.

Shortly after the Revolution, George Mason chaired the Mount Vernon Compact at the estate of his friend, George Washington. In 1784, the Mount Vernon Compact between Virginia and Maryland bridged many of obstacles between the two colonies. Tolls were reduced for Maryland vessels passing though the Virginia Capes at the mouth of the Chesapeake Bay. Tariffs and foreign currency evaluations were harmonized between the two colonies to reduce smuggling across the Potomac. Virginia agreed to let Maryland have a land route to the western frontier. Fishing was becoming more important on the Potomac by the end of the century. Maryland held sovereignty over the Potomac, but the Marylanders gave the Virginians equal access to the Potomac fishery domain. The colonies understood that their mutual interests lay in tobacco plantations. This was a high point of unity between Maryland and Virginia!

On the Potomac today, we have many reminders of this colonial period -- Mason Neck, Smith Point, Cornwallis Neck, Brent Point, Neale Sound, Leonardtown, and others.

TRADITIONAL AGRICULTURE

For about two centuries, tobacco or "sotte weed" was the foremost crop in the economies of both sides of the river. Aided with several ferry crossings, commerce between these two states thrived. Tobacco was also used as currency and called the "cash crop."

Along the entire East Coast, a series of inland port towns developed on the "fall line," the delineation between the flat coastal plain and the hilly piedmont region. There were usually rapids on the river at the fall line and ocean-going commerce could not travel further inland. Richmond was established on the James River, Fredericksburg on the Rappahannock River, Baltimore on the Patapsco River, and, of course, Georgetown on the Potomac. Downriver from Georgetown, the Potomac ports of Alexandria, Dumfries, Port Tobacco, and Leonardtown also shipped tobacco to Europe.

Before the Revolution, tobacco shipped to Britain was re-exported to markets all around the world. British merchants reaped large profits while the Virginia and Maryland planters were subject to price vagaries and had to contend with the agricultural risks. Tobacco growing was labor intensive and, near the end of the 18th century, tobacco planters were facing many problems. European markets were shrinking, soil was becoming depleted of nutrients, and there was tremendous pressure to reduce production costs. This encouraged the exploitation of African slaves.

Before the Civil War the Virginia economy clung to tobacco although some agricultural land had moved from tobacco to grain, wheat, and timber. Other southern states also relied on tobacco and cotton. Southern Maryland's economy was also in tobacco, but other parts of the state's economy was in coal, industry, and railroads. During the War, southern Maryland, including the three Potomac counties, was sympathetic to the Confederacy and felt its region was being occupied by Unionists. In less than a century the Potomac River had gone from a mutual trading artery to a bloody dividing line between the North and the South. General Robert E Lee's Army of Northern Virginia and the Union Army of the Potomac crossed the river several times before the War ended. Most army crossings were north of the wide tidal Potomac. The tidal Potomac saw less action. Civil War forts, battery emplacements, a few skirmishes, and even two prisoner-of-war compounds along the tidal Potomac are addressed in later chapters.

After the Civil War, another type of interstate tension developed on the Potomac. Virginia and Maryland watermen fought each other over oysters. On the eastern shore of the Chesapeake Bay, Virginia watermen started assertively dredging (or drudging) for oysters while the Maryland watermen were restricted to hand-tonging. Dredging -- mechanically scraping the oysters off the bed with a towed metal, rake-like contraption -- was more productive, as well as more destructive to the oyster bed. Virginia oyster dredgers sneaked into the Maryland waters on the Chesapeake. Hence, Maryland watermen took matters into their own hands. The conflict spread from the eastern shore of the Bay to the Potomac. As late as 1959, blood was shed on the Potomac in this two-state war. The "oyster wars" were not officially ended until 1962, when President Kennedy signed the Potomac River Fisheries Bill.

BOATING CHRONICLES

In 1787, the Potomac River was the site of the first steam-powered boat in the United States. The boat was propelled by a stream of water forced aft by a steam-powered piston pump. Steam engines later evolved to turn paddle wheels and much later to screw propellers similar to those on the *Titanic*. Commercial steamboats appeared after the War of 1812. Unlike the Mississippi River's rear-mounted paddle wheelers, Chesapeake and Potomac paddle wheelers were side-mounted.

In the late 19th and early 20th centuries, excursion steamboats became very popular, and some ships carried as many as 2,500 passengers on Chesapeake Bay routes. Earl Jenkins, the storied owner of Sandy Point Marina on the Yeocomico River, can recollect hauling lumber from the lower Potomac to Baltimore aboard steamships. Steamboats revolutionized water transportation and industry, but the ships were dangerous. In 1842 a steam boiler exploded on the *Medora* and dozens of people were killed.

In the earlier part of the 20th century, the safer and smaller internal combustion engine appeared commercially. This engine had a great impact on steamboats, as small internal combustion engines in automobiles reduced the need for steamship travel.

The tidal and navigable Potomac ends in Georgetown. However, 120 years ago, water-borne commerce traveled from Georgetown for 184 miles west-northwest to Cumberland, Maryland. Finished products and store goods were shipped to Cumberland. Coal, lumber, grain, produce, and cement were shipped from Cumberland to Georgetown. On the Maryland side, the **Chesapeake and Ohio (C&O) Canal** paralleled the Potomac and emptied into Rock Creek near the creek's confluence with the Potomac. The canal raised the water from sea level to 605 feet in Cumberland. There were 74 locks, 11 aqueducts, and a tunnel of more than one half mile through a mountain near Paw Paw, West Virginia. All the locks were 98 feet long by 15 feet wide. With no room to spare, canal boats were made 92 feet long and 14 and one-half feet wide and could carry 120 tons. Many canal boats were family operated.

In the 1870s, the C&O Canal was at its heyday, and more than 500 mule-pulled boats plied the canal. Besides housing the family and crew, the canal boats quartered a spare mule team. A one-way trip took five to seven 18-hour days. The wooden canal boats lasted about 25 years and were primarily built at a handful of boatyards in Cumberland.

As the railroads and highways improved, commerce on the C&O Canal became less competitive. Habitual Potomac floods also wreaked havoc with the canal. Commerce on the canal ceased for good after a bad flood in 1924. Today, much of the big ditch is dry, but there are some sections containing water. The C&O Canal is run by the US Park Service and has been a national historic park since 1971. Many of the old locks and lock houses still stand, as well as the 3,118-foot Paw Paw tunnel. The old mule towpath is maintained in superb condition and is very popular with today's hikers and bicyclists.

DOMAIN

The boundary between Maryland and Virginia is not in the middle of the river as is usual for many other state-river boundaries. The official boundary is the high-water line on the Virginia shore. Except for the Virginia tributaries, the Potomac is in Maryland. This has created anomalies and problems. Because Maryland's gaming and liquor laws have usually been more lax than Virginia's, enterprising Virginia businessmen have built taverns and gaming houses out from the Virginia shore on pilings over the river to be technically located in Maryland.

Management of fishery resources was another major problem that culminated in the bloody oyster wars. Historically, at reports of dwindling supplies of oysters, crabs, and other fishery resources, Maryland has been more prone to regulate and restrict fisheries while Virginia has been more laissez-faire. Virginia watermen often didn't like abiding by the Maryland laws (and many Maryland watermen didn't particularly care for them either). Today, in the lower Chesapeake, the Virginia fishing season sometimes lasts longer. Some Maryland watermen and charter fishing boat captains feel disadvantaged.

In December 1993, after the Maryland rockfish season closed, a southern Maryland-based fishing headboat, *El Toro*, made a longer-than-usual trip to fish in Virginia waters off Smith Point VA. In rough weather, the *El Toro* foundered, and three lives were lost. An inconsistency in jurisdictional laws did not create the disaster but may have helped set the stage for it. In my opinion, if any one of many sensible steps had been taken (e.g., maintaining the boat in better condition, heeding earlier gale forecasts, returning earlier to Maryland waters at the onset of deteriorating weather, seeking an alternate safe harbor before it was too late), this tragedy could have been averted. Nonetheless, the disparate statutes of the two states add to many legalities and restrictions that I hear watermen and charter captains grumble about.

Beginning in late spring Maryland and Virginia watermen set crab pots. In the summer they pull and rebait crab pots or tend fish traps. In the fall they start oystering. In the winter they repair boats and all of their other equipment. Their income is tenuous, but they probably wouldn't trade places with you. Their reward is being independent and catching the sunrise in a small boat on a big river as the workday begins! Like the Indians of yesteryear, the watermen were here before us. At times, a few may show an understandable resentment to the Johnny-come-lately recreational users of the river. Whether you are in a sailboat or a powerboat, show some courtesy to the watermen and give them the right of way, especially while they are doing their arduous work.

WATERSHED

Beyond Georgetown, the nontidal Potomac drains a four-state area of 11,800 square miles. This area is second only to the main Chesapeake Bay basin or the Susquehanna channel. The Potomac drains one-fifth of the entire Chesapeake Bay watershed and supplies one-sixth of all the bay's freshwater. If taken by itself, the Potomac drains the fourth largest watershed on the entire East Coast!

The Shenandoah River, about 60 miles northwest of Georgetown, is the largest nontidal tributary on the Potomac. The Shenandoah enters the Potomac near Harpers Ferry, West Virginia. The South Branch of the Potomac River, another large tributary, dumps into the Potomac about 105 miles beyond Harpers Ferry. Both the Shenandoah and the South Branch flow north-northeast in enchanting river valleys, paralleling Appalachian ridges in Virginia and West Virginia before mixing with the Potomac. Regularly occurring floods along either of these tributaries are often felt as high water on the tidal Potomac a couple of days later. Beyond the fork with the South Branch, the Potomac River, also referred to as the North Branch, forms the border between Maryland and West Virginia. The North Branch has its headwaters near the Fairfax Stone. The Fairfax Stone marks the southwestern tip of Maryland's western panhandle. Nearly all of the watershed west of the Fairfax Stone (i.e., much of West Virginia) drains westward into the Ohio and Mississippi River basins before flowing into the Gulf of Mexico.

In 1900, five million people lived in the entire Chesapeake Bay watershed, in contrast to about 15 million living here today. There are estimated to be 18 million by 2020. The Chesapeake Bay and Potomac River have taken a lot of abuse from humans, especially over the past 350 years. The Potomac truly is a resilient river and can take much misuse. But the river should never be taken for granted.

Chapter 2
TIDES AND WEATHER

Gravitational Tides
Sketch 2-1, The Potomac River Segmented by Tidal Hours
High Water and Flooding
Thunderstorms
Lightning
Hurricanes
Tornadoes
Fog
Winter Weather
Sunny Days

GRAVITATIONAL TIDES

The highest range between the high and low tide in all the Chesapeake estuary occurs on the upper Potomac River. In Washington Channel, a four-foot swing between high and low tide is typical. The four-foot tidal range generally lessens south of Washington. Around Smith Point VA, the tidal range is less than two feet. When the tide is rising, it is flooding. When it's falling, it's ebbing. The tidal current is slack near times of both high and low tide.

On the Potomac, as along the East Coast, the time required for a tide to go from high to low, or vice versa, is a little more than six hours. This tide cycle is known as semidiurnal -- two high tides and two low tides occur almost every day. If a high tide occurs at 8 PM tonight, it will be close to high tide tomorrow night at 9 PM at that same location (i.e., two high tides away). On an almost weekly schedule, there is another pattern. If you regularly go boating every Saturday and the first Saturday at 9 AM happens to be at high tide, the following Saturday (i.e., seven days later) at 9 AM will be almost at low tide.

There is about a seven-hour differential between the time of high (or low) tide in Washington and the time of high (or low) tide at Point Lookout MD and about an eight-hour differential between Washington and Smith Point, VA. The high or low tide in Washington occurs Later than the tide on all other places on the river. Actually, the Low tide at Washington takes place *seven and a half* hours after the Low tide at Point Lookout, and the High tide at Washington takes place only *six and a half* hours after the High tide at Point Lookout. This pattern holds for much of the Potomac because the tidal river is constantly being fed by freshwater upstream. The ebbing tide lasts longer and has a slightly stronger current than the flooding tide.

Many tidal prediction tables present the average time difference between high and low tide. For example, the high (or low) tide at Point Lookout is an average of seven hours ahead of that same tide in Washington. This should be adequate for most of us. Sketch 2-1, near the end of this section, depicts the river at one-hour tidal difference intervals.

About one-half of the swing in tidal range (a possible two-foot change) takes place in the middle two hours of the six-plus hour tidal interval. For more than an hour during slack high or slack low tide, the tidal rise or fall is insignificant. An overall four-foot tide range in Washington reduces to half of that range (i.e., two feet) at Point Lookout. However, the lessening range downriver is not uniform. For example, at Maryland Point, the high tide is only 41 percent (i.e., 1.6 feet) of the Washington tidal range, but, for the next 30 miles downriver, the tidal range acts erratically. At Cobb Island, the tide range increases to 69 percent of

Washington's range (i.e., 2.7 feet).

You will note from the tidal sketch that there is about a three-hour tidal difference in a short 20-mile stretch of the Potomac between northwest of Maryland Point and northwest of Colonial Beach. The average cross-sectional area of the Potomac (i.e., average depth times average width) in this section of the river is relatively small compared to adjoining sections of the river. When the tide is at maximum flood or maximum ebb (i.e., in the middle two hours) the tidal current can be quite strong. If you are in a slow-moving sailboat, it behooves you to take advantage of the tidal current (or at least try not to catch it adversely) in this section of the river. The tidal current here can run close to a couple of knots.

Since salt water is denser than fresh water, saltwater supports your weight better. Hence, there is more saltwater at lower layers in the river and more freshwater at upper layers in the river. On flooding tides, the saltier water moving up the river travels closer to the bottom, while the fresher water moving down on an ebbing tide travels closer to the water's surface. Many animals that require saltwater, such as crabs and jellyfish start thinning out north of the US Route 301 bridge as the Potomac becomes more of a freshwater river.

HIGH WATER AND FLOODING

The gravitational semidiurnal high tide is not the only thing that causes high water. The Potomac drains a large watershed reaching well into Virginia, all of the large eastern panhandle of West Virginia, nearly all of central and western Maryland, and a portion of southern Pennsylvania. When heavy, prolonged rains fall in these areas, the tidal Potomac is affected. In Washington, I've seen the river several yards above the mean high-tide line. Also, if you have to navigate the tidal river during these times, as I have on a few occasions, you'll encounter much floating debris. During floods, much of the debris is lifted off the nontidal river's bank on the high water and carried down the river. This debris may be large tree trunks and branches. An encounter with a boat would likely be destructive. You might encounter other debris too. On one day, in the course of 20 miles, I must have counted more than 40 tennis balls. Another time, I encountered a bloated deer carcass near Hains Point. It's not advisable to be boating during these conditions, especially if going upriver and bucking a strong current. Also, the water temperature will be colder than normal because the temperature of the runoff is cooler.

Steady winds from one direction will also have a localized effect on the water level. Such winds can actually blow the top off the water on a particular part of the river and pile that water up in another part of the river. For example, a day or more of strong northwest wind can blow the water out of Washington Channel as well as curb a normally flooding semidiurnal high tide. Where does the water go? In this case the water is blown down the river, and if the river is wide enough, its displacement effect downstream may be minimal. Contrarily, a strong south wind could pile the water up in Washington and slow down the naturally occurring ebb of the tide.

The combination of a high semidiurnal tide, flooding in the panhandle of West Virginia two days before, and a strong and steady south wind for the past day will be *Additive*. This scenario, mostly dependent on the severity of flooding in West Virginia, could create a high water level in Washington, which would be yards above the normal high-tide line. Good marina people are well aware of impending high or low waters, but beforehand is the time to be closely monitoring your dock lines and boat fender situation. Generally, as the river flows southeast from Washington, the severity of the high water decreases. But even downriver, the wind "piling up" or "blowing out" phenomenon still occurs, and it is especially noticeable in small and mid-size creeks and bays.

7

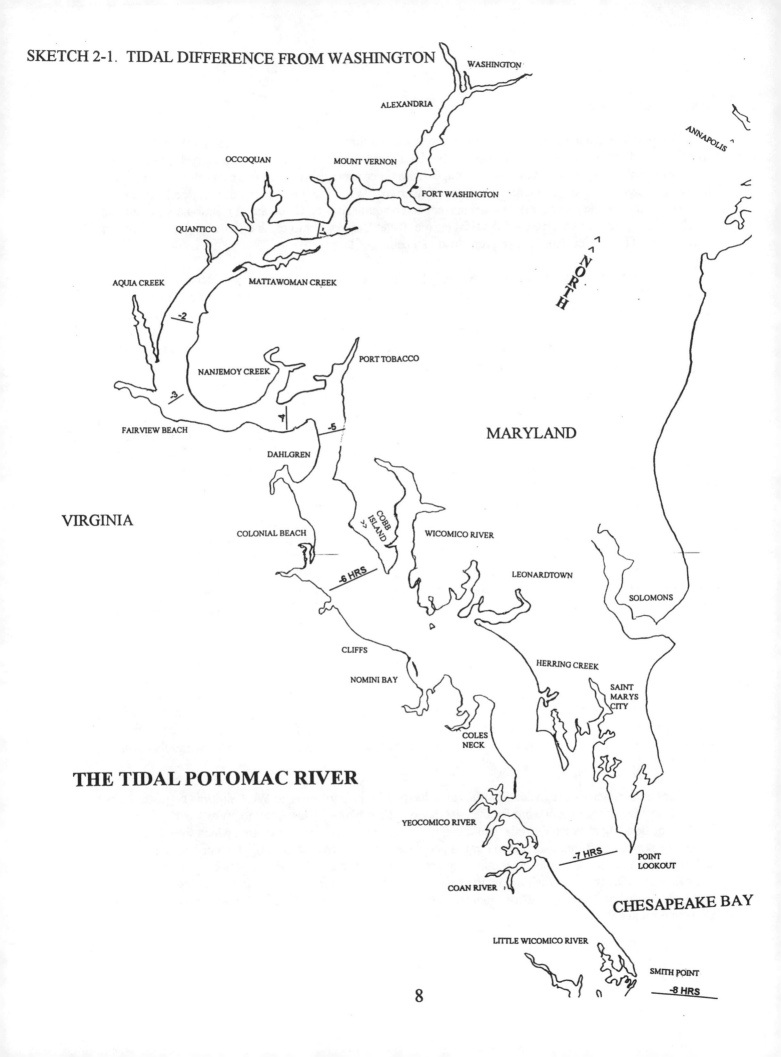

SKETCH 2-1. TIDAL DIFFERENCE FROM WASHINGTON

WASHINGTON

ALEXANDRIA

ANNAPOLIS

OCCOQUAN

MOUNT VERNON

FORT WASHINGTON

QUANTICO

NORTH

AQUIA CREEK

MATTAWOMAN CREEK

-2

PORT TOBACCO

NANJEMOY CREEK

-3

MARYLAND

-4

FAIRVIEW BEACH

-5

DAHLGREN

VIRGINIA

COBB ISLAND

COLONIAL BEACH

WICOMICO RIVER

LEONARDTOWN

SOLOMONS

-6 HRS

CLIFFS

HERRING CREEK

NOMINI BAY

SAINT MARYS CITY

THE TIDAL POTOMAC RIVER

COLES NECK

YEOCOMICO RIVER

-7 HRS

POINT LOOKOUT

COAN RIVER

CHESAPEAKE BAY

LITTLE WICOMICO RIVER

SMITH POINT

-8 HRS

8

THUNDERSTORMS

Summertime Chesapeake (and Potomac) thunderstorms, or honkers, usually approach from anywhere between the southwest and the northwest. The wind during a thunderstorm can quickly accelerate to 70MPH, threatening a boat knockdown. These storms usually don't last long enough to cause sizeable seas to buildup. Thunderstorms are most common from May through September and from 3 PM till dusk. However, I've also been caught during the morning and well after dark. If caught by a thunderstorm, don't panic and keep your composure.

The average thunderstorm is 6-10 miles wide and travels forward at 25 MPH. A thunderclap can be heard about four miles away. Beforehand, you can hear the crackling of distant thunder and lightning as static on the radio. Often you can see the storms in the distance. In a powerboat, it's not difficult to outrun or turn in a direction away from the storm's path. Even in a slow-moving sailboat, I have changed my direction on seeing a thunderstorm and averted an encounter. Usually, but not always, the weather reports predict them. A rapidly falling barometer is also an indication of an approaching thunderstorm. Sometimes thunderstorms come in clusters.

If thunderstorms are forecast, it may be prudent to remain in port or at least return to port before the anticipated "weather." If an encounter with a thunderstorm is eminent, do everything to reduce windage (i.e., put all sails and canvas down) beforehand, and keep your motor running. But be mindful that, if your engine intake water thru-hull fitting isn't far below the waterline, and the boat takes a severe heel because of the wind, air could get sucked into your raw water system making your engine overheat. If this occurs, you obviously need to shut the engine down.

If I can't reach a safe harbor before the onslaught, I prefer "sea room." Your survival impulse may suggest getting closer to land, but I contend that there are more options and a better chance to minimize personal injury and boat damage if you have room to maneuver. Being caught close to land in a confined channel, near treacherous shoals, jetties, the shore, or other boats hightailing to port, may be more ruinous. With 360-degree sea room, you can keep your bow pointed to the fearsome wind. It's also likely that the winds may shift throughout the ordeal. You could run (i.e., taking the winds on your stern) before a thunderstorm too, but you'll be through the ordeal quicker if you keep your bow into the wind. Try to stay collected; it will be over before you know it.

A few uncommon thunderstorms can contain microbursts. A microburst is a downburst of wind traveling very fast, sometimes more than 100 MPH. As the wind strikes the ground, it fans out in all directions. It was likely a microburst knocked down and capsized the first *Pride of Baltimore* in the southwest North Atlantic in May 1986, resulting in four deaths.

LIGHTNING

Lightning accompanies thunderstorms. The thunderclap we hear is the explosion of super-heated air near the lightning bolt. Sound (i.e., a thunderclap) travels about a mile in five seconds. If there is a five second interval between the sighting of a lightning flash (relative to sound, light travels at an instantaneous speed) and the sound of the thunderclap, the lightning is only one mile away!

The intense heat in a lightning bolt can be five times hotter than the surface of the sun. About 90 percent of all lightning activity never touches the earth and remains within the clouds. Nonetheless, about 20 million strikes hit the United States every year. The United States receives more than its proportional share of the world's lightning strikes, and some areas of the country attract more hits than others. Lightning is the second biggest "natural" killer in the United States, behind only floods. About one-half the people struck by lightning can be revived.

The clouds that produce lightning are huge cumulonimbus thunderheads. These clouds may be swirling vertically upward. The anvil-shaped top of these thunderheads may extend close to the stratosphere. As water and ice particles swirl around within the cloud, a negative electrical charge develops near the bottom of the cloud, and a positive charge develops near the top of the cloud. The ground is positively charged. When a lightning strike finds land, usually the positive charge from the ground, in the form of an upward-moving streamer, makes contact with the downward-moving negative spike, or stepped leader from the bottom of the cloud. After the two charges meet, the thunderbolt continues its downward destructive path to the ground. This "up-down" process happens instantaneously and can repeat itself several times in a millisecond.

Although much has been written about lightning, it is still not fully understood. Precautions advising boaters seem to have changed somewhat as we learn more about lightning. A lightning de-ionizing rod installed at the masthead purports to dissipate the positive ground charge your boat is presenting to the negatively charged clouds, and thereby reduce the probability of taking a hit. Some boaters bond everything metallic together in order to dissipate a damaging electrical charge into the water as quickly as possible. With this approach, if you do take a lightning hit, your damage will be considerably less than in a unbonded boat. The lightning's path to the ground (i.e., the water) is faster and less damaging if the strike has a bonded conduit to follow. I've also heard the rationale of boaters purposely not bonding or grounding anything because a well-grounded boat is a more enticing "target" for a lightning strike. But even if you're poorly grounded, you could still have an unlucky day, and receive a direct and very damaging jolt. In lightning or thunderstorms, don't touch, and avoid being near, any metal parts of a boat. Your chance of survival is reasonable unless your body becomes part of the lightning's path to the water. Also heed the latest advice your insurance company provides on lightning defensive measures.

Interestingly, most lightning fatalities occur not during the periods of heaviest rain, but either after or before the most intense part of a storm. Late and early in the life of a passing thunderstorm have proven to be the most fatal.

HURRICANES

The Atlantic hurricane season lasts from June through November with the highest probability for occurrence being August though October. Most hurricanes that threaten the eastern seaboard form off the coast of Africa as low pressure troughs. A tropical depression develops and generally moves westward. If the depression's winds exceed 48 knots, the depression is classified as a tropical storm. If wind speeds exceed 64 knots (i.e., 74 MPH), it becomes a hurricane. The extreme low-pressure system of a hurricane has winds swirling counterclockwise and inward in the northern hemisphere. Ninety percent of the fatalities occurring during hurricanes are drownings during the storm surge.

Hurricanes affecting the Potomac are infrequent, although remnants of some have visited in the not-too-distant past. More often than not, the damage associated with a hurricane is not inflicted by hurricane force winds, but by the weather spawned from the receding depression, such as heavy rains, floods, and tornadoes. In 1972, the Potomac sustained untold flood damage from heavy rains falling in the watershed from hurricane *Agnes,* which inflicted an unheard of $7.5 billion in damage. In November 1985, hurricane *Juan* struck the southeastern United States and traveled as a tropical depression across the eastern seaboard. Northeast of this area, the depression re-formed as a nor'easter, swerved back inland, and inflicted serious flooding on the

Potomac basin, especially in West Virginia.

Hurricanes (or the remnants of) *Gloria* (1985), *Charlie* (1986), *Bertha* (1996), and *Fran* (1996) made appearances in the Chesapeake or Potomac. Winds and chop from hurricane *Fran* damaged two inadequately tied-up boats in Aquia Creek. In the middle of the night, the eye of hurricane *Bertha* passed over the mouth of the Potomac. I recollect missing work a few times in the past decade to better secure my boat and waited restlessly for a hurricane on the Potomac's doorstep. Hurricanes *Hugo* (1989), *Bob* (1991), and *Emily* (1993) flirted with our region but eventually settled on other areas. Often before an impending hurricane, naval ships go out to sea to avoid being battered against the docks during the predicted high winds. In 1993, in advance of hurricane *Emily*, some navy vessels from Norfolk scrambled into the Potomac River and anchored in order to get out of the way of the eye of that very powerful storm.

With today's excellent weather forecasting, no boater should be caught unaware of an oncoming hurricane. There is invariably time to take action to either get away from the storm's path or holeup somewhere. Don't wait until last hours to make hurricane preparations. Marina personnel will have their hands full well beforehand. Pulling your boat out of the water is probably the most preferred alternative, although boats have been blown off marina boat stands in hurricane force winds. If hauling out is impractical, reduce the boat's windage as much as possible (i.e., remove all sails, canvas, and like material) and add more dock lines. Your normal dock line complement, if it is on the thin side, should be beefed up prior to any bad weather. There may be a much wider tidal fluctuation than normal during a storm, so when you beef up your dock lines, consider a potentially unusual tidal range. At a marina in the upper Chesapeake in 1985, I witnessed hurricane *Gloria* produce an extremely low tide. The uncommonly low water indirectly damaged some boats. As boats floated several feet beneath the normal low-tide line, if there was not enough slack in dock lines, something would break, under the extreme tensile load.

Under extreme loads, a nylon dock or anchor line could easily chafe at a point of friction. Chafing occurs when a line rubs on chocks, stanchions, forestay, bobstay, or even the side of the boat. Old pieces of plastic water hoses, slit down the middle, can help. Everyone fittingly carries duct tape these days. Duct tape could be used in conjunction with plastic hose pieces, or it could be deployed by itself to minimize chafe.

There is something to be said about leaving a marina and Anchoring in a "hurricane hole" before the storm. The boat's bow will always be into the "weather," and the boat isn't as rigid when confronting the high winds. Hopefully the hurricane hole anchorage isn't crowded with other people of like mind. Allow for the likely 360-degree wind shift. Anchoring with three heavy anchors down is not unreasonable. Preparing a boat for a hurricane is no time to be stingy. If the boat in the next slip (or the same anchorage) is inadequately prepared, there's a reasonable chance that boat could flail into your vessel and damage both. Once the boat is prepared, it is highly recommended you leave the vulnerable boat for an area where your chance of personal injury or drowning is less.

TORNADOES

Unlike tornadoes on the Great Plains, tornadoes in this area are less common and much smaller. Their contact on the ground is usually less than a mile long, sometimes much less. Tornadoes vary greatly in their destructiveness. Winds in the vortex of a tornado are anywhere from 40 to 300 MPH. The months of likeliest incidence are April and May. Since 1990, annually five to seven tornadoes touch down around Washington. Atmospheric conditions for tornadoes are ripest between 3 PM and 9 PM and, to a lesser extent, from noon until midnight. Tornadoes often occur in the middle of other storms, such as thunderstorms and hurricanes.

Precursor signs of a tornado are a greenish tinge to a darkened sky, large hail, and roaring winds. A "tornado watch" means that the atmospheric conditions are ripe for a tornado. A "tornado warning" means that one has been spotted on radar.

A tornado on the water is a waterspout. I've heard that if you are facing a waterspout head-on, it is more likely to swerve to your right than to your left, because it is spinning with a counterclockwise rotation. If this is true, you may have a higher chance of "a near miss" by turning left than turning to your right. But this may be just barroom advice.

FOG

As fog poses a threat to motorists on land, it also poses a threat to boaters. Fog occurs when ground-level warmer humid air cools. Warmer air is capable of holding more water vapor than cooler air. If the warm air cools, the once "invisible" water vapor in the warm air condenses from a gas to a suspended liquid. These small suspended liquid droplets actually obstruct visibility.

In foggy conditions, two recreation boats could easily collide. A barge could run over a boat in fog. Visibility in fog is worse than nighttime visibility. At night, if it's not foggy, you can usually see the lights of another ship at a distance. This isn't true in fog. In July 1956, the Italian liner *Andrea Doria* was broadsided by the *Stockholm* in fog outside of New York harbor. The luxury liner sank, and 51 lives were lost. Radar provides a boat another sense of perception in fog, but both the *Andrea Doria* and the *Stockholm* had radar in 1956.

The fall months produce the conditions most conducive for fog formation. But I recollect encountering some serious fog banks on the Potomac in spring and summer. Many times it may be clear over the land but dangerously foggy over the water. The radiant heat from the sun will usually "burn off" early morning fog. Another pair of eyes near the bow, sound-producing devices and slowing the boat speed are good ideas in foggy conditions.

WINTER WEATHER

The river will generally only freeze in the upper freshwater portions. For the river to freeze, it must be cold for several days, and it cannot be windy. Wind will create choppy water, which is incapable of freezing. But once the surface has frozen over, the windiness factor will have little effect on lessening the freeze. Even when the river freezes solid, there is tidal action beneath the ice layer. Anything in the water, including the ice, will move up and down with the tides. This means that there will usually be a ring of water in the ice around boats and pilings. I've never seen a floating boat "stuck" to an ice pack on the river. Forced air bubblers, and propeller water-churning devices are sold at boat stores with the notion that disturbed water will prevent freezing around your boat. This is true but, even without one of these devices, you'll likely still have that "tidal ring" of water around your boat during the times the river is solidly frozen. Where these bubblers and churners do have merit is during a windy condition after a hard freeze which could blow a boat against the frozen portion of ice and abrade the hull.

In Washington Channel, in barely half of the recent winters, a sheen of ice strong enough to support a convention of sea gulls has appeared. In December 1989, the Potomac north of the Wilson Bridge froze so solid and deep that it took many weeks for it to thaw. The winters in this area are unpredictable. In 1998, the coldest, nastiest month was March. But it could be December, January, or February next year. Strong snowstorms have occurred in November, and extended warm spells have occurred in January and February.

God only knows what April may bring each year.

Boats remaining in the water during winter are susceptible to more damage than in other seasons. There are a myriad reasons for this (e.g., boaters staying away from their boats more, freezing water lines, the added weight of snow or ice atop boats, and neglected electrical systems). You can take precautions for many potential winter mishaps. Most precautions are common sense. Close all of your thru-hull fittings. This is a good idea also in the summer if you leave the boat for any extended period of time. Drain all the water lines or replace the water with environmentally friendly antifreeze. As you would for hurricane preparation, remove unnecessary items that create windage. And please don't forget to winterize your engines.

SUNNY DAYS

This is boating time. Nonetheless, misery will find you if you get sunburned. The sun's rays on the reflective water are more dangerous than the sun's rays on the land. Biminis, sun shades, and other ways to shade are good and perhaps essential to you and to your crew. Broad-brimmed hats protect your ears from sun. It's a good idea to have a clip or chin strap for your hat or it will soon be blown into history. Of course, sun screen should always be on hand. Also, make sure you have plenty of drinkable water or nonalcoholic drinks aboard to combat dehydration.

Many boating accidents occur on beautiful sunny days. Impaired judgment due to the consumption of alcohol is often a culprit behind the scenes. The exhilaration of a calm sunny day on the water (if you're a powerboater) or a windy sunny day (if you're a sailboater) is hard to beat. But there are always some who want to take it a step further by imbibing alcohol while boating. Look at the statistics and see how many boating accidents are alcohol related. Save the alcohol for the anchorage or after returning to the marina at the end of the day. The postponement will be worthwhile.

Chapter 3
NAVIGATION AND OTHER HELPFUL SKILLS

Navigation Aids and Entering Tributaries
Supplemental Navigational Updates
Communications
Global Positioning System (GPS) units
Etiquette in Traffic
Degrounding
Reading Depths
Avoiding Crab pots
Avoiding Fish Traps
Duck Blinds
Hydrilla
Anchoring

NAVIGATION AIDS AND ENTERING TRIBUTARIES

Across the Potomac's mouth, from Smith Point VA to Point Lookout MD, the river is about 10 miles wide. The river maintains no less than four miles of width from its mouth to Colonial Beach. A good portion of the lower river is more than 30 feet deep, with a handful of large areas more than 60 feet deep. If you're not close to the shore in the lower river, with the possible exception near Ragged Point and Heron Island Bar, you likely have enough deep water for most large boats. It is still advisable to follow the NOAA charts.

Five NOAA charts cover the tidal Potomac River. Four charts are scaled 1:40,000. The other chart, 12287, is scaled 1:20,000 and covers a small section of the river south of the US Route 301 bridge, including the approaches to Dahlgren. This section of the river is also covered on NOAA chart 12286 at the larger scale. Chart 12233 covers the lowest portion of the Potomac (i.e., mostly southeast of Piney Point MD). Chart 12286 covers the next section, northwest of Piney Point MD to Lower Cedar Point MD (i.e., near the Route 301 bridge). Chart 12288 covers the section of river from the Route 301 bridge to Mattawoman Creek. Chart 12289 covers the northernmost tidal section, from Mattawoman Creek to Georgetown. The mean low-water (MLW) depth posted on NOAA charts is far from infallible.

Like all of North America, the buoyage system on the Potomac and Chesapeake is the IALA Maritime Buoyage System for Region B. To stay in the channel, **RED** navigation aids should be passed (remain) on your **RIGHT** side while **RETURNING** (i.e., going up the river or up a tributary), and green aids should be passed (remain) on your left side. Red navigation aids are even-numbered and have a triangular shape (i.e., a triangular placard on a post or a pointy-tipped floating "nun" buoy). Green navigation aids are odd-numbered and have a square shape (i.e., a square placard on a post or a flat-topped floating "can" buoy).

The easternmost (i.e., first) Potomac buoy is a Green can, numbered "1" -- "G1". "G1" is about a mile northeast of Smith Point VA. Following "G1" upriver in a missing-numbered sequence of mostly floating buoys, you'll reach "G35" before the Route 301 bridge (i.e., about 50 miles upriver). On the other side of this bridge, the numbering starts over again with another "G1". Likewise, the last buoy encountered south of the Woodrow Wilson Bridge, 45 miles upriver from the Route 301 bridge is "R90". The first buoy encountered north of the Wilson Bridge is "R2".

While it is important to adhere to Rules of the Road, there are places in the river where it might even be preferable to navigate outside of the buoyed channel. Unless you have a mega-yacht or Scandinavian newsprint ship, many places south of Occoquan Bay, the water is deep enough for small boat navigation. Outside the channel, you won't be in the way of a tug and barge, a seagoing newsprint ship, or mega-yacht that Does need to remain in the channel. Nearly everywhere south of the Route 301 bridge, a deep-draft sailboat can comfortably navigate outside the channel. Between the Wilson Bridge and the Route 301 bridge, there are a handful of places to navigate outside the channel. However, there are almost no places north of the Wilson Bridge to navigate outside the channel for a vessel of size.

If the water is shallow enough, daymarks (immoveable posts with plywood placards) will likely be used instead of floating buoys. You invariably see daymarks in creek entries along the shallower edges of deeper creek channels. Like the taller towers, daymarks will depict a "foot" element on a NOAA chart. Most daymarks are no taller than 14 feet. They may be either lighted or unlighted. It would be easy for an inattentive boater to strike an unlighted daymark at night. Last year, there was a boating fatality on the Potomac when a powerboat struck a daymark. The accident occurred at night, and the daymark was a lighted aid flashing at two and a half seconds.

Near the middle of the river, and farther from shore in deeper water, you'll find the floating buoys anchored to the bottom. On NOAA charts, floating buoys might be labeled something like "C9" "G11" "N6" or "R8". A "C" or "G" navigation aid will be GREEN in color while an "N" or "R" aid will be RED in color. UNLIGHTED floating buoys will be labeled either "C" (can) or "N" (nun). There are two huge (i.e., about half the size of a Volkswagen) unlighted can buoys (i.e., "C"s) on each side of the Route 301 bridge.

If a floating buoy has the "G" or "R" designation on a NOAA chart, it is likely a LIGHTED buoy and will have more information such as "4s" or "2.5s." The "integer plus s" indicates a lighted aid and the flashing interval in Seconds. The "2.5" or "4" indicates a light that flashes every 2.5 or 4 seconds. "Q" means "quick," with the lighted aid "quickly" flashing on and off. In addition to "Q" "2.5" and "4" seconds, 6- and 10-second flashing lights are common on the Potomac. At night, red lights are easier to find than green lights from the same distance away. On NOAA charts, lighted aids usually have a purple exclamation mark. The number in quotes on a NOAA chart is the number of that particular aid.

Going upriver from Smith Point, there are three Morse code "A" (i.e., mid-channel) buoys. The last one is off Saint Clements Island (about 35 miles upriver). These mid-channel buoys are exactly that (i.e., placed close to the center of a very wide channel) and can be safely passed on either side. At night these buoys emit a distinctive white light pattern flashing the Morse code "A" -- a dot and then a dash (i.e., a quick white light followed by a longer white light). On a NOAA chart they will be indicated by "Mo(A)". A 24-foot-deep shipping channel starts northwest of Saint Clements Island flanked by green and red floating buoys.

Originally, there were 11 lighthouses on the Potomac. Today only three remain -- Jones Point, the Fort Washington Bell Tower, and Piney Point. Fort Washington is the only one emanating a signal -- a six-second light. Piney Point's lighthouse has become part of an interesting museum.

At certain places downriver from Potomac Creek, about 10 tall steel girders stand. Usually, but not always, they mark a protruding land hazard or a cluster of rocks in the river. The structures could emit white, green, or even red light patterns. These structures are colloquially referred to as "spiders," "crabs," or "towers." See the appropriate NOAA chart for the light color and interval for a particular tower. On a NOAA chart, if you notice neither an "R" (for red) nor a "G" (for green), you can generally assume the color flashed from the tower is white (e.g., Ragged Point tower flashes a 6-second white light).

The light tower in the middle of the river off Maryland Point, the structure off Cobb Island, and the

15

Smith Point Light have "red sectors." A red sector is found on a light that rotates through both a white and a Red lens. If you're at an angle from which you're viewing the light through the white part of the lens, it appears white. You could travel less than 20 yards on a line perpendicular to the light rays, and that same light could appear red. You have crossed an unseen line into the red sector. Generally, the white sector is preferable. You should look at your NOAA chart to interpret what's going on, especially if you find yourself in the red sector of one of these light towers. On NOAA charts, these dangerous light towers will also have information giving away their height. If you see a lighted aid on a NOAA chart that reads "44ft" "39ft" or even "29ft" in height, you know you're not looking at an ordinary 14-foot daymark! You're likely looking at one of these tall steel towers.

There are more than a few junction buoys (two colored can buoys) found on the river. Going upriver, a buoy with a green band over a red band can be passed on either side, but the predominant channel is indicated by the topmost band. In this example, the green band dominates, and to enter into the predominant channel the buoy should be passed on your left (e.g., at the junction of Washington Channel and the Potomac River). Likewise, when traveling upriver, a red band over a green band indicates that the predominate channel goes to the left and the secondary channel upriver heads toward the right (e.g., at the junction of Washington Channel and the Anacostia River). Like solid red or green buoys, junction buoys may or may not be lighted. If they are lighted, they generally have a unique flashing pattern called a "group flash." They usually flash the preferred channel color but the pattern will be a less regular set of flashes (e.g., two quick flashes followed by one longer flash).

Near the mouth of many tributaries, you'll see daymarks that begin with "PRM" or "PRV" followed by a number (e.g., "11"), then suffixed by either an "A" or a "B". These marks divide the river into three of the four fishing jurisdictions. "PRM" daymarks indicate the boundary between the Maryland and the Potomac River fisheries and will be found near the Maryland shore. Likewise, "PRV" daymarks indicate the boundary between the Virginia and Potomac River fisheries and will be found near the mouth of Virginia tributaries. The middle part of the River is under the jurisdiction of the Potomac River fisheries.

Commercial activities along the river (e.g., power plants, petroleum terminals, and even bridges) may have their own peculiar navigational light nuances. You can usually decipher their meaning from a NOAA chart. Remember, any one navigation aid could fail. A lighted aid could burn out or become very dim. A daymark could get knocked over. Storms play havoc with navigation aids. Aids can also change locations due to dredging or similar river operations. Navigation aids, though not foolproof, are of great help, unlike so many places in Latin America where they are totally absent or seriously inadequate. There is still much more to learn about navigation aids (e.g., sounds, radar reflecting capabilities, and range lights). You can learn more from the small print on NOAA charts or from the *Chapman Piloting* book (see appendix E).

Even though I have spent more than 13 years on navigating experience, I sometimes go through a quick mental block when coming across an unexpected navigation aid. I quickly note that it is red (or green); I am returning (or departing); then on what side should I leave it? By taking this thoughtful second or two, I might avoid impulsively jumping to the wrong side of the aid and running aground.

Just because you "find" a tributary navigational aid, don't automatically assume it is the most seaward. I've learned though mistakes that the first aid *seen* on a creek, especially in daylight, may not be the FIRST aid. The course to this "second" aid can often result in a grounding. At night, lighted navigational aids can reduce the potential. Occasionally turning around and looking behind you can reduce the chance of missing that first aid. I also think too few boaters look behind them. Glancing backwards, you might find that surprising first aid, an overtaking vessel, or even a helpful "reverse range" set of landmarks.

SUPPLEMENTAL NAVIGATIONAL UPDATES

The US Coast Guard Fifth District publishes a monthly edition of *Notice to Mariners* with additional weekly supplements, to which you could subscribe. This *Notice to Mariners* contains numerous updates, such as faulty lights on navigational aids, dredging operations, channel changes, NOAA chart updates, notices of regattas, and other water-confining events. The Potomac River is in the Coast Guard Fifth District, headquartered in Portsmouth VA. Within the Fifth District, the Potomac River falls under the jurisdiction of Coast Guard Activities Baltimore. Activities Baltimore irregularly transmits the *Marine Safety Broadcast* over the VHF radio. The *Marine Safety Broadcast* transmits some of the information found in the *Notice to Mariners*, but some detail may be missing. Activities Baltimore will initially alert listeners on VHF 16 of a *Marine Safety Broadcast* and will advise listeners to switch to VHF 22A for receiving the actual transmission of the broadcast. The *Coast Pilot* is another source found at nautical stores. Among other things, the *Coast Pilot* contains bearings, ranges, coordinates, and a detailed description of various channel and harbor approaches.

COMMUNICATIONS

There are well more than 50 MARINE VHF RADIO CHANNELS available to recreational boaters, but we'll limit our concerns to the major channels. VHF Channel 16 is the International Distress and Hailing Channel. This is the most important channel. All vessels should be monitoring VHF 16, and very few vessels should be transmitting on it. When you use channel 16 to hail another vessel, be punctual and don't interrupt other radio traffic. If your party doesn't respond after three hails, please don't keep trying and trying. In my opinion, too many boaters do this when it's obvious to everyone except the transmitter that the other party, for whatever reason, is not reachable. Foremost, VHF 16 should be reserved for boating emergencies and Coast Guard priority traffic. The Coast Guard moves off channel 16 as soon as possible and recreational boaters are required to do likewise. VHF channel 16 is the hailing channel, but once contact is made, the radio traffic should quickly move to a "noncommercial working channel."

There are three levels of urgency on the VHF radio. A MAYDAY is broadcast when there is an immediate life-threatening situation and FOR NO OTHER REASON. If the Coast Guard is responding to a Mayday, stay off channel 16 until the situation is resolved. Once the Coast Guard has garnered pertinent information concerning a Mayday call, even the Coast Guard moves that situation off VHF channel 16 to another channel in case there is another Mayday that needs to be heard on VHF 16. The second level of urgency is PAN-PAN (pronounced "pon-pon"). A Pan-Pan is used when the safety of a boat is in jeopardy. The lowest level of urgency is a SECURITE (pronounced with four syllables). The Coast Guard often uses Securite to pass navigational information or weather warnings. The Notice of an upcoming Securite, or Pan-Pan broadcast is on VHF 16. But the broadcast itself does not transmit on channel 16. The actual broadcast is on the another Coast Guard working channel, VHF 22A. Coast Guard *Marine Safety Broadcasts* are also on VHF 22A. Besides VHF 16 and 22A, the Coast Guard may conduct radio traffic on VHF 23A, 82A, 83A, or other VHF channels.

VHF 13 is another important channel. If your radio has a dual-watch capability, as many do, monitoring VHF 13 along with VHF 16 is a prudent idea. VHF channel 13 is a predominant navigational channel (also known as the bridge-to-bridge channel). Tugboats, large ships, drawbridges, and canal locks monitor VHF 13. It is preferable to contact them on VHF 13 rather than on VHF 16.

Certain channels are reserved for marine radio telephone operators. You could call one of these channels and patch through, at a cost, to a land line (telephone) and call anywhere you would on a normal telephone.

Collect calls aren't much of a problem for these marine operators (though they might be for the recipient!). The VHF channels reserved for marine operators are VHF 24, 25, 26, 27, 28, 84, 85, 86, and 87. The Point Lookout Marine Operator, KAQ383, can be hailed on VHF 26. The Washington Marine Operator, KTA463, can be hailed on VHF 28. If they need to reach you, the marine operators hail your vessel, by name, on VHF 16. Any correspondence over the airwaves is not secure, so don't give your credit card number over the airwaves for the call.

If you want to talk to another vessel, and you made initial contact on VHF 16, you should quickly carry your traffic to a noncommercial working channel. Your choice of noncommercial working channels is limited to VHF 9, 68, 69, 71, 72, and 78. Many marinas are starting to use VHF 9 regularly. Most of the other VHF channels not addressed are used by commercial ships and port operations, and you should stay off of them. Generally, the lower power setting (i.e., 1 watt) is adequate for VHF radio transmissions. The lower transmitting wattage is absolutely required on VHF 13.

Perhaps one of the more regularly used features of your marine VHF will be to RECEIVE weather information. Three channels are generally used -- WX1, WX2, and WX3. If you aren't able to receive one channel, try the other two. Every place on the East Coast should be in the range of at least one weather channel. Sometimes you can receive a weather forecast on two and possibly all three of the weather channels. KHB-36 on WX1 is transmitted from Manassas VA and is well received on the upper Potomac River. WXM-57 on WX2 is transmitted from Heathsville VA and is well received on the lower river. On WX3 you may receive WXF-65 transmitted from Richmond VA or KEC-2 transmitted from Salisbury MD. Always listen to one of these NOAA radio weather stations for about 10 minutes while preparing your boat and before you take it out. Changing plans due to a last-minute negative weather forecast may not be what you wanted but may prove to be the most prudent thing to do.

Cellular Phones are common, and they have a certain practicality for boaters. With a cellular phone you can call folks ashore apprising them of your always fluid boating plans. If you decide to have a cellular phone aboard, consider the providing company's coverage range. Coverage may not extend to Smith Point, Point Lookout, or even perhaps many parts of the lower or middle Potomac River.

In no way does a cellular phone replace a VHF radio. You can't call the nearest boater (unless he or she is a friend also carrying a cellular phone). The nearest boater cannot call you in an emergency. You cannot receive important *Marine Safety Broadcasts* on a cellular phone; nor can you receive important intra-boat radio traffic transmitted over the VHF radio.

For long-range communications, *Single Sideband Radios* (SSB) have become increasingly popular. You really don't need one on the Potomac or Chesapeake, and they are an expensive accessory and easy to get hooked on. With an SSB radio, you don't need to take the lengthy training that is required for a HAM radio license. Your radio call sign will be the same as your VHF. With a SSB radio you can converse anywhere around the world. Like VHF channel 16, SSB channel 2182 is monitored by the Coast Guard for "vessel in distress" transmissions. Many SSB channels have duplex capability like talking over a telephone (i.e., both parties can speak and be heard at the same time). You'll need a very long antenna (at least 23 feet) or use an isolated backstay on a sailboat as an antenna. You'll also need a very-well grounded boat and likely an automatic tuner. With more expensive accessories, you can get weatherfaxes (i.e., charts with the locations of weather fronts and other useful information).

With an SSB radio, you can receive the National Weather Service *High Seas Weather Report*. Unlike NOAA weather radio, this forecast is for beyond 25 miles offshore and covers the Atlantic as far east as

35°W. In Portsmouth VA, station NMN broadcasts the Atlantic weather four times daily. Besides providing you a good handle on upcoming weather, you can also use your SSB to listen to the Voice of America, the British Broadcasting Corporation, the Christian Science Monitor, and Armed Forces Radio from anywhere on the globe. You can find the broadcasting frequencies in the latest edition of *Reed's Nautical Almanac* (see appendix E).

The SSB radio will also allow you to talk to an AT&T high-seas marine operator. Marine operators will patch you through a telephone land line and you can talk to anybody in North America. Comprehensive lists of channels and frequencies can be found in the "Communications and Weather Services" Chapter of *Reed's Nautical Almanac*. When I purchased a used SSB, I had every intention of reselling the unit after two cruises to Central America. Notwithstanding, it expanded my horizons nicely, and I decided to keep it.

GLOBAL POSITIONING SYSTEM (GPS) UNITS

GPS units are great, but they are not foolproof. Facilitating your Potomac River navigation, appendix D contains 43 useful GPS waypoints. You should not rely solely on your GPS unit for navigation. Your unit can give bad readings. Mine has many times. Once in the middle of the Gulf of Mexico, and for the better part of a day, my GPS unit kept placing me in the Pacific Ocean off the coast of Peru! Another time in the Potomac, off Coles Point, a different unit placed me in the lower Chesapeake off Cape Charles. Every year, in this age of electronic positioning, I read of needless vessel mishaps because the captain or crew were over-relying on precise electronic instruments. It's always a good idea to keep your dead reckoning skills honed.

I am of the opinion, especially for Potomac navigation, that you should NOT use GPS units to navigate from one waypoint to the next waypoint. Hence, my GPS waypoints are NOT intended to be used for "along the shore" navigation. These waypoints are solely intended to assist your "focus" on a particular creek or harbor from well in the center of the river. There may be a bulge in the shoreline or an island between two adjacent GPS waypoints. When traveling between two adjacent creeks with GPS waypoints, proceed beyond the exiting creek's GPS waypoint and go well into deep water before gradually arcing your way toward the next desired GPS waypoint. My GPS waypoints can usually be approached from a "deep-water cone," but in some cases that cone may have an arc of as little as 90 degrees (e.g., in Nomini Creek which is in Nomini Bay).

Generally, my GPS waypoints are intended to position you off the first creek navigation aid. However, there are a few exceptions. The GPS waypoint for the Occoquan River is well into Occoquan Bay and about a mile seaward of the first daymark. This waypoint makes more sense for a vessel heading downriver. The GPS waypoint for Monroe Bay, Colonial Beach, is off the second mark, "R4" versus the first mark, "R2". Coming from the southeast, or downriver, a vessel need not aim for the first mark, "R2" but can aim for the second mark, "R4". If you are coming into Monroe Bay from the opposite direction, the northwest, you should clear the rounded head of land around Colonial Beach anyway and should not focus on any GPS waypoint, even "R2" until you clear this head of land. Likewise, I think, in most scenarios, the best GPS waypoint for the Coan River is the second buoy, "R4". The purpose of my GPS waypoint is to position you near the first creek markers in the deepest water with a few exceptions (e.g., Occoquan Bay, center spans of the Route 301 bridge, and Wilson Bridge). Once you spot the creek's navigational aids, forget the GPS waypoint and rely on your visual cues and skills.

My GPS latitude/longitude waypoints were calibrated to Degrees/Minutes/<u>and Hundredths of Minutes</u>. Beware! Instead of hundredths of minutes, some folks calibrate their GPS units to seconds. A second is a sixtieth of a minute. The difference between 39°00.59N in hundredths of minutes and 39°00.59N in seconds is nearly 800 yards, or about 0.4 of a nautical mile!

There are many instances when it is more prudent to put your GPS unit aside and let your eyeballs do the navigating. A second, or even third, set of eyeballs near the bow is even better. These times include heavy vessel traffic, anywhere north of the Wilson Bridge, or when your undivided attention is needed elsewhere (e.g., on the depthfinder, when there are a lot of distractions, and in fog). Technology is great, and although many are trying, I doubt, and I earnestly hope, that there will NEVER be a day when high technology fully replaces good human judgment and instinct. You will develop good instinct if you spend time on the water. Very few things in life are more satisfying than confronting and partially mastering mother nature's challenges on the water.

ETIQUETTE IN TRAFFIC

The US Inland "RULES OF THE ROAD" are thorough and address many caveats. This section will attempt to distill a few of them for some of the more likely situations that might be encountered on the Potomac. If two vessels are approaching head-on in a "meeting" situation, more often than not both should swerve to their right, or starboard side, thereby passing port-to-port. The change in direction should be pronounced. A slight gradual turn might not be discernible to the other vessel. This action can be supplemented by horn signal blasts. One horn blast means "I intend to leave you on my port side." If the second vessels concurs, it should reciprocate with the same signal -- one horn blast.

A starboard-to-starboard meeting is safe and reasonable if two vessels are meeting slightly off center and each is slightly to the other's starboard side. One vessel should fire two horn blasts, which means "I intend to leave you on my starboard side." The second vessel should reciprocate with two blasts, in effect relaying that a starboard-to-starboard meeting is fine. If the second vessel has any problems with the signal sounded by the first vessel, the second vessel should sound FIVE blasts and start the horn-blast process all over again. The second vessel should fire only the same number of horn blasts as the first vessel or five blasts. Never should one blast be responded to with two blasts or vice versa.

If one vessel is "overtaking" another, the same sound signal logic used in a meeting situation applies. A fast-moving overtaking tug may sound two blasts, signaling its intent to "leave you (the vessel being passed) on his starboard side." Again you would either respond with two or five blasts. If you respond with two blasts, you acknowledge his intent to leave you on his starboard (in an overtaking situation, this will be your port side). Etiquette, if the channel permits, is to make a noticeable turn to your starboard, giving the vessel a tad more room on your port side. Even a sailboat under sail, if overtaking a slow-moving powerboat, is an overtaking vessel and should abide by these rules. Technically, an overtaking situation arises when a vessel is approaching another from slightly abaft of abeam (i.e., 22 degrees behind amidship). If the vessel's projected paths are forward of this, it's a "crossing" situation.

If two power vessels are crossing paths, the vessel that has the other vessel on its starboard side should yield the right of way. A vessel that has the other on its port side should assume, as least initially, that it has the right of way and should maintain his present course for a little while longer. If the supposed-to-yield vessel doesn't seem to be yielding, the other privileged vessel should alter course to avoid a collision well beforehand.

A motoring sailing vessel, even if its sails are hoisted, abides by these powerboat rules. For two sailing vessels meeting under sail, another set of rules applies. If the wind is on different sides of the two sailboats, the vessel on the starboard tack (i.e., the wind is coming across the starboard side of the boat and the sails are blown off to the port side) has the right of way. You'll often see racing boat skippers coyly trying to position themselves on a starboard tack at the start of a sailboat race for this reason.

If two sailing boats are both on the same tack (e.g., the wind on each boat is coming from the port side and blowing the sails to the starboard side), there is another rule. The second boat receiving the wind, the downwind or leeward boat, has the right of way over the upwind or windward boat. Why would an avowed powerboater ever care to know about this? If two sailboats and one powerboat are converging, and this does happen, a crafty powerboater could figure out which of the two sailboats has to yield to the other and then which way the burdened sailboat will have to turn (usually by tacking or by turning downwind). The powerboater, anticipating the moves of the sailboats, can pick a way though this entanglement with crew-impressing dexterity.

Generally, a vessel under sail has the right of way over a power-driven vessel, unless overtaking it. But sailing vessels (and power vessels) should give way to certain power vessels engaged in fishing. These fishing vessels are employing nets, trawls, and other gear that restrict the fishing vessel's maneuverability. On the Potomac, this inexactly translates to watermen and possibly charter headboats. A weekend powerboat trolling a line or two generally does not have the right of way over a sailboat under sail. There's a lot of misunderstanding here. I recollect many times sailing close-hauled (i.e., as close as a sailboat can force itself into the wind), trying to clip a point of land ahead me and then being forced to make a time-consuming tack (a cumbersome 90-degree turn through the eye of the wind on the opposite tack) because a small powerboat trailing a couple of fishing lines wouldn't make a slight turn and give the sailboat the right of way. It would be nice if more powerboaters understood the sailboaters' range of maneuverability. Likewise, sailboaters should understand the powerboaters' point of view and try to stay out of their fishing grounds. The watermen trying to earn a livelihood on the river should be afforded the right of way by both the sailboaters and the powerboaters.

There are other common sense points. At night, all vessels should burn the proper lights as well as know what they are seeing. For example, viewing both a red and a green light on another vessel means you're probably approaching a collision! Don't ever exceed a safe speed. The safe speed relates to your ability to handle your boat while factoring other boating traffic, visibility, the sea choppiness, and even the water depth. A smaller vessel should never cut off a larger vessel confined by draft. Of course, there are exceptions to all of the Rules of the Road. It is the responsibility of all skippers to avoid **immediate danger** (of a collision) even if that means deviating from the prescribed Rules in order to do so. And assume not all skippers know the Rules as well as you.

DEGROUNDING

If you spend any time on the Potomac or Chesapeake, you will probably run aground someday. Luckily, the user-friendly Potomac bottom is soft mud in the upper reaches and soft sand, a bit harder than mud, near the Potomac's mouth. It could be a combination of the two in middle sections. It is different in other areas. In the Caribbean the bottom is often coral; in New England there are many treacherous rocks; and in Florida many of the bottoms are hard sand.

If When you run aground, first ask yourself, is the tide rising or falling? If you can, you should try to avoid navigation near times of high tide through areas with a dicey grounding potential. If you do ground, there is almost a 50 percent chance that the tide is rising. If you can wait and nothing is imperiled, why not let the rising tide lift you off? You should know the time of high tide somewhere on the river. With sketch 2-1 of this book in hand, you can figure when it will be close to high at your present location.

If you don't want to wait for the rising tide, there are a few things you can do. First, determine where the deeper water is. Not always, but more often than not, it is behind you (i.e., the path you took to get into this predicament). If heavy motor assistance is going to get you off, it has been my experience that four out of five times, it will be in reverse gear. So generally try reversing first. There are times when it may be better to work yourself off in a port, starboard, and occasionally even a forward direction. Take the time to find out where the deeper water is located by either wading in or using a dinghy and some sort of depth-measuring pole (e.g., a boathook).

Kedging is a method of deploying a heavy anchor, usually aboard a dinghy, and dropping it in the deeper water and then winching or pulling your boat toward that anchor to deground. I've tried this a few times in the Chesapeake and Potomac and the results have been marginal. In the Caribbean, where I could get the anchor to bite down hard onto something like a rock or hard sand, kedging worked better. I've even successfully kedged with multiple anchors to extricate the vessel from a menacing situation off Mexico. A kedging anchor line can be deployed from the top of the sailboat's mast and the main halyard. This method also induces a list in the vessel, lessening the draft requirement, while pulling the vessel toward the deeper water. If you have a sailboat, you may consider the merits of hoisting a sail if with it you can be blown toward deeper water. You can assist a kedging or a sail-assisted operation by running the engine. If you have been running your engine hard, don't forget to check that raw water strainer for stirred-up sucked-in debris. Enough stirred-up debris collected in your raw water system could restrict the flow of raw water and lead to an engine overheating problem.

Running aground in the Potomac is seldom a panic situation. Figure out where the deeper water is. You could wait for a rising tide to lift you off. If you choose not to be patient, try motoring in the direction of deeper water. If that doesn't work, you could try kedging or sail assistance (if in a sailboat). If none of the above methods work, call one of the four Potomac River Boat/US towboat operators (covered in chapter 4).

READING DEPTHS

Had you been reading your depthfinder assiduously, you probably wouldn't have run aground in the first place. You can almost never see the bottom in the Potomac. You need a depthfinder, and one with an audio alarm than can be set and reset is preferred. Don't hesitate to reset the depth alarm based on the anticipated bottom. In some places in the Florida Keys, my depth alarm was set to as little as one foot beneath the keel, and it still sounded often. In that shallow water, if it were set at two feet beneath the keel, it would have been useless because it would have been alarming all of the time. Conversely, while sailing around the Bay Islands of Honduras where huge coral formations and ledges rise from out of nowhere, my depth alarm was set deep (i.e., 15 feet or more, depending on the normal bottom depth) in order to give me an adequate early warning of these massive underwater structures.

AVOIDING CRAB POTS

In the Potomac, the crabbing season is from April 1 to November 30. After that, the recreational crabbers take a break, but the watermen keep working -- tonging for oysters. Crab pots are wire mesh cubical cages baited in the center with a foul piece for meat attractive to blue crabs. The crabs find their way into the cage, but the trap is designed so that, once in, the crabs cannot easily get out. The cage, resting on the bottom, is tethered to a float. Watermen usually identify their individual traps by painting a distinctive pattern on their floats. Often a stick or handle will be protruding through the float for ease in retrieval. However, sometimes the float is nothing more than a plastic bleach bottle. In the summertime, some areas are inundated with crab pots -- Judith Sound, Saint George Bar, and Mathias Point Bar.

Although it may not appear obvious, crab pots and their floats are almost always in a line. The watermen set them that way. Moving slowly forward in his workboat, the waterman gets in "his line," hauls a trap, shakes out any crabs, rebaits the trap, drops the trap back on the bottom, and then hauls up the next trap in line. Often he is doing this work singlehandedly while simultaneously moving his boat forward. If you keep running into the same color-patterned floats, offset yourself a bit to get out of that waterman's deployment line. Crab pots are not usually found in water more than 20 feet deep; nor are crab pots placed in only a few inches of water. I've heard that while negotiating real shallow water (in a shallow-draft boat), if you stay near the crab pots, you'll probably find the relatively deeper water.

Many times, the floats and the tether line are angled away from the pot by the current. If you snag a crab pot tether line on your keel, prop, or prop shaft, you will have to unravel the line. This usually means putting on a dive mask and taking a swim.

AVOIDING FISH TRAPS

Fish traps are often found near tributary mouths. Fish stake traps or pound nets are usually found in 8-20 feet of water. The stakes may remain in the same place for many years or may deteriorate after only a few seasons. These fish traps consist of many stakes and heavy netting strung between the stakes. The stakes are made of pine and the pointed tips are fire-hardened. One waterman told me that the stakes may last a couple of years or a bad season of worms can significantly shorten their life. The watermen hammer the stakes into the bottom and lay them in a line perpendicular to the shore. At the "seaward end" of the trap, the stakes are more densely planted so that a maze or a fish "pound" is created to trap fish (see picture).

As fish swim parallel to shore, they encounter the underwater netting supported by the stakes. Instinctively the fish turn seaward (i.e., away from the shore), paralleling the netting, and soon find themselves caught in the "maze net" at the end of the fish trap. The fish remain in the maze or pound section until the watermen collect them. You'll often see cormorants (black, fair-sized, fish-eating, diving birds) perched atop stakes at the seaward part of a fish trap looking for easy pickings.

Don't try to go between fish trap stakes because you may get entangled by a heavy underwater netting strung between the stakes. At night, it is easy to accidentally bump into a fish trap. Almost all have no lighting, although a few have bicycle reflectors to help your spotlight identify them. If you navigate at night, you should already know the area from daylight boating and be able to avoid areas where fish traps are located. You'll likely find fish traps near the mouth of the Potomac near Smith Point and near the mouth of other Potomac tributaries (e.g., Saint George Bar in the Saint Marys River, at the mouth of Nomini Bay, near Breton Bay).

Besides fish stakes, there are other less permanent fish traps on the river. Lighter gill nets are sometimes strung between anchored or unanchored floats. The floats usually have pennants or other warning symbols atop. The weighted gill nets may be at any water depth. To avoid encountering the underwater net, do not split any conspicuous pair of floats.

DUCK BLINDS

Duck blinds are found in many of the Potomac's creeks and dot the shoreline in a few places. Duck and geese hunters build these camouflaged shacks, usually on stilts, for wintertime perches. Sometimes they are indicated on NOAA charts, but often the location is imprecise. Furthermore, they are not permanent. After a few seasons, they may be in a badly dilapidated condition with only their stilts remaining.

Out in the water and in the shadows, it is easy to mistake a duck blind for a navigational aid (e.g., a daymark or even a spider tower). This could be a big mistake. Unlike navigational aids, duck blinds are often surrounded by SHALLOW water. Wherever you find a duck blind, even if there is much water around it, it's reasonable to assume that the duck blind was erected in shallows. Once you have determined that you're looking at a duck blind instead of a navigation aid, it is advisable to turn away from the blind before getting too close and running aground.

HYDRILLA

Hydrilla is an introduced aquatic plant, with many stringy stems. It grows rampant in some of the Freshwater parts of the Potomac River. It can't survive in the saltier water. It usually builds up in shallow water in places where there is no strong tidal current. Large mats of vegetation will be seen floating on or near the surface. There are places where you'll see it only at low tide. Besides clogging certain areas of the river, hydrilla can easily clog your engine water intake. Broken pieces of vegetation could get sucked into your raw water system and constrict the flow. If this happens, your engine will overheat. Always have a functional engine temperature gauge. Hydrilla does have some merit. It improves water quality and clarity.

ANCHORING

Unlike many other nautical guides, this guide doesn't contain the "anchor" symbols for the better anchorages. There are too many great anchorages on the Potomac! Justice is not served by broadcasting my top 50 or so. Besides, how would you feel if I happen to have "flagged" your personal favorite unspoiled cove? Study the NOAA charts, especially in the creeks and coves, and you'll likely find many good anchorages. From the mouth of the river to Colonial Beach, there are more than a dozen large enchanting rivers. Each of these large rivers contain many smaller creeks loaded with great anchorages! From Colonial Beach northward, there are about another dozen tributaries deep enough for all but some deep-draft vessels. The northern tributaries, with exceptions, have fewer deep anchorages than their lower river counterparts.

The bottom holding for almost all of the tidal Potomac is soft mud. In the very lower reaches, close to the bay and especially not far into some of the lower rivers, the bottom is a sandy mixture. Both mud and a sandy mixture make good holding conditions. Hard sand is generally not a great holding bottom.

The only official anchorage is near the head of Washington Channel on the Southwest Waterfront (see appendix C). The Harbor Police request you anchor off the bow and stern to minimize your swinging radius in Washington Channel. Most of Washington Channel is more than 20 feet deep. At night, whether in an official anchorage or elsewhere, you should display a 360-degree white anchor light. Often, I hear of an underway vessel striking an anchored boat at night. Sometimes the results involve injuries. In the lower reaches, many bleary-eyed watermen pull out before daybreak, and they least expect to find a newly anchored boat on their creek.

I am a firm believer in having multiple anchors aboard, though a second anchor may be used less than 1 percent of the time. That 1 percent could save your boat. In the Caribbean aboard my 33-footer, I carried five, used four, and deployed as many as three anchors at once on more than a few occasions. A powerboat or sailboat on the Potomac doesn't need that many, but you ought to have at least two.

A heavier anchor is generally better, although its weight is limited by your ability to easily retrieve it. A light "lunch hook" anchor can nicely complement situations where you don't want to drop that cumbersome "overnight" anchor. You should set your anchor by backing down gently with the transmission in reverse

Excerpt 6-1. Washington Channel. From NOAA Chart 12289. Reduced to 69%.

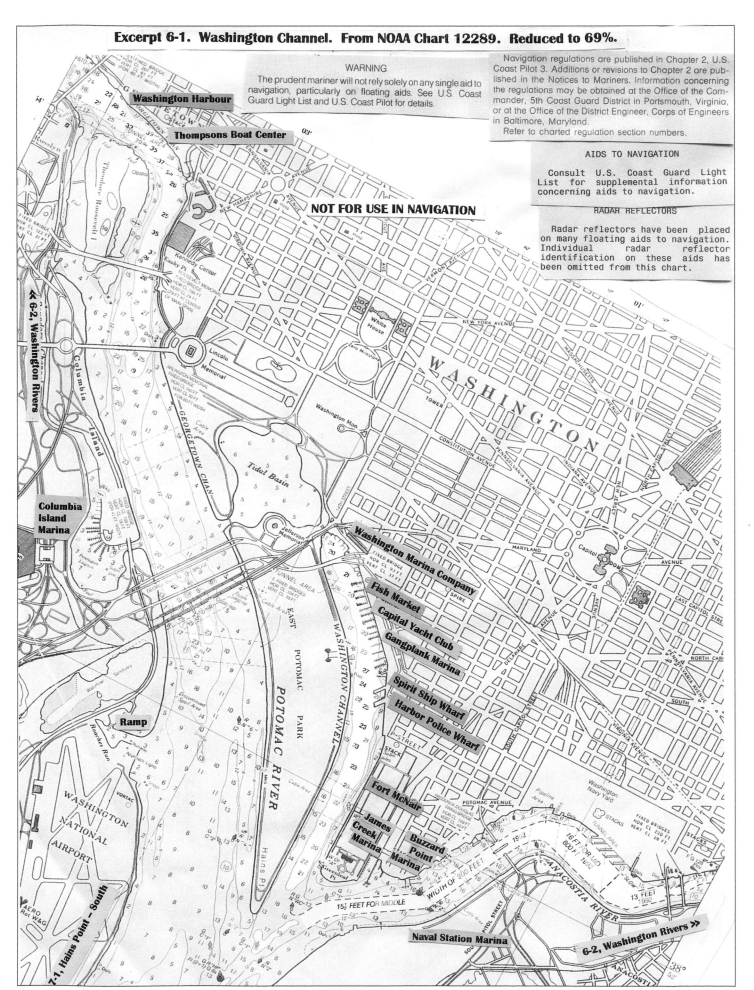

WARNING
The prudent mariner will not rely solely on any single aid to navigation, particularly on floating aids. See U.S. Coast Guard Light List and U.S. Coast Pilot for details.

Navigation regulations are published in Chapter 2, U.S. Coast Pilot 3. Additions or revisions to Chapter 2 are published in the Notices to Mariners. Information concerning the regulations may be obtained at the Office of the Commander, 5th Coast Guard District in Portsmouth, Virginia, or at the Office of the District Engineer, Corps of Engineers in Baltimore, Maryland.
Refer to charted regulation section numbers.

AIDS TO NAVIGATION

Consult U.S. Coast Guard Light List for supplemental information concerning aids to navigation.

RADAR REFLECTORS

Radar reflectors have been placed on many floating aids to navigation. Individual radar reflector identification on these aids has been omitted from this chart.

NOT FOR USE IN NAVIGATION

Washington Harbour

Thompsons Boat Center

Columbia Island Marina

Ramp

Washington Marina Company

Fish Market

Capital Yacht Club

Gangplank Marina

Spirit Ship Wharf

Harbor Police Wharf

Fort McNair

James Creek Marina

Buzzard Point Marina

Naval Station Marina

6-2, Washington Rivers ≫

≪ 6-2, Washington Rivers

7-1, Hains Point – South

25

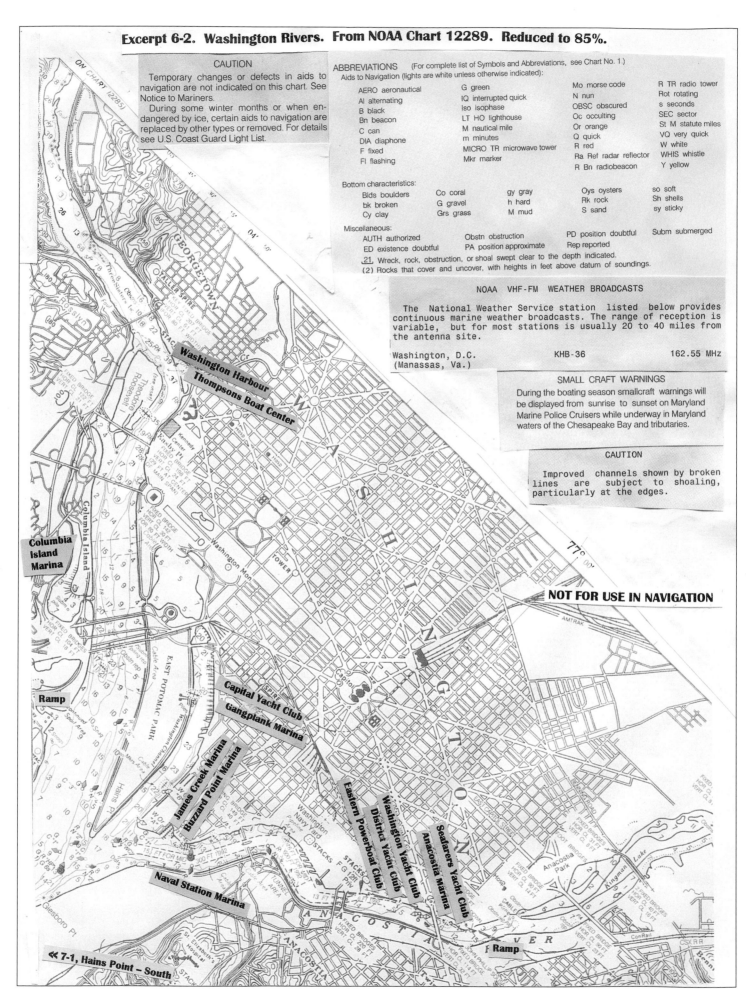

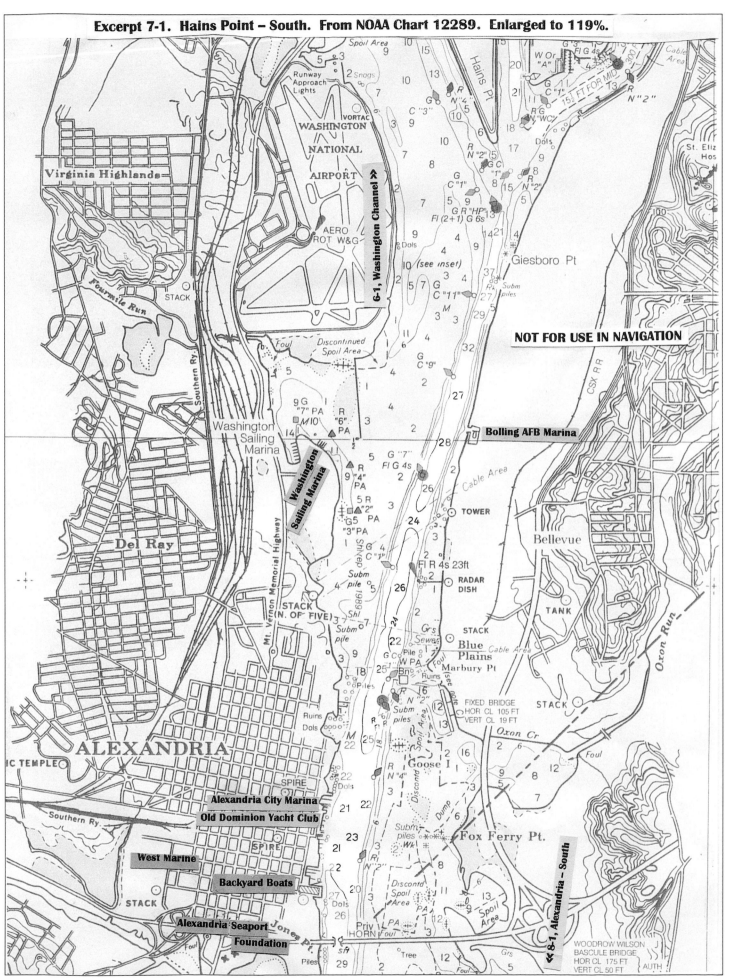

Virginia Highlands

Fourmile Run

STACK

VORTAC
WASHINGTON
NATIONAL
AIRPORT

AERO
ROT W&G

6-1, Washington Channel ≫

Runway
Approach
Lights

Spoil Area

2 Snags

Hains Pt

W Or
"A"

FI G 4s

Cable
Area

St. Eliz
Hos

Giesboro Pt

NOT FOR USE IN NAVIGATION

CSX R R

Washington
Sailing
Marina

Discontinued
Spoil Area

Foul

9 G
"7" PA

M 10

R
"6"
PA

Washington Sailing Marina

Mt. Vernon Memorial Highway

Southern Ry.

Del Ray

STACK
(N. OF FIVE)

Subm
pile
1989

Subm
pile

Ruins
Dols

Piles

ALEXANDRIA

IC TEMPLE

SPIRE

Alexandria City Marina

Old Dominion Yacht Club

Southern Ry.

West Marine

SPIRE

Backyard Boats

STACK

Alexandria Seaport
Foundation

Jones Pt.

HORN Foul

Dols

G "7"

FI G 4s

R
"4"
PA

5 R
"2" PA

G5
"3" PA

G C "1"

G C "1"

WPA
Bn

N "6"

R
"6"
Subm
piles

M
22

Dols

R
N "4"

Goose I.

Subm
piles
Wk

R
N "2"

Priv
LPA

Bolling AFB Marina

Cable Area

TOWER

FI R 4s 23ft

RADAR
DISH

Gr's
Sewer

STACK

Blue
Plains

Cable Area

Marbury Pt.

Ruins
(see note)

FIXED BRIDGE
HOR CL 105 FT
VERT CL 19 FT

Oxon Cr.

16

Dump

Discontd
Spoil
Area

PA

Submpiles

Fox Ferry Pt.

Foul

Tree

Bellevue

TANK

STACK

Oxon Run

Spoil
Area

8-1, Alexandria – South ≫

WOODROW WILSON
BASCULE BRIDGE
HOR CL 175 FT
VERT CL 50 FT
AUTH

Entry to Quantico Marina

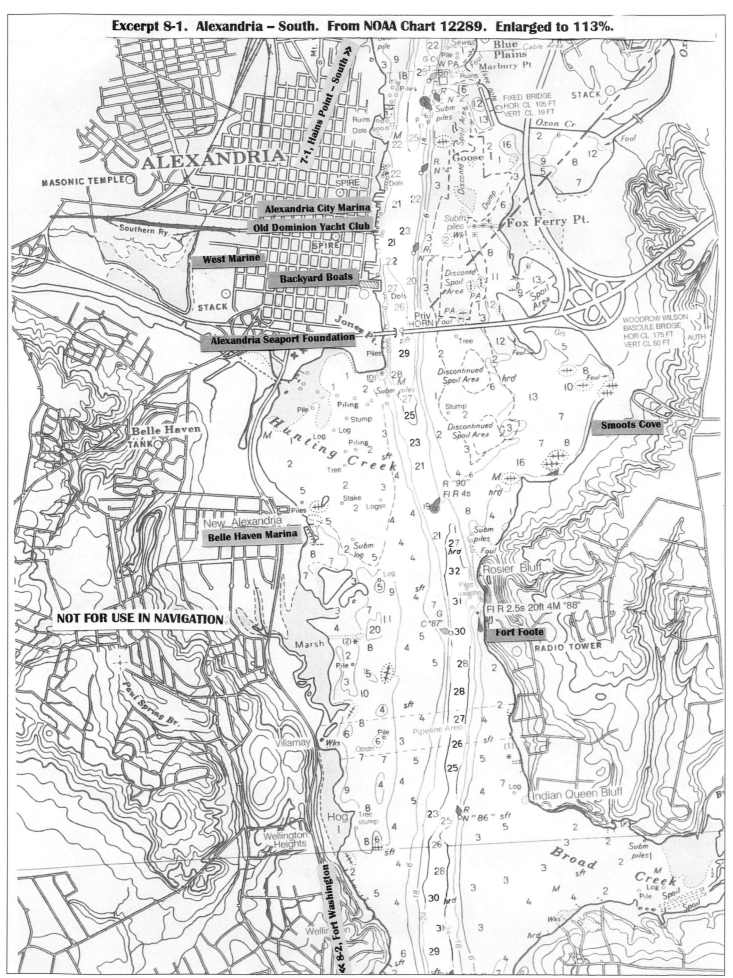

ALEXANDRIA

MASONIC TEMPLE

7-1, Hains Point – South ➤➤

Southern Ry.

SPIRE

Alexandria City Marina

Old Dominion Yacht Club

SPIRE

West Marine

Backyard Boats

STACK

Jones Pt.

Alexandria Seaport Foundation

Blue Plains

Marbury Pt.

FIXED BRIDGE
HOR CL 105 FT
VERT CL 19 FT

STACK

Oxon Cr

Goose I.

Fox Ferry Pt.

WOODROW WILSON
BASCULE BRIDGE
HOR CL 175 FT
VERT CL 50 FT

Smoots Cove

Hunting Creek

Belle Haven
TANK

New Alexandria

Belle Haven Marina

NOT FOR USE IN NAVIGATION

Rosier Bluff

Fort Foote

RADIO TOWER

Marsh

Paul Spring Br.

Villamay

Pipeline Area

Indian Queen Bluff

Hog I.

Wellington Heights

◄◄ 8-2, Fort Washington

Broad Creek

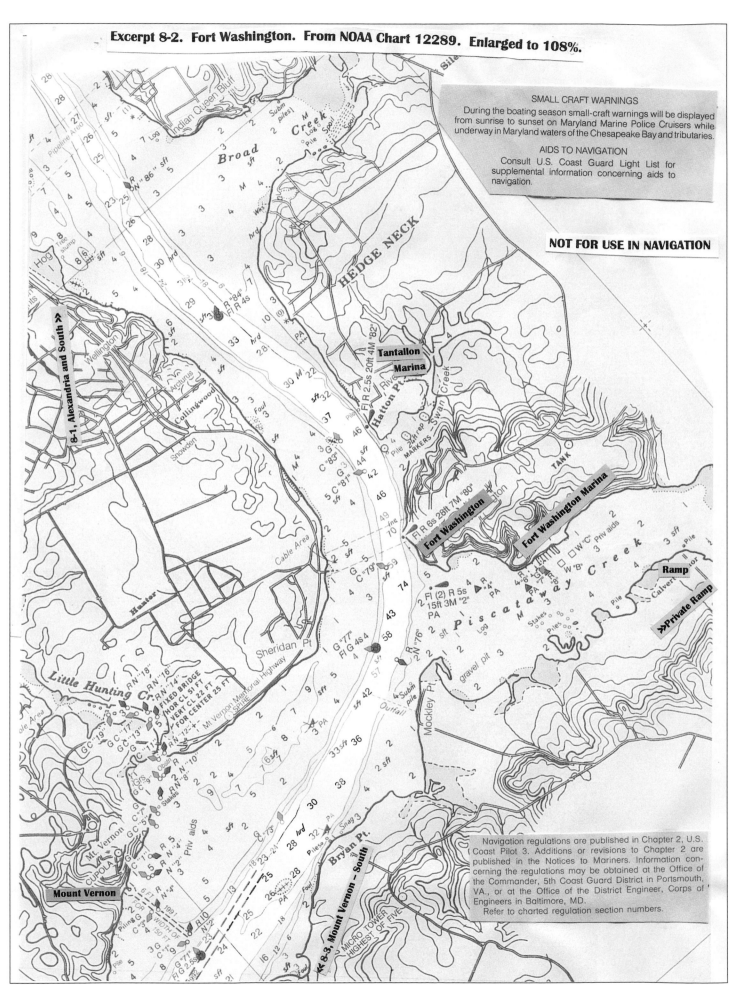

SMALL CRAFT WARNINGS
During the boating season small-craft warnings will be displayed from sunrise to sunset on Maryland Marine Police Cruisers while underway in Maryland waters of the Chesapeake Bay and tributaries.

AIDS TO NAVIGATION
Consult U.S. Coast Guard Light List for supplemental information concerning aids to navigation.

NOT FOR USE IN NAVIGATION

Navigation regulations are published in Chapter 2, U.S. Coast Pilot 3. Additions or revisions to Chapter 2 are published in the Notices to Mariners. Information concerning the regulations may be obtained at the Office of the Commander, 5th Coast Guard District in Portsmouth, VA., or at the Office of the District Engineer, Corps of Engineers in Baltimore, MD.
Refer to charted regulation section numbers.

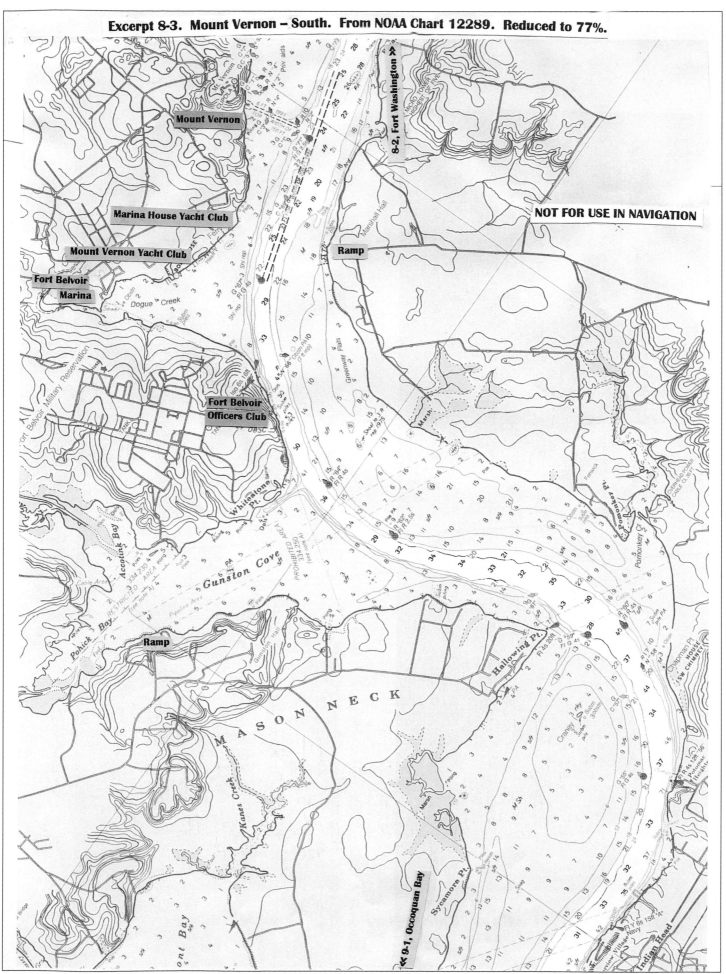

Excerpt 8-3. Mount Vernon – South. From NOAA Chart 12289. Reduced to 77%.

NOT FOR USE IN NAVIGATION

31

Locals on Nanjemoy Creek

Marine Railway at Point Lookout Marina

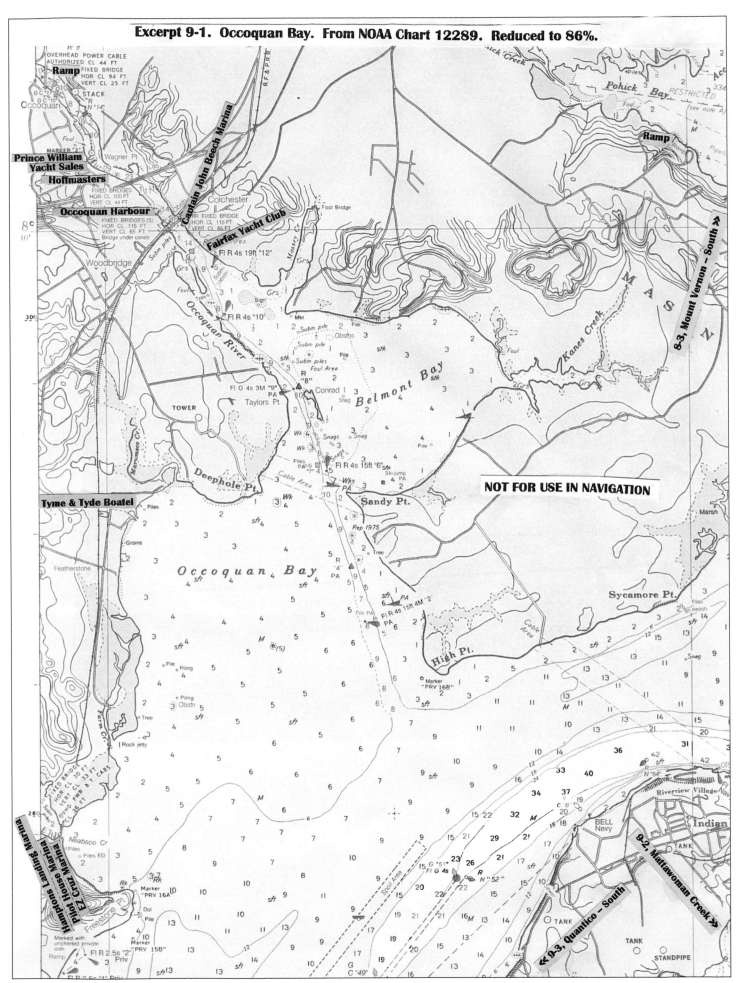

Excerpt 9-1. Occoquan Bay. From NOAA Chart 12289. Reduced to 86%.

Ramp

STACK

Occoquan

MARKER "2"

Prince William Yacht Sales

Hoffmasters

Occoquan Harbour

Wagner Pt.

Captain John Beach Marina

Colchester

Massey Cr.

Foot Bridge

Fairfax Yacht Club

Fl R 4s 19ft "12"

Woodbridge

Fl R 4s "10"

Occoquan River

Belmont Bay

Kanes Creek

MASON

8-3, Mount Vernon – South

Pohick Bay RESTRICTED (see note A)

Ramp

Fl G 4s 3M "9"

Conrad

Taylors Pt.

TOWER

Deephole Pt.

Cable Area

Fl R 4s 15ft "6"

Ski jump

Sandy Pt.

Rep 1975

NOT FOR USE IN NAVIGATION

Tyme & Tyde Boatel

Occoquan Bay

High Pt.

Marker "PRV 16B"

Sycamore Pt.

Marsh

Featherstone

Tree

Rock jetty

Hamptons Landing Marina
Pilot House Marina
EZ Cruz Marina

FIXED BRIDGE HOR CL 30 FT VERT CL 33 FT OVHD PWR & T CABS

Freestone Pt.

Neabsco Cr.

Marker "PRV 16A"

Fl R 2.5s "2" Priv

Marker "PRV 15B"

Spoil Area

BELL Navy

Riverview Village

Indian

9-2, Mattawoman Creek

Fl G 4s G "51"

R N "52"

9-3, Quantico – South

TANK

TANK

STANDPIPE

33

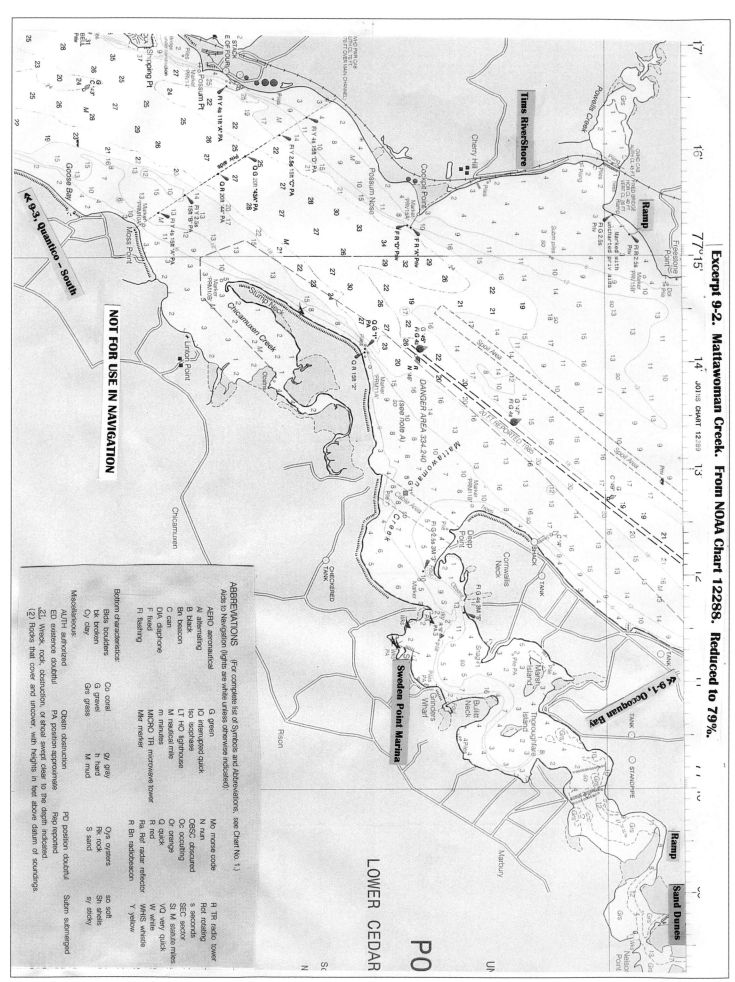

Excerpt 9-2. Mattawoman Creek. From NOAA Chart 12288. Reduced to 79%.

Tims RiverShore

Ramp

9-3, Quantico — South

NOT FOR USE IN NAVIGATION

Sweden Point Marina

9-1, Occoquan Bay

Ramp

Sand Dunes

LOWER CEDAR

PO

ABBREVIATIONS

Aids to Navigation (For complete list of Symbols and Abbreviations, see Chart No. 1):

AERO	aeronautical		G	green		Mo	morse code		R TR	radio tower
Al	alternating		IO	interrupted quick		N	run		Rot	rotating
B	black		Iso	isophase		OBSC	obscured		s	seconds
Bn	beacon		LT HO	lighthouse		Oc	occulting		SEC	sector
C	can		M	nautical mile		Or	orange		St M	statute miles
DIA	diaphone		m	minutes		Q	quick		VQ	very quick
F	fixed		MICRO TR	microwave tower		R	red		W	white
Fl	flashing		Mkr	marker		Ra Ref	radar reflector		WHIS	whistle
						R Bn	radiobeacon		Y	yellow

Bottom characteristics:

Blds	boulders		Co	coral		Oys	oysters		so	soft
bk	broken		G	gravel		Rk	rock		Sh	shells
Cy	clay		Grs	grass		S	sand		sy	sticky
			h	hard					
			M	mud					

Miscellaneous:

AUTH authorized
ED existence doubtful
Obstn obstruction
PA position approximate
PD position doubtful
Rep reported
Subm submerged

(1) Wreck, rock, obstruction, or shoal swept clear to the depth indicated.
(2) Rocks that cover and uncover, with heights in feet above datum of soundings.

JOINS CHART 12289

DANGER AREA 334,240 (see note A)

20 FT REPORTED 1985

34

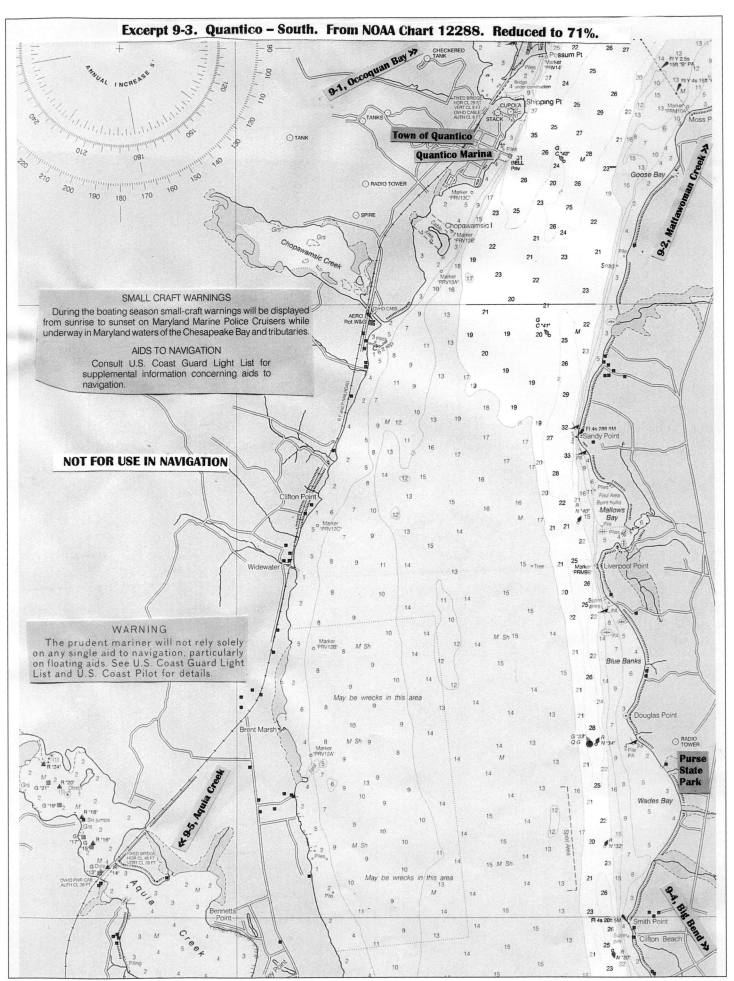

SMALL CRAFT WARNINGS

During the boating season small-craft warnings will be displayed from sunrise to sunset on Maryland Marine Police Cruisers while underway in Maryland waters of the Chesapeake Bay and tributaries.

AIDS TO NAVIGATION

Consult U.S. Coast Guard Light List for supplemental information concerning aids to navigation.

NOT FOR USE IN NAVIGATION

WARNING

The prudent mariner will not rely solely on any single aid to navigation, particularly on floating aids. See U.S. Coast Guard Light List and U.S. Coast Pilot for details.

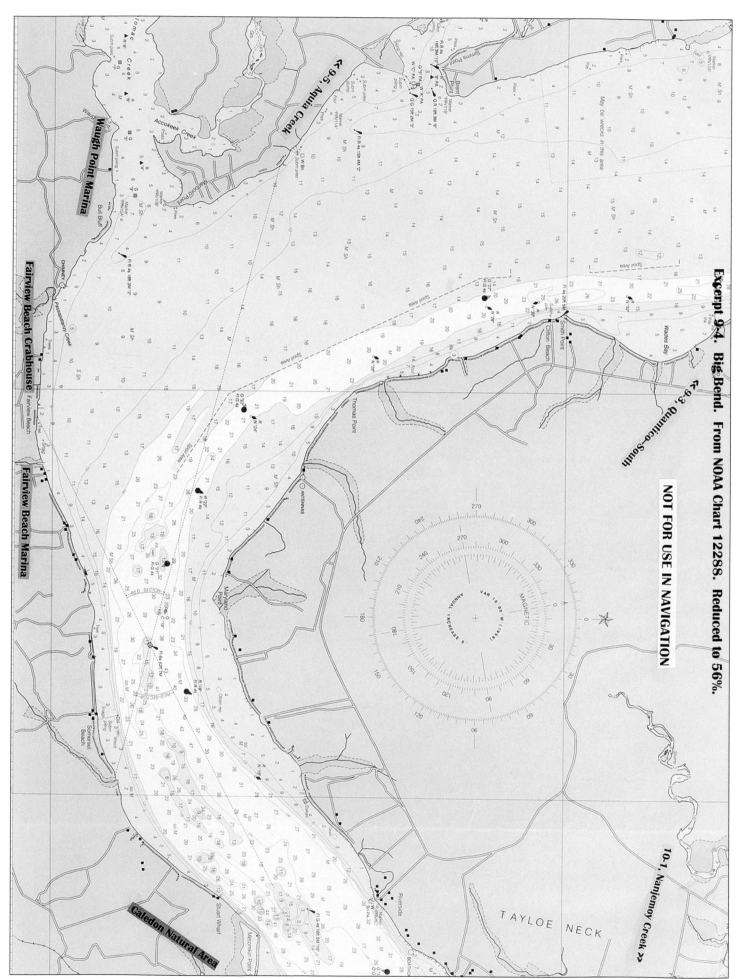

Excerpt 9.4. Big Bend. From NOAA Chart 12288. Reduced to 56%.

NOT FOR USE IN NAVIGATION

← 9-5; Aquia Creek

← 9-3; Quantico-South

10-1; Nanjemoy Creek ≫

Waugh Point Marina

Fairview Beach Crabhouse

Fairview Beach Marina

Caledon Natural Area

TAYLOE NECK

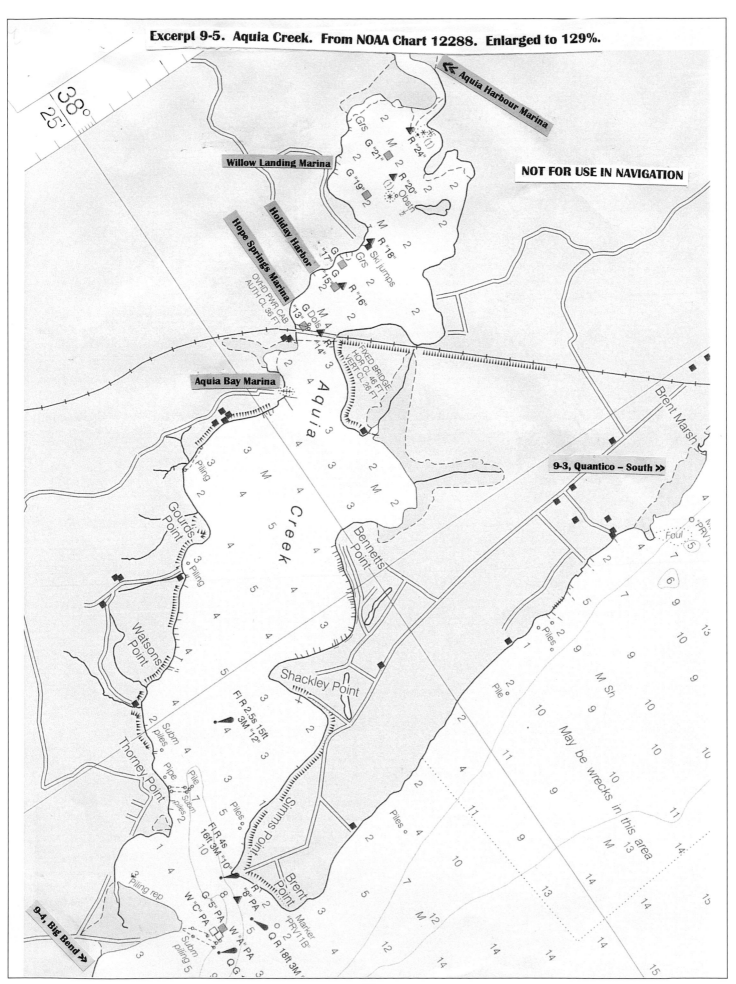

38°
25'

Aquia Harbour Marina

Willow Landing Marina

NOT FOR USE IN NAVIGATION

Holiday Harbor

Hope Springs Marina

OVHD PWR CAB
AUTH. CL. 36 FT

Aquia Bay Marina

Aquia Creek

Ski jumps

FIXED BRIDGE
HOR CL 46 FT
VERT CL 26 FT

9-3, Quantico – South »

Brent Marsh

Gourds Point

Bennetts Point

Watsons Point

Shackley Point

Foul

Thorney Point

FI R 2.5s 15ft
3M "12"

Simms Point

Brent Point

May be wrecks in this area

Piling rep

FI R 4s
16ft 3M "10"

Marker "PRV11B"

9-4, Big Bend »

W "C" PA

W "A" PA

G "5" PA

R "8" PA

Q R 16ft 3M

QG

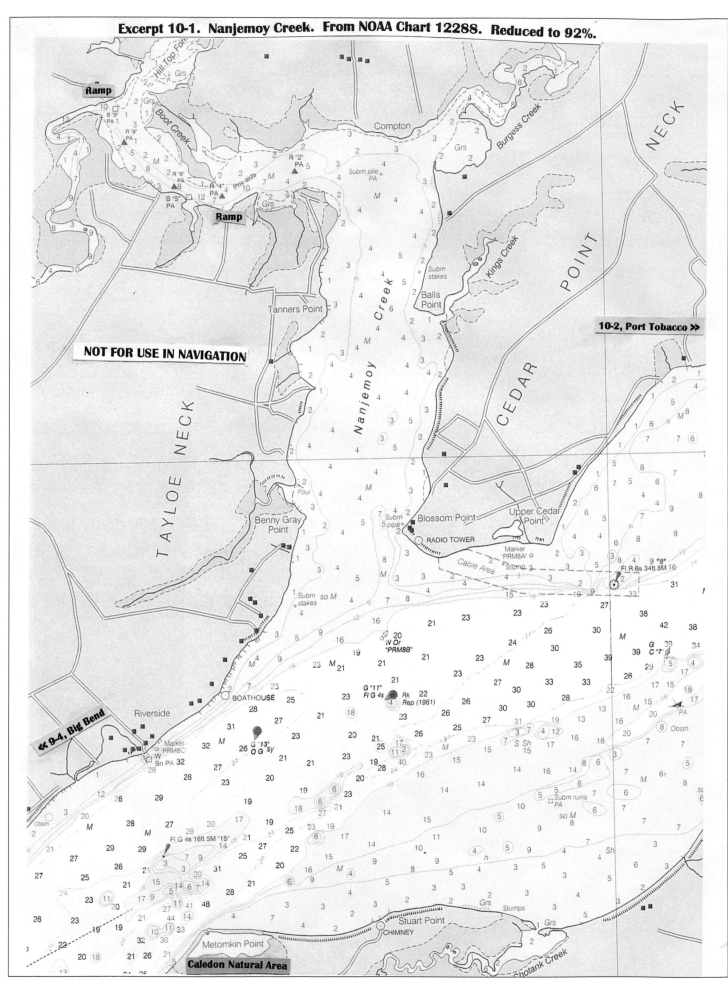

Ramp

Ramp

NOT FOR USE IN NAVIGATION

10-2, Port Tobacco »

« 9-4, Big Bend

Caledon Natural Area

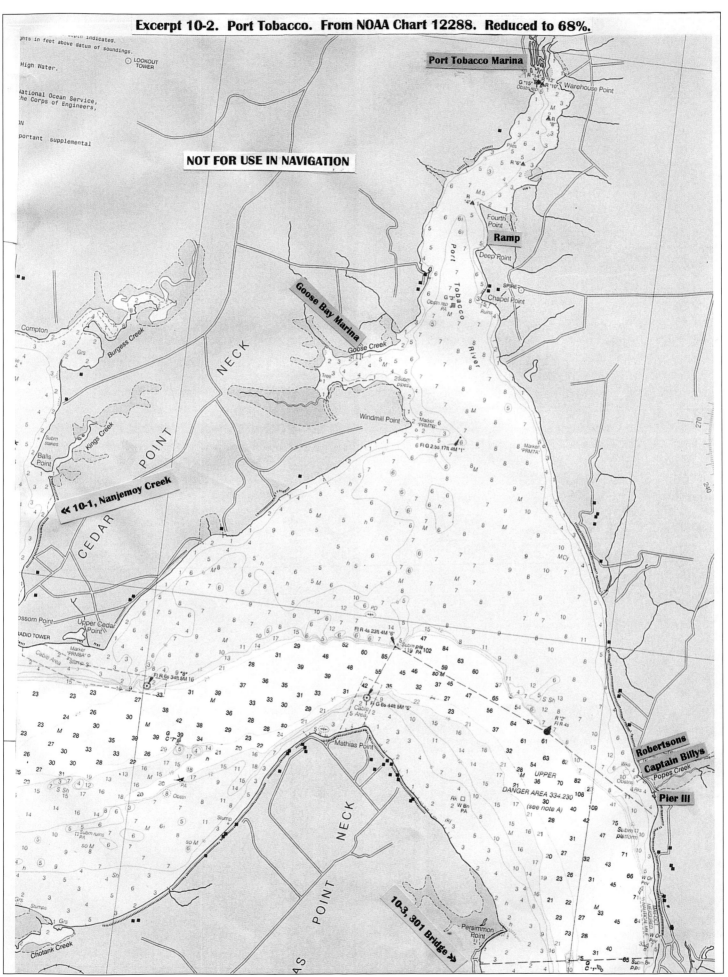

Excerpt 10-2. Port Tobacco. From NOAA Chart 12288. Reduced to 68%.

Port Tobacco Marina

Warehouse Point

NOT FOR USE IN NAVIGATION

Ramp

Goose Bay Marina

Goose Creek

Deep Point

Chapel Point

SPIRE

Windmill Point

◄◄ 10-1, Nanjemoy Creek

CEDAR POINT NECK

Compton

Burgess Creek

Kings Creek

Balls Point

Blossom Point

Upper Cedar Point

RADIO TOWER

Mathias Point

MATHIAS POINT NECK

Chotank Creek

UPPER DANGER AREA 334.230 (see note A)

Robertsons

Captain Billys

Popes Creek

Pier III

Persimmon Point

10-3, 301 Bridge ►►

39

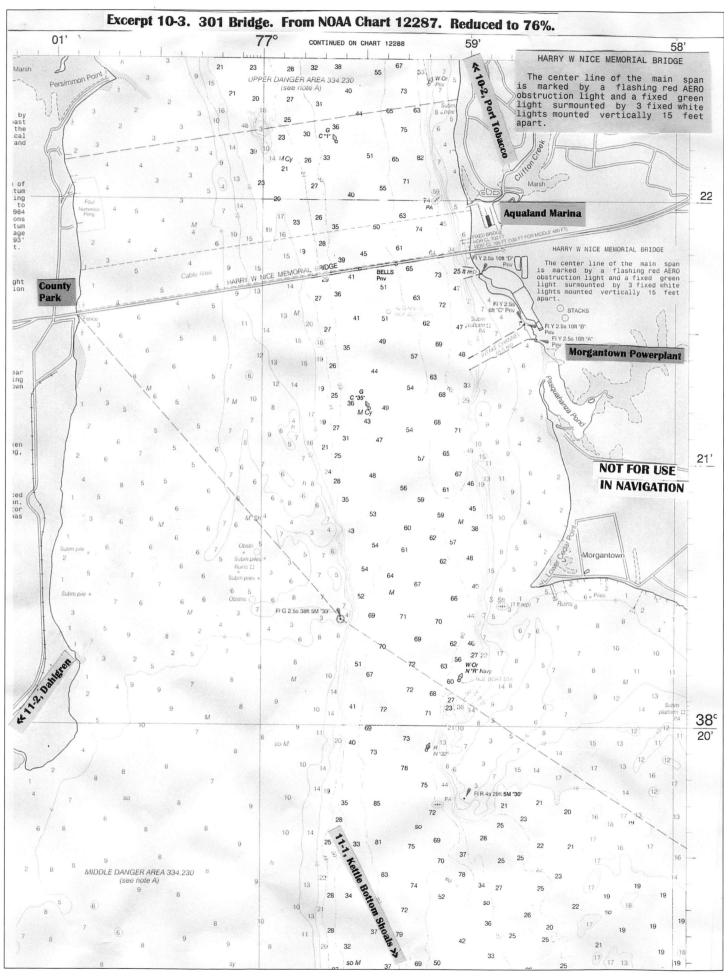

CONTINUED ON CHART 12288

HARRY W NICE MEMORIAL BRIDGE

The center line of the main span is marked by a flashing red AERO obstruction light and a fixed green light surmounted by 3 fixed white lights mounted vertically 15 feet apart.

UPPER DANGER AREA 334.230
(see note A)

Aqualand Marina

FIXED BRIDGE
HOR CL 700 FT
VERT CL 105 FT (135 FT FOR MIDDLE 480 FT)

HARRY W NICE MEMORIAL BRIDGE

The center line of the main span is marked by a flashing red AERO obstruction light and a fixed green light surmounted by 3 fixed white lights mounted vertically 15 feet apart.

County Park

HARRY W NICE MEMORIAL BRIDGE

Cable Area

BELLS
Priv

Morgantown Powerplant

NOT FOR USE
IN NAVIGATION

Morgantown

MIDDLE DANGER AREA 334.230
(see note A)

40

gear, in the orientation your boat will lie at anchor. Usually the orientation is not hard to figure out from cues in the area (e.g., other boats at anchor, the tidal flow, or wind direction). Don't hesitate to up the anchor and try again if you're not where you want to be. Remember, when you drop your anchor, you'll likely need a 360-degree swinging radius atop the anchor, especially when anchoring overnight.

More anchor rode (i.e., anchoring line) is better, limited to the size of your swinging radius. You don't want to swing into other boats or the shore when the tide or wind changes. At least a 7:1 (i.e., horizontal deployed line-to-anchoring depth) ratio is recommended for most conditions. For stormy conditions, a 10:1 ratio or even more scope is highly recommended.

The last 6 to 12 feet at the end of the anchor rode should be a piece of chain. The chain will weigh down the stock of your anchor, reducing the pull angle from three-dimensional space to a two-dimensional plane. A section of chain also provides an abrasion-resistant element on the bottom. Who knows what may be down there -- oyster shells, a rock, sharp discarded boat parts? Any anchoring or docking system is only as good as its weakest link (e.g., the anchor fluke's ability to hold, the strength of the chain-nylon anchor rode, the shackle connections in the rode, the boat's cleat, or the cleat's backing plate). The cleat backing plates on a few stock production vessels are substandard or even nonexistent.

Chapter 4
SAFETY, WELFARE, AND LEISURE

Safety Equipment and Vessel Management
Towboats
Boating Associations and Sailing Clubs
Sailing Schools
Swimming and Jellyfish
Phiesteria
Flying Critters
Fishing
Crabbing
Bird Watching

SAFETY EQUIPMENT AND VESSEL MANAGEMENT

The US Coast Guard has established minimum requirements for recreational vessels. These requirements are complex and change with the size of the vessel. Many Coast Guard requirements change as vessels go over 16 feet, 26 feet, and 40 feet. Generally, more is required on larger vessels. Furthermore, state jurisdictions may apply overlying requirements. Everyone aboard or waterskiing should have access to a class I, II, or III personal floating device (PFD) i.e., a life jacket. In Washington waters, if the vessel operator is under 18 years old, he or she and all aboard under 18 years old must WEAR their PFDs. In Maryland waters, all water skiers and personal water craft (PWC) operators must WEAR PFDs. In Virginia waters, PWC users and all under 16 years old must WEAR PFDs. Any vessel over 16 feet in length is also required to carry a throwable (i.e., class IV) life preserver.

The Coast Guard requires that visual distress signals (i.e., flares and smoke signals) to be carried at all times for vessels over 16 feet. Vessels under 16 feet are required to carry visual distress signals only at night. Visual distress signals have a expiration date stamped on them. The Coast Guard often fines vessel operators carrying outdated flare kits.

One USCG-approved fire extinguisher, type B-1, is required on vessels of less than 26 feet. Two fire extinguishers are required on vessels of 26 feet to 40 feet in length. Vessels over 40 feet in length are required to carry three B-1 fire extinguishers. In some instances, substituting a B-II fire extinguisher for a B-1 fire extinguisher can reduce the total complement of fire extinguishers required.

Vessels over 39.4 feet in length are required to carry both a whistle and a bell. Vessels less than 39.4 feet need only one sound-producing device.

Except on outboards, each gasoline engine carburetor is required to have a back-fire flame arrestor. Vessels built after 1980 need two ventilation ducts for the gas/engine/tank compartments, with some exceptions.

For night operations, your vessel is required to have functioning navigation lights. Minor cuts, abrasions, and burns periodically visit boaters so a GOOD FIRST AID KIT is almost a necessity. The Coast Guard Auxiliary often conducts courtesy inspections and can be very helpful in finding your vessel's deficiencies. As captain, I strongly believe in training your crew in as many aspects of vessel operations and nuances as possible. There are many sad examples of all perishing because the captain became incapacitated and nobody was capable to replace him or her.

The captain should be in charge and capable of making hard decisions (e.g., "The vessel is staying in port today"). That doesn't mean there is no consultation with competent crew members. I like to consult with crew, but, after weighing their input, I make the decision. Once a decision is made, sometimes it makes sense not to be intractable. If you made a bad decision, admit it and be willing to change your plans to rectify or improve the situation. Every day on the water you make many decisions and some are bound to be less than perfect. Less than ideal decisions don't need to be costly if you don't continue compounding one bad decision.

TOWBOATS

Four different Boat/US towboat operations work the Potomac. Two outfits have more than one boat. One company is solely devoted to towboat operations, and two other towing operations are an aside to marina activities. The more dutiful towboat operators monitor VHF 16 twenty-four hours a day. If somehow you can't reach a towboat, radio the Coast Guard Station Saint Inigoes on VHF 16. Saint Inigoes will relay the message to the nearest towboat operator.

Captain Bob Knight, (T 301 872-5144 (VHF Knight Life)) is based near Point Lookout in Smith Creek. Bob has two towboats, a 25-footer and a 42-footer. Living aboard his 42-footer, powered with twin 671 Detroit diesels, Bob monitors his VHF radio 24 hours a day. Most of Bob's tows are in the lower Potomac and the middle Chesapeake, but he has towed boats as far as Washington. Terry Hill (Potomac Marine) has a fleet of six towboats, ranging from 20 feet to 34 feet, in the upper Potomac. These six boats are located at various locations along the upper river -- Alexandria, Fort Washington, Neabsco Creek, and possibly Aquia Creek (late summer of 1998). Terry's phone number at Hampton's Landing Marina in Neabsco Creek is T (703) 221-4915. The two smaller, more marina-integrated Boat/US towers are situated in between Bob and Terry. Dennis Point Marina (T 301 994-2288) is in Carthagena Creek in the Saint Marys River, and Cather Marine (T 301-769-335) is based in Saint Patrick Creek near Saint Clements Island.

"Smith Point to the Rescue" (T 804 453-4551 or VHF 16) is a very commendable and volunteer organization assisting boaters in need. They operate a 30-foot Bertram from Smith Point Marina in the Little Wicomico River and two boats further south in the Great Wicomico River (i.e., Reedville VA). They'll assist distressed boaters around Smith Point and travel into the Potomac about as far as the Coan River. They might not be as flexible (as to where they can tow a vessel) or able to respond as quickly as one of the professional Boat/US towers.

The four Potomac River towboats are affiliated with the Boat/US's towboat insurance program. This is an excellent program, and it is recommended that you enroll in it. If you are in the program and your towed cost is within your coverage limits, all you have to do is sign and exchange some paperwork with the towboat operator who is a professional captain. If you're not in the Boat/US program, you may be required to pay heavily after a tow. You may or may not be able to get a reimbursement, depending on your boating insurance coverage. For more information on the Boat/US towboat program call T (703) 461-2866.

Never hail a Mayday if your boat is grounded, out of fuel, has an engine failure, or is in a similar non-life-threatening situation. Please reserve the Mayday calls for immediate life-threatening situations (a boat on fire, unrecovered man overboard, life-threatening injury, or an imminent sinking). If it is a non-life-threatening situation, call a towboat and wait patiently. It's usually not too long before a professional towboat captain arrives. It is a good habit to monitor VHF 16 and be ready to offer assistance, if ever needed, to a distressed vessel needing immediate Mayday help. If the professionals (i.e., towboat captains or

Coast Guard personnel) arrive in a timely manner, let them provide the assistance. However, you can still be a very helpful player on a distress scene, by locating the craft, describing the circumstances to the Coast Guard, or by offering assistance when time is of the essence.

BOATING ASSOCIATIONS AND SAILING CLUBS

There are many boating associations and clubs on the Potomac. Every year, new ones form and old ones abandon. A few of the larger and some smaller marinas are exclusively yacht clubs (e.g., Capital Yacht Club, Old Dominion Yacht Club, Mount Vernon Yacht Club, Corinthian Yacht Club, and Dahlgren Yacht Club, and several more). You cannot be a slipholder at those marinas unless you are a member of the club. However, some of these marina-yacht clubs allow transients to use their facility. Some marinas host yacht club(s) as a large part of their marina operation but do not limit marina use to yacht club membership (e.g., Tantallon Yacht Club, National Potomac Yacht Club at Colombia Island Marina, as well as others). If there are both a marina and a yacht club on the premises, many times it's confounding to pigeonhole the relationship between the two.

Washington Sailing Marina, just south of National Airport, hosts several boating organizations. The Sailing Club of Washington (SCOW), (T 202 628-7245), with many activities, is one of the more active sailing clubs around Washington and has five boats for their members -- three Flying Scots, a Yankee Dolphin, and a 25-foot Catalina -- harbored at Washington Sailing Marina. During the boating season, SCOW has social sails every Thursday evening at the marina. The Potomac River Sailing Association (PRSA) is also hosted at Washington Sailing Marina. PRSA promotes racing and has a fleet of Albacores, Lightnings, Hobie Cats, and other one-design boats that race on the Potomac and beyond. For the Washington Sailing Club, also hosted at Washington Sailing Marina, you need your own boat. The Daingerfield Island Cruising Fleet is another club hosted at Washington Sailing Marina and uses boats over 20-feet. The National Yacht Club, also at Washington Sailing Marina, is oriented to such as children's regattas. Other groups meeting at Washington Sailing Marina include the Georgetown University Rowing and Sailing Team and the Saint George's Episcopal Sea Scouts.

There are powerboating and sailing organizations along the river, including a few smaller ones on the lower river (e.g., Potomac Yacht Club and X-Priates). Many boat models also have their own regional organizations. The Potomac River Yacht Club ASSOCIATION (PRYCA) has been around for 27 years and comprises 19 Potomac River yacht clubs. The PRYCA encourages boating safety and the advancement of yachting clubs on the Potomac. The National Potomac Yacht Club, based at Colombia Island Marina, has been in existence for 33 years.

SAILING SCHOOLS

There are three sailing schools on the Potomac. In the Washington area, the Mariner Sailing School at Belle Haven Marina offers a low student-to-instructor ratio aboard 14-foot Sunfish and 19-foot Flying Scots and a cruising course on one C&C 34-footer. Belle Haven's phone number is T 703-768-0018. Washington Sailing Marina also has a sailing school. It has some Hobie Cats, several 14-foot Sunfish, five 19-foot Flying Scots, and a Catalina 25-footer. The school's phone number is T 703 548-9027. Quantico Marina (T 703 784-2359), about 25 miles downriver, has a sailing school that employs three 14-footers and two 19-footers. Their primary "adult class" takes two full weekends.

SWIMMING AND JELLYFISH

During the summer, swimming and cooling off in the lower Potomac would be great if it weren't for jellyfish. These primitive invertebrates, colloquially called nettles, have been around for more than 400 million years. They exist everywhere on the globe and there are numerous varieties. Some, such as those found off Australia, can be deadly. There are several varieties in the Potomac. None are deadly; most are aggravating. The larger varieties with "more drippy" tentacles are worse. Once they beach themselves, they quickly die, and most people can safely handle them without itchy repercussions.

Jellyfish may arrive en masse in the Potomac as early as late spring or as late as early July. Their arrival time depends mostly on the salinity of the water which depends mostly on spring rains. They cannot tolerate the fresher Potomac waters, and you'll see very few jellyfish north of Fairview Beach. They grow larger and potentially become more painful as the summer progresses.

I usually don't allow jellyfish to disrupt my summer swimming plans, but I sometimes get nailed. Meat tenderizer, baking soda, diluted ammonia, vinegar, alcohol, or lemon juice can ease the itchy stings. For most people, an untreated sting quickly mellows to a reddish itch, which soon dissipates completely. Unless you are allergic, there is no need to panic if a jellyfish brushes you while swimming.

Jellyfish drift at the mercy of the tidal currents. In the lower reaches, they seem to be greater in number at the head of small bays and creeks than in the middle of the river. Hence, if I want to swim during hot August with a lower probability of being nailed by jellyfish, I take the boat to the middle of the Potomac, drift a while (if it's not too windy or choppy), look in the water until I observe few or no jellyfish, and then jump overboard for that refreshing jellyfish-free swim.

If you are in the water swimming near your drifting or anchored boat, etiquette is to hoist a "diver down" flag, alerting other boaters of people in the water.

PFIESTERIA

Pfiesteria is a one-celled microorganism that can become lethal to fish, usually attacking menhaden. The pfiesteria microorganism goes through several different life stages. In a few stages, of its many-faceted life, it is toxic and creates ugly lesions that eventually kills fish. Pfiesteria's effects on humans are not fully known. A few watermen working in pfiesteria-infected waters on the Eastern Shore have complained of various ill effects.

In 1997, pfiesteria was found in a couple of rivers on the eastern shore of the Chesapeake Bay, but no outbreaks of pfiesteria were recorded in the Potomac. The eastern shore rivers and estuaries are notably saltier than the Potomac and other western shore rivers of the Chesapeake. Some people are pointing a finger at high levels of nutrients in the water, making it very conducive for pfiesteria outbreaks.

A high-nutrient loading in the water has negative effects in other ways. Once washed into the bay or river, these nutrients encourage tremendous growth of algae. The algae, being relatively heavy, settle near the bottom of bays and rivers. Most fish can swim over the settling algae to clearer water. However, the immobile oysters and, to a lesser extent, crabs, cannot. The algae consume much of the oxygen and minerals that these bottom dwellers need for life. Heavy nutrient loads mostly come from over-fertilized farm runoff. The chicken and vegetable farmers on the eastern shore may be indirectly contributing to the demise of Bay oysters and crabs, the lifeblood of watermen.

45

FLYING CRITTERS

In the summer months, flies, mosquitos, and small gnats can be a nuisance on windless days and nights on the river. In most Potomac River localities, mosquitos are seldom encountered in large numbers. There are very few mosquitos in Washington Channel or nearby. Besides only female mosquitos bite. North American mosquitos are most active during dusk and dawn. If you are boating to other parts of the river, fitted mosquito netting, around hatches and companionways will generally keep them out of the boat. It is easy to make custom-fitted mosquito netting using glue and Velcro strips for the hatches you wish to remain open during the night.

If you leave your boat unoccupied for any length of time during the late spring and summer months, you may discover mud daubers, hornets, and wasps starting nests when you return. This can create a dicey situation. Find their nest and spay it with a can of flying insect spray. You need to be a dead-eye shot with that spray; otherwise a second-place finish means a painful sting.

Smaller gnats or no-see-ums can be a minor irritation at times. Again they seem to be localized. Some places along the river may have none while other areas might have a few. Many of these smaller critters can pass through mosquito netting. Insect repellent containing DEET (N,N-diethyl meta-toluamide) will keep them off. However, don't apply concentrations of DEET greater than 35 percent on adults. A concentration of 6-10 percent is recommended for children. Many of these smaller insects are most active at dusk.

During the daytime, there are biting flies or tabanids. Biting flies generally breed in wet areas and are active during the summer and early fall months in our area. They include horseflies, deerflies and another vicious little critter masquerading as a simple house fly until it bites. You shouldn't encounter any horseflies, but deerflies and those vicious little flies can sometimes be prevalent on the Potomac on non-windy days. Like mosquitos, only female fly bites. The housefly-looking critter is much more rampant on the eastern shore of the Bay than on the Potomac. DEET insect repellant will dissuade them. If you don't want to apply DEET, you can seek retribution with the ol' flyswatter and make a game of it by challenging your hand-eye coordination skills. I recall, cruising the lower eastern shore for a few windless days with one hand on the tiller and the other on the flyswatter for the better part of the day. At the end of the day, the cockpit was strewn with dead bloody flies. The fly-biting activity ceases as the sun dips below the horizon. Despite these past encounters as well as the threat of future frays, I still often have a great night's sleep lying in the open cockpit, watching the Milky Way whirl across the night sky while the boat gently swings at anchor. Then, in the morning...buzzzzzzzz.

FISHING

Potomac River fish aren't as overflowing as in the days of Captain John Smith, but they are still plentiful. In the saltier lower reaches, you will find rockfish (striped bass or rock), bluefish, sea trout (weakfish), summer flounder, spanish mackerel, white perch, croaker, norfolk spot, channel bass, black sea bass, and black drum. In Saint Marys County MD, about a dozen and a half fishing charter boats and headboats operate in the lower Potomac.

You will also see eel traps in the lower Potomac. The largest eel-processing plant in the United States is in Nomini Creek, near Montross VA. Eels are not popular on American plates, so they are packed and exported to Europe and Japan. Eels are fish, not snakes, born in the Sargasso Sea (i.e., in the southern North Atlantic Ocean). As juveniles, eels travel up the Potomac, and then return to the Sargasso Sea to spawn as adults. Commercially, eels are caught in baited cages, called "pots." Eel pots are cylindrical whereas crab pots are cubical.

In the fresher waters north of the US Route 301 bridge, you will find largemouth bass, perch, and catfish. Even in Washington you can find catfish, carp, and rockfish. A 36-pound catfish was landed near Fort Washington in 1996. Landing a 20-pound-plus catfish is not that uncommon.

Fishing on the Potomac is regulated by four jurisdictions. Each of the jurisdictions has the authority to enforce rules dealing with seasons, size limits, creel limits, and licensing. When you are fishing, it is important to know which jurisdiction you are in. If you are fishing north of the Woodrow Wilson Bridge, you are in the District of Columbia's jurisdiction and need a District fishing license. The Virginia tributaries are under the jurisdiction of Virginia. The Maryland tributaries are under the jurisdiction of Maryland. The vast middle part of the river is under a Potomac River Fisheries Commission, a two-state commission. The commission does a good job in placing daymarks at the mouths of tributaries on both sides of the river between their boundary and the individual state jurisdictions. These daymarks are white with an orange border and have black lettering, reading something like "PRM7A" or "PRV2B." The "M" or "V" will indicate the state border and the integer will indicate the ascending-numbered tributary.

Generally, if you are fishing from a boat, south of the Wilson Bridge, you need either a Potomac River Sport Fishing license, a Virginia Saltwater Recreational license, or a Maryland Tidal Sport fishing license. The Potomac River Sport Fishing license gives you the widest coverage. You can call the Potomac River Fisheries Commission in Colonial Beach VA at ☏ (800) 266-3904 or ☏ (804) 224-7148. For Virginia licensing information, call ☏ (804) 247-2200 (for below the Route 301 bridge) or ☏ (804) 367-1000 (for above the Route 301 bridge). For Maryland licensing information, call ☏ (800) 688-FINS.

CRABBING

The crabbing season in the Potomac runs from April 1 to November 30. The minimum size for taking a hard crab is five inches, point-to-point (i.e., across the width of shell) and for a soft-shelled crab (i.e., one that has just molted) three and a half inches. The laws concerning recreational crabbing are somewhat convoluted and should be thoroughly understood before crabbing in a particular area. Generally, recreational crabbers can crab 24 hours a day using baited handlines and dipnets. Recreational crabbers can also crab from boats from 5:30 AM until sunset. There are a few restrictions for crabbing off docks, piers, and shorelines. These restrictions limit the number of traps a recreational crabber can employ. Recreational crabbers can also use trotlines and collapsible hand traps, but there are few other crabbing restrictions. Trotlining in Maryland, you can keep a bushel of "legal" crabs per day but not more than two bushels per boat. You should release any egg-bearing female crabs recognizable by an orange-brown sponge-mass of eggs. Female crabs also have an underside shelled apron resembling the shape of the US Capitol Dome. The underside apron on male crabs resembles the shape of the Washington Monument. It is a criminal offense to tamper with commercial crab pots.

BIRD WATCHING

If you spend any time on the River, besides seeing cormorants, you'll see blue and green herons, osprey, hawks, and bald eagles. A small green heron regularly perches on one of my dock lines at the Capital Yacht Club in Southwest Washington. Blue herons are plentiful and found everywhere on the River. Osprey are migratory birds traveling as far as South America during the winter and returning to the Potomac each March. These fish-eating birds build their nests near water and many times right atop navigational daymarks. Woody osprey nests sometimes occlude lighted daymarks, and the osprey will squawk loudly at you if you come too close to "their" daymark.

Each weekend I took my sailboat out on the lower Potomac last year, I saw at least one bald eagle. Various species of ducks abound on the river. In the mid-spring, mallard duck hatchlings follow their mother around, sometimes disrupting marina activities. In the water, small duck hatchlings are extremely vulnerable to being eaten from beneath by large fish. Canada geese are prevalent, especially in the wintertime.

Chapter 5
PREAMBLE TO BOATING SUPPLIES AND SERVICES ALONG THE POTOMAC

This reference chapter presents lists of (1) boating facilities, (2) restaurants, (3) gasoline locations, (4) diesel locations, (5) some hardware stores, (6) some grocery stores, (7) some lodging, (8) haul-out facilities, and (9) small boat launching ramps. These nine lists are organized in four columns. The left two columns refer to the Virginia shore and the right two columns refer to the Maryland or Washington shore. The lists are further ordered from upriver to downriver along that particular shore. The first and third columns refer to the NOAA chart excerpt containing the specific facility. You can look at the appropriate NOAA chart excerpt and usually pinpoint a specific facility's location along the river. The first number of the NOAA chart excerpt is usually the chapter that covers the details on that facility.

The boating facilities listed all have wet slips and are primarily marinas. However, a couple of campgrounds with wet slips fall in this category. Marinas that are Boat/US cooperating marinas are noted. There are many restaurants along the river. Some are connected to marinas and others are not. Some areas have several restaurants (e.g., Central Colonial Beach has eight) and are so indicated by a note. Please read the appropriate chapter for a better evaluation of the particular restaurants or restaurant areas. The gasoline and diesel locations are also listed from upriver to downriver. Not all marinas have gasoline, and even fewer marinas carry diesel fuel. There are a few other nonmarina facilities which are accessible to boaters that do carry gasoline or diesel fuel.

The next three lists present hardware stores, grocery stores, and lodging close to the Potomac. This list is not exhaustive, and "close" is a relative term, and there may be other like facilities in the area. The name of the town or city follows the establishment in parentheses.

The next list contains 50 haul-out yards. Again, most are marinas previously mentioned but there are many marinas with no capability to haul vessels. There are a few other facilities, which are not marinas, that can haul vessels. These facilities are incorporated onto this list. On the Potomac, haul-out facilities can "pull" vessels in at least one of six ways, using (1) open-end marine travel lifts, 2) closed-end marine travel lifts, (3) marine railways (see picture), (4) forklift trucks, (5) large hydraulic trailers, or (6) cranes. The appropriateness of the particular "hauling method" is lightly addressed in a section prior to the list. Every haul-out facility is supplemented with no less than one footnote characterizing its method(s) of hauling vessels. For more information on a haul-out facility and the haul-out yard, please read the appropriate sections in the relevant chapters, or telephone the particular facility.

Eighty-six launching ramps were counted on the Potomac. Many are at marinas, but again many marinas have no launching ramps. There are also many unattended boat-launching sites on the Potomac and they are included on this list as well as on the appropriate NOAA chart excerpts. A handful of launching ramps are private and are thus indicated with a footnote. Even some launching ramps at marinas have restrictions. Like all the other lists in this chapter, the launching ramps go from upriver to downriver along the appropriate shoreline. For more information addressing the nuances of a particular launching ramp, please read the appropriate chapter.

BOATING FACILITIES WITH WET SLIPS (MOSTLY MARINAS)

VIRGINIA SIDE

Location [1]

6-1	Columbia Island Marina [2]
7-1	Washington Sailing Marina [2]
7-1	Alexandria City Marina
7-1	Old Dominion Yacht Club
8-1	Belle Haven Marina [2]
8-3	Mount Vernon Yacht Club
8-3	Fort Belvoir Marina
9-1	Fairfax Yacht Club
9-1	Captain Johns Beach Marina
9-1	Occoquan Harbour Marina
9-1	Hoffmasters Marina
9-1	Prince William Yacht Sales
9-1	Tyme n' Tyde Boatel
9-1	E-Z Cruz Marina
9-1	Pilot House Marina
9-1	Hampton's Landing Marina [2]
9-3	Quantico Marina
9-5	Aquia Bay Marina
9-5	Hope Springs Marina [2]
9-5	Holiday Harbor RV Park & Marina
9-5	Willow Landing Marina
9-5	Aquia Harbour Marina
9-4	Waugh Point Marina
9-4	Fairview Beach Marina
11-2	Dahlgren Yacht Club
11-2	Dahlgren Marine Works
11-4	Colonial Beach Yacht Center
11-4	Parker's Marina
11-4	Stanford's Marine Railway
11-4	Winkiedoodle Marina
11-4	Monroe Bay Yacht Club
11-4	Hop's Marine
11-4	Nightingale's Marina
11-3	Stepp's HarborView Marina
11-8	Branson Cove Marina
11-8	North Point Marine
11-8	Lower Machodoc Marina
11-8	Coles Point Plantation
15-1	Sandy Point Marina
15-1	White Point Marina
15-1	Port Kinsale Marina [2]
15-1	Kinsale Harbour Yacht Club
15-1	Krentz's Marina (Yeocomico)
15-1	Olverson's Marina [2]
15-2	Lewisetta Marina
15-2	Coan River Marina
15-3	Smith Point Marina
15-3	Leroy's Marina
15-3	Smith Island KOA Campground and Marina
15-3	Krentz's Marine Railway (Little Wicomico)
15-3	Cockrell's Marine Railway

MARYLAND (WASHINGTON) SIDE

Location [1]

6-1	Washington Marina Company
6-1	Capital Yacht Club
6-1	Gangplank Marina
6-1	James Creek Marina
6-1	Buzzard Point Marina
6-2	Eastern Powerboat Club
6-2	District Yacht Club
6-2	Washington Yacht Club
6-2	Anacostia Marina
6-2	Seafarers Yacht Club
6-1	Anacostia Naval Station Marina
7-1	Bolling AF Base Marina
8-2	Tantallon Marina
8-2	Fort Washington Marina
9-2	Sweden Point Marina
10-2	Goose Bay Marina
10-2	Port Tobacco Marina
10-3	Aqualand Marina
12-1	Yacht Club at Swan Point
12-2	Saunder's Marina
12-2	Shymansky's Marina
12-2	Cobb Island Marina
12-2	Captain John's Marina
12-3	Cather Marina
12-3	Kopel's Marina
12-4	Fitzies
12-4	Combs Creek Marina
12-5	Tall Timbers Marina
12-5	Cedar Cover Marina
13-2	Sea Fruit
12-5	Curley's Marina
13-3	Dennis Point Marina [2]
14-1	Point Lookout Marina
14-1	Corinthian Yacht Club
14-1	Phil's Marina
14-1	Seaside View Campground

---

[1] The location is the NOAA chart excerpt. With few exceptions, the first number of the excerpt is also the chapter number referencing that facility.

[2] Denotes a Boat/US-Cooperating Marina. Some services are discounted to Boat/US members. For more information on this program phone ᴛ 888 333-BOAT.

RESTAURANTS AND CAFES NEAR THE POTOMAC

VIRGINIA SIDE		MARYLAND (WASHINGTON) SIDE	
Location [1]		Location [1]	
6-1	Colombia Island Marina Cafe	6-2	Washington Harbour [2]
7-1	Potowmack Landing	6-1	Le Rivage
7-1	After Deck Cafe	6-1	Phillips Flagship
7-1	Old Town Alexandria [2]	6-1	Hogates
8-3	Mount Vernon Inn	6-1	H.I. Ribsters
9-1	Geckos	6-1	Pier 7
9-1	Old Town Occoquan [2]	6-1	L'Enfant Plaza Delis [2]
9-1	Pilot House Restaurant	6-1	Waterfront Metro [2]
9-2	Tim's RiverShore	7-1	Slip Inn Cafe (Bolling)
9-3	Quantico [2]	8-2	Galley Cafe
9-4	Fairview Beach Crabhouse	10-2	Turf Club Restaurants
11-2	Dahlgren [2]	10-2	Robertson's Crab House
11-3	Wilkerson's	10-2	Capt. Billy's Crab House
11-3	Happy Clam	10-2	Pier III Crab House
11-4	Dockside	10-3	Aqualand Truck Stop
11-4	Parker's	12-2	Shymansky's
11-4	Monroe Bay Landing	12-2	Captain John's
11-3	Central Colonial Beach [2]	12-1	Quade's Country Store
11-6	Mount Holly Steamboat Inn	12-3	Frank Morris Carryout
11-8	Driftwood II	12-4	Fitzies
11-8	Pilot's Wharf Restaurant	12-4	Harbor View Inn
15-1	Moorings	12-5	Reluctant Navigator
		12-5	Cedar Cove
		12-5	Oakwood Lodge
		13-2	Evan's
		13-3	Still Anchors
		14-1	Courtney's
		14-1	Scheible's
		14-1	Spinnaker's

---

[1] The location is the NOAA chart excerpt. With few exceptions, the first number of the excerpt is also the chapter number referencing that facility.

[2] More than one restaurant in this area.

GASOLINE LOCATIONS

Location [1]

6-1	Columbia Island Marina	6-1	James Creek Marina
8-3	Mount Vernon Yacht Club	7-1	Bolling AFB Marina
9-1	Captain Johns Beach Marina	8-2	Fort Washington Marina
9-1	Occoquan Harbour Marina	9-2	Sweden Point Marina
9-1	Hoffmasters Marina	10-2	Goose Bay Marina
9-1	Prince William Yacht Sales	10-2	Port Tobacco Marina
9-1	Tyme n' Tyde Boatel	10-3	Aqualand Marina
9-1	E-Z Cruz Marina	12-2	Captain John's Marina
9-1	Pilot House Marina	12-2	Shymansky's Marina
9-1	Hampton's Landing Marina	12-1	Quade's Store
9-3	Quantico Marina	12-3	Cather Marina
9-5	Aquia Bay Marina	12-3	Kopel's Marina
9-5	Hope Springs Marina	12-3	Frank Morris Carryout
9-5	Willow Landing Marina	12-4	Fitzies
9-5	Aquia Harbour Marina	12-5	Tall Timbers Marina
9-4	Waugh Point Marina	12-5	Cedar Cover Marina
9-4	Fairview Beach Marina	13-1	Swann's General Store
11-2	Dahlgren Marine Works	13-3	Dennis Point Marina
11-4	Colonial Beach Yacht Center	14-1	Scheible's Fishing Center
11-4	Hop's Marine	14-1	Point Lookout Marina
11-3	Stepp's HarborView Marina	14-2	Point Lookout State Park
11-5	Westmoreland State Park		
11-8	Branson Cove Marina		
11-8	Coles Point Plantation		
15-1	Sandy Point Marina		
15-1	White Point Marina		
15-1	Port Kinsale Marina		
15-1	Kinsale Harbour Yacht Club		
15-1	Olverson's Marina		
15-2	Lewisetta Marina		
15-2	Coan River Marina		
15-3	Smith Point Marina		

DIESEL LOCATIONS

Location [1]

9-1	Occoquan Harbour Marina	6-1	James Creek Marina
9-1	Prince William Yacht Sales	8-2	Fort Washington Marina
9-1	Pilot House Marina	10-3	Aqualand Marina
11-2	Dahlgren Marine Works	12-2	Shymansky's Marina
11-4	Colonial Beach Yacht Center	12-3	Kopel's Marina
11-8	Branson Cove Marina	12-4	Tall Timbers Marina
11-8	Coles Point Plantation	13-3	Dennis Point Marina
15-1	Sandy Point Marina	14-1	Scheible's Fishing Center
15-1	White Point Marina	14-2	Point Lookout Marina
15-1	Kinsale Harbour Yacht Club		
15-1	Port Kinsale Marina		
15-1	Olverson's Marina		
15-2	Lewisetta Marina		
15-2	Coan River Marina		
15-3	Smith Point Marina		

---

[1] The location is the NOAA chart excerpt. With few exceptions, the first number of the excerpt is also the chapter number referencing that facility.

VIRGINIA SIDE	MARYLAND (WASHINGTON) SIDE
FACILITY (LOCATION)	FACILITY (LOCATION)

BOATING HARDWARE AND NONMARINA BOAT STORES

Boat/US (Alexandria)	Washington Marina Company (SW Wash.)
Fischer's Hardware (Springfield)	Frager's Hardware (SE Washington)
West Marine (Alexandria)	Boater's World (Waldorf)
Backyard Boats (Alexandria)	Mattingly's Hardware (Leonardtown)
West Marine (Woodbridge)	Loffler Marine (Lexington Park)
Rankin's Hardware (Colonial Beach)	Dyson's Building Supply (Great Mills)
Jett's Hardware (Reedville)	Dyson's Building Supply (St. Inigoes)
	True Value Hardware (Ridge)

LARGER GROCERS NEAR THE POTOMAC

Safeway (Old Town Alexandria)	KOC Deli (L'Enfant Plaza -- SW Wash.)
Food Lion (Colonial Beach)	Safeway (SW Waterfront)
	Grocery (Cobb Island)
	Food Lion (Leonardtown)
	Swann's (Saint George Creek)
	Raley's (Ridge)

LODGING NEAR THE POTOMAC

Best Western (Alexandria)	Channel Inn Hotel (SW Washington)
Holiday Inn (Alexandria)	Loew's L'Enfant Plaza Hotel (SW Wash.)
Nightingale's (Colonial Beach)	Holiday Inn (SW Washington)
Days Inn (Colonial Beach)	Relax Inn (Leonardtown)
Wakefield Motel (Colonial Beach)	Swann's (Piney Point)
Potomac Inn (Colonial Beach)	Oakwood Lodge (Piney Point)
Westmoreland Motel (Colonial Beach)	Scheible's Fishing Center (Ridge)
Doc's Motor Court (Colonial Beach)	

HAUL-OUT FACILITIES

There are about 50 locations on the Potomac where large vessels can be hauled out of the water for emergency or routine maintenance. By the method of hauling-out, these facilities can be grouped into six categories: (1) open-end travel lifts, (2) closed-end travel lifts, (3) marine railways, (4) forklifts, (5) hydraulic trailers, and (6) cranes. Some of the larger facilities have more than one method to haul a vessel. Marine railways are mostly used to haul heavier wooden boats. A carriage on rails goes into the water, and the floating boat nuzzles onto the carriage. The carriage and vessel are pulled on rails out of the water. The open-end travel lift is most preferred for fiberglass sailboats. In the travel lift bay, the open-end lift can surround the sailboat and its mast(s). Heavy-duty sling webbing is strung beneath the vessel before hoisting it out of the water. A closed-end lift is similar, except structural beams on BOTH the front and back of the lift connect to the sides of the lift. Hence, a sailboat's tall mast usually cannot fit underneath a closed-end lift. Closed-end lifts, as well as open-end lifts, are good for fiberglass powerboats. A few closed-end lifts can handle modest-size sailboats with the mast remaining unstepped (i.e., not removed). Some closed-end lifts are pulled by a separate unit, usually the marina tractor. Large hydraulic trailers are pulled by a heavy-duty marina vehicle. A good long sloping ramp in the marina is also required for hydraulic trailers. Forklifts are seen in a few marinas and are best suited for large BOATELS that handle up-to-modest-size powerboats.

HAUL-OUT FACILITIES

---

[1] With a few exceptions, the first number of the excerpt is also the chapter number referencing that facility.
[2] Travel Lift -- open-end.
[3] Travel Lift -- closed-end.
[4] Marine Railway.
[5] Forklift.
[6] A crane visits the marina twice a year.
[7] A large hydraulic trailer is used to haul powerboats.

SMALL BOAT LAUNCHING RAMPS

<u>VIRGINIA SIDE</u>

Location

6-1	Columbia Island Marina
6-1	Gravelly Point Ramp
7-1	Washington Sailing Marina
8-1	Belle Haven Marina
8-3	Marina House Yacht Club [2]
8-3	Mount Vernon Yacht Club
8-3	Fort Belvoir Marina
8-3	Pohick Bay Park Ramps
9-1	Captain Johns Beach Marina [2]
9-1	Occoquan Harbour Marina
9-1	Hoffmasters Marina
9-1	Prince William Yacht Sales
9-1	Occoquan Regional Park
9-1	E-Z Cruz Marina
9-1	Pilot House Marina
9-1	Hampton's Landing Marina
9-2	Leesylvania State Park Ramp
9-5	Aquia Bay Marina [2]
9-5	Hope Springs Marina
9-5	Willow Landing Marina
9-5	Aquia Harbour Marina
9-5	Waugh Point Marina
9-5	Fairview Beach Marina
11-2	Dahlgren Yacht Club
11-2	Dahlgren Marine Works
11-4	Colonial Beach Yacht Center
11-4	Gum Bar Point Ramp
11-4	Monroe Bay Campground Ramp
11-4	Westmoreland Shores Ramp [2]
11-3	Stepp's HarborView Marina
11-5	Westmoreland State Park
11-6	Currioman Landing Ramp
11-6	Robberecht's Packing House
11-8	Branson Cove Marina
11-8	Lower Machodoc Marina
11-8	Glebe Creek Ramp [2]
11-8	Coles Point Plantation
11-8	Bonum Creek Ramp
15-1	Shannon Park Ramp [2]
15-1	Sandy Point Marina
15-1	Port Kinsale Marina
15-1	Kinsale Harbour Yacht Club
15-1	Olverson's Marina
15-1	Lodge Landing Ramp
15-2	Lewisetta Marina
15-2	Coan River Marina
15-2	Forrest Landing Ramp
15-2	Rowe's Landing Ramp
15-3	Smith Point Marina
15-3	Smith Island KOA Campground and Marina
15-3	Cockrell's Marine Railway Ramp

<u>MARYLAND (WASHINGTON) SIDE</u>

Location

6-2	Anacostia Park Ramp
6-1	Buzzard Point Marina [1]
7-1	Bolling AFB Marina
8-2	Fort Washington Marina
8-2	Calvert Manor Ramp [2]
8-2	Farmington Landing Ramp
8-3	Marshall Hall Ramp
9-2	Sweden Point Marina
9-2	E F Mattingly Park Ramp
10-1	Tayloe Landing Ramp
10-1	Friendship Landing Ramp
10-2	Goose Bay Marina
10-2	Port Tobacco Marina
10-2	Chapel Pt State Park Ramp
10-3	Aqualand Marina
12-1	Yacht Club at Swan Point [2]
12-2	Saunder's Marina
12-2	Shymansky's Marina
12-2	Captain John's Marina
12-1	Bushwood Wharf Ramp
12-1	Chaptico Wharf Landing
12-1	Wicomico Shores Park Ramp
12-3	Whites Neck Creek Area
12-3	Cather Marina
12-3	Kopel's Marina
12-4	Combs Creek Marina
12-4	Leonardtown Ramp
12-5	Tall Timbers Marina
12-5	Cedar Cover Marina
13-2	Saint George Creek Ramp
12-5	Curley's Marina
13-3	Dennis Point Marina
13-3	Feldman's Marine Railway
14-1	Kitt's Point Ramp
14-1	Phil's Marina
14-1	Seaside View Campground
14-2	Point Lookout State Park

---

[1] Cable launching. Prearrangement required.
[2] Private Ramp. Restricted use.

A NOTE FOR ENSUING CHAPTERS

The following chapters divide our tidal Potomac into 10 regions. The sketch at the end of this chapter, sketch 5-1, presents this division geographically.

One to eight COLOR NOAA chart excerpts accompany each chapter. Thirty-five NOAA chart excerpts cover the entire 10 chapters. Twelve NOAA charts were enlarged, while 22 were reduced from the original NOAA scale. All reductions, except one, are more than 54 percent. Accompanying chapter chart excerpts are found in one of three places in this guide. The borders of each NOAA chart excerpt were carefully selected to give you the most useful viewpoint. A helpful overlap area was designed when developing these excerpts. So that the chart excerpts can be maximized, they are not all oriented due north. This top orientation ranges anywhere from northwest to northeast. Eight chart excerpts are presented in wider landscaped orientation (versus the vertical portrait format like this page). A comprehensive list of all the NOAA chart excerpts and their short title names are found in appendix A.

Chapter 6 starts with Washington. Chapter 7 covers Old Town Alexandria and the Potomac north to Hains Point. Chapter 8 covers from the Wilson Bridge to Craney Island. Chapter 9 covers from Occoquan Bay to Fairview Beach. Chapter 10 goes from Nanjemoy Creek to near Lower Cedar Point Maryland including the US Route 301 bridge and Cuckold Creek. Chapter 11 covers from Dahlgren to slightly beyond Ragged Point, focusing on the Virginia shore. Chart excerpts for the middle of the Potomac near this area are included in chapter 11. Chapter 12 covers from Cobb Island to Piney Point MD. Chapter 13 focuses on the Saint Marys River in Maryland. A lower Potomac chart excerpt for the middle of the river is found in chapter 13. Chapter 14 remains in Maryland covering the area east of the Saint Marys River. Chapter 15, the last chapter, returns to the Virginia shore, covering the lower Northern Neck of Virginia.

The locations of marinas, restaurants, launch ramps, and other points of interest have been added to these color chart excerpts. Marinas, restaurants and boating facilities are tagged in orange. Other points of interest are labeled in pink. Launch ramps are tagged in green, while information on adjoining NOAA chart excerpts are labeled with blue tags. Forty-three useful GPS waypoints are also found throughout the text as well as in appendix D. Thirty-one marina dock sketches are found in appendix B. Waterfront locality street sketches of Southwest Washington, Old Town Alexandria, Colonial Beach, Leonardtown, and Saint Marys City are found in appendix C.

Please don't rely exclusively on any one single approach to navigation on this river or anywhere.

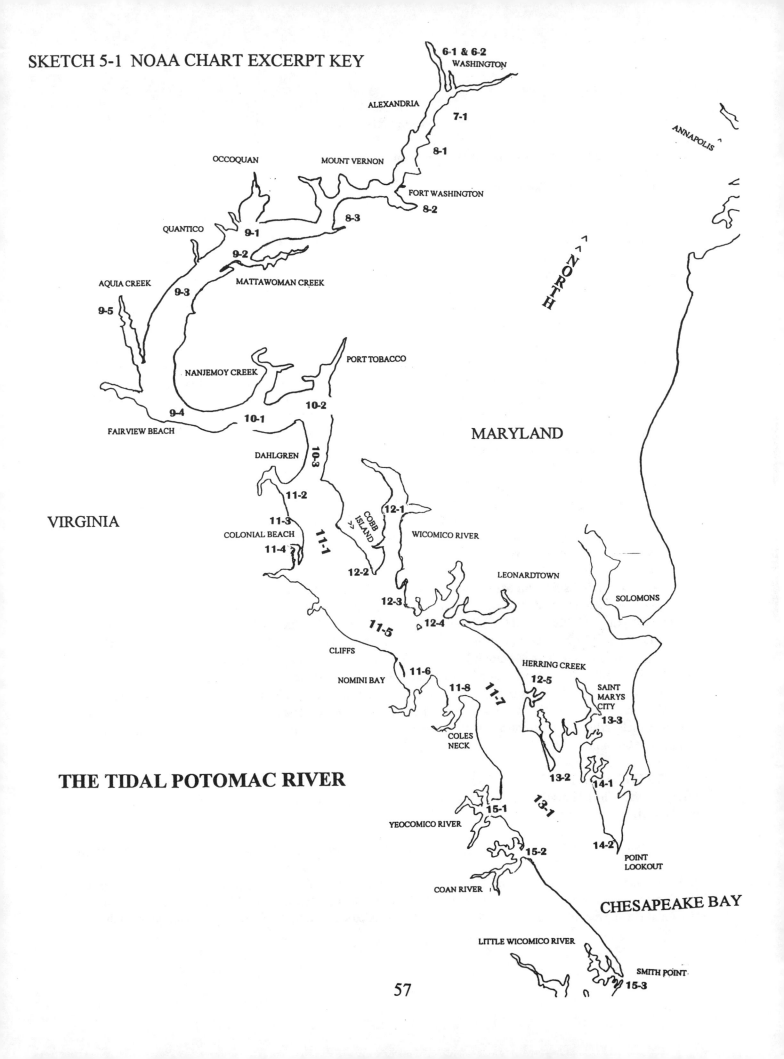

SKETCH 5-1 NOAA CHART EXCERPT KEY

6-1 & 6-2
WASHINGTON

ALEXANDRIA

ANNAPOLIS

7-1

OCCOQUAN   MOUNT VERNON   8-1

FORT WASHINGTON

8-2

NORTH

QUANTICO   8-3

9-1

9-2

AQUIA CREEK   MATTAWOMAN CREEK

9-3

9-5

PORT TOBACCO

NANJEMOY CREEK

MARYLAND

10-2

9-4   10-1

FAIRVIEW BEACH

DAHLGREN   10-3

11-2

VIRGINIA   11-3

COLONIAL BEACH   12-1

COBB   WICOMICO RIVER
ISLAND

11-4   11-1   LEONARDTOWN

12-2   SOLOMONS

12-3

11-5   12-4

CLIFFS   HERRING CREEK

11-6   12-5   SAINT
NOMINI BAY   MARYS
11-8   CITY
11-7   13-3

COLES
NECK   13-2

14-1

THE TIDAL POTOMAC RIVER   13-1

15-1

YEOCOMICO RIVER   14-2

15-2   POINT
LOOKOUT

COAN RIVER

CHESAPEAKE BAY

LITTLE WICOMICO RIVER

SMITH POINT
15-3

57

Chapter 6
WASHINGTON

Washington Channel and Southwest Washington
Anacostia River
Washington Channel to Georgetown

Washington DC was established in 1791 as the world's first planned national capital. This city came into existence later than the nearby tobacco ports of Georgetown and Alexandria. Today, beside being the nerve center of the democratic world and the stage for assorted blowhards, it is a city of monuments and memorials. Some of the larger monuments -- such as the Washington Monument (see front cover picture), Lincoln Memorial, and the Jefferson Memorial -- are best beheld from on or across the water. Even the US Capitol Building is a good bearing point when heading northbound up the Potomac River from Alexandria. No building in Washington can be more than 12 stories high, potentially masking the view of a monument.

Viewing a Washington **Fourth of July** celebration by boat is very popular. A dazzling and spectacular fireworks display is launched near the base of the Washington Monument. In just about any patch of water around Washington, many boats will be anchored during the Fourth. After the fireworks, the more prudent boaters will remain anchored for the night, thereby avoiding the congested mass exodus of boats heading downriver. There are a few other Fourth of July fireworks celebrations visible on the Potomac -- at Colonial Beach VA, Leonardtown MD, and occasionally at a few marinas.

A **blessing of the fleet** takes place in Washington Channel usually on the third weekend in May. The marinas and yacht clubs have an organized parade for this gala, and awards are presented in various categories. There is also a less formal blessing of the fleet off Saint Clements Island, about 70 miles downriver, during the first weekend in October. The pre-Christmas **Festival of Lights** is another Washington Channel favorite event.

The 555-foot **Washington Monument** (T 202 426-6840) towers over everything in Washington. The cornerstone was laid in 1848, but the monument was not completed until 1884. You can ride an elevator to the top. The **Lincoln Memorial** (T 202 426-6841), at the west end of the mall, houses a 19-foot marble statue of a seated Lincoln gazing out over the reflecting pool. The Lincoln Memorial was dedicated in 1922. The brand new **Korean War Memorial** (T 202 619-7222) is less than one quarter mile southeast of the Lincoln Memorial. The Korean War Memorial has 19 ground troops in a "V" formation. The **Vietnam Memorial** (T 202 634-1568) is one quarter mile northeast of the Lincoln Memorial. This wall was dedicated in 1982 with the names of 58,202 casualties etched in black marble. The National Park Service Information Center, which furnishes information on all the monuments, is located on the south side of the Washington Monument Grounds.

The **White House** (T 202 456-7041) is one half mile north of the Washington Monument. The tourist office for the White House is located one block east of the White House at 1455 Pennsylvania Ave NW. This tourist office phone number is T (202) 208-1631.

The impressive **Jefferson Memorial** (T 202-426-6822) is on the south side of the Tidal Basin almost on the Potomac River. Inside the circular colonnaded monument are some profound quotes from Thomas Jefferson as well as a 19-foot bronze statue. The Jefferson Memorial was dedicated in 1943. Another one of Washington's newest memorials, the **Franklin Delano Roosevelt Memorial** (T 202-426-6841) is also along the Tidal Basin west of the Jefferson Memorial. This shaded walk-though of dark stones and quiet pools

58

contains many of FDR's inspiring quotes. The memorial is partially occluded by the Japanese cherry trees, but the Tidal Basin is quite attractive from the memorial.

Arlington National Cemetery (☏ 703 607-8052) is on the opposite side of the Potomac in Arlington VA. Arlington cemetery's 612 acres is home to the tombs of the unknown soldier as well as the hallowed resting place of more than 100,000 known revered heros. Robert E. Lee's Custis Mansion is also on the grounds. The cemetery was started during the Civil War as a burial place for Union soldiers. They were to be buried on General Lee's property! By the end of the Civil War, 16,000 soldiers were interned at Arlington. Adjacent to and at the north end of Arlington cemetery is the **Iwo Jima Marine Corps Memorial** (☏ 703 285-2598), bronze edifice of four members of the Marine Corps immortally raising our flag over Mount Suribachi. The **Netherlands** 49-bell **Carillon**, a gift from the Dutch after World War II, is adjacent to the Marine Corps Memorial.

The most recognized symbol of democratic government in the world and arguably the most recognized building in Washington is the **US Capitol**. For tours, phone ☏ (202) 225-6827. Notwithstanding being torched by the British in 1814, the Capitol has housed Congress since 1800. Near the Capitol are the **US Supreme Court** (☏ 202 479-3211) and the three **Library of Congress** buildings (☏ 202 707 9956). This is the world's largest library, with 532 miles of shelves! Both the Library of Congress and the Supreme Court are open to the public and offer tours.

For performing arts, the **Kennedy Center** (☏ 202 467-4600) and **Arena Stage** (☏ 202 488-3300) are practically on the Potomac. The gargantuan Kennedy Center is one half mile upriver from the Lincoln Memorial and Arena Stage is about one block behind the Gangplank Marina. The infamous Watergate Complex, forever placing the word "gate" into any new Washington scandal vocabulary, is just north of the Kennedy Center.

Guided ground tours of Washington range from $10 to $36 per adult. Some tours last all day, while others are just a few hours. Companies offering tours are Tourmobile (☏ 202 554-7950), Old Town Trolley Tours (☏ 202 832-9800), All About Town, Inc. (☏ 202 393-3696), and Gray Lines Tours (☏ 301 386-8300). A few outfits offer tours on the Potomac. DC Ducks (☏ 202 966-3825) uses converted World War II amphibious vehicles combining a street and a river tour. Two large *Spirit* ships, the *Spirit of Washington* and *Potomac Spirit* (☏ 202 554-8000) cover the waterfront and travel downriver as far south as Mount Vernon, serving lunch or dinner. The low-clearance *Odyssey III* (☏ 202 488-6000) offers dinner and lunch cruises and can travel northbound under some of Washington's lower Potomac bridges. Many guided tours are seasonal only, especially many of those on the Potomac. Some federal buildings are also open to the public and available for guided tours.

WASHINGTON CHANNEL AND SOUTHWEST WASHINGTON

Northbound, **Washington Channel** is the preferred Potomac channel at Hains Point. See NOAA chart excerpt 6-1. At Hains Point, Washington Channel forks to the north (right), while the Potomac River forks northwest (left) to Georgetown. Another channel fork is just after Hains Point. At this second junction, the preferred Washington Channel forks left (north) and the Anacostia River forks right (northeast). Hains Point is the tip of East Potomac Park, where much of the spoil material was placed when Washington Channel was dredged. The National Park Service's Capital Region Headquarters (☏ 202 619-7222) is at the western end of East Potomac Park. The headquarters houses the Public Affairs office for all of the national parks around Washington. East Potomac Park also has tennis courts, a golf course, and an unusual half-statue called the "Awakening." All of the Washington Channel is a no-wake zone.

Fort McNair Army Base extends from Greenleaf Point northward for more than a half mile almost to the Washington Harbor Police docks in Washington Channel. Fort McNair is home to the Military District of Washington (MDW). Every four years, the MDW staff is tasked to seeing that the presidential inauguration goes off without a hitch. The base is the third oldest in continuous use in the country. In 1791, the fort was built to defend the new capital city. Later until 1881, the post served as an arsenal. After the Spanish-American War, the Army War College sprouted to train senior officers. In 1946, the Army War College evolved into the National War College. In 1948, the post was renamed for the highest ranking officer killed by friendly fire during World War II, Lt General Lesley McNair. In 1962, the Inter-American Defense College opened training for many senior officers throughout the Americas. Many high-ranking generals reside on the post. On the waterfront, there are 15 homes which comprise "Generals' Row."

Northwest of Fort McNair, the southernmost wharf in Washington Channel is home to the **Washington Harbor Police** (☎ 202 727-4582) and the fireboat (☎ 202 673-3200) *John Glenn*. The harbor police monitor VHF channel 17 as well as VHF 16. You'll often see their Boston Whaler out on the water, but they have about another dozen boats. Boaters in the District are required to take a boating safety class. During boating season, these classes are frequently offered by harbor police.

At the second large wharf, you might see the two *Spirit* ships -- the *Potomac Spirit* and the *Spirit of Washington*. The Gangplank Marina and the Capital Yacht Club are next to and before the 37-foot vertical clearance Case Bridge over Washington Channel. The **Washington Fish Market** is nestled between the Capital Yacht Club and the Case Bridge. The fish market wharf is a crowded and noisy place, especially in the summer months. About a half-dozen hustling seafood vendors in their floating fish houses add color to the wharf.

If you wish to anchor in the channel, you can, but there are some precautions you should take. Anchor across from either the Capital Yacht Club or the Gangplank Marina and use their dinghy docks. You should favor the East Potomac Park side (i.e., the southwestern side) of the channel for anchoring. The large *Spirit* ships and other large tour boats ply the channel as far as the Case Bridge on a daily basis, or more often. These boats pilot closer to the marina side of the channel and need some turning room before the Case Bridge. The channel is deep (i.e., 20 feet or more) in most places. Hence, you must drop sufficient anchor rode. To offset a potentially wide swinging circle in this sometimes crowded channel, the harbor police require that you drop two anchors. You should contact the harbor police to get specific anchoring instructions. The holding in Washington Channel is not very good because the bottom is a thick layer of soft silt.

The Channel Inn Hotel and five nice restaurants sit right on the channel. The restaurants, from northwest to southeast along the channel, are Le Rivage, Phillips Flagship Seafood Restaurant, Hogates, H.I. Ribsters, and the Pier 7 (Channel Inn) Restaurant. Phillips, Hogates, and H.I. Ribsters have seasonal outdoor seating. H.I. Ribsters is generally the most economical. The Pier 7 serves a nice breakfast buffet. All of these establishments are on Water Street, the frontage street to Maine Avenue. Taxis are plentiful on Water Street. See appendix C for a street layout of Southwest Washington.

Four Metrorail (subway) stations are within easy walking distance of Washington Channel. These are indicated by a large "M" on the street sketch in appendix C. A small shopping center with a Safeway grocery store, drug store, liquor store, Pizza Hut, Jenny's Chinese Restaurant, and a few more eateries, is located at the Waterfront metro rail stop. This metro stop is at 4th and "M" Streets, SW. A public library is adjacent to and on the northeast side of the shopping center.

The metrorail stop near 7th and "D" Streets, SW is L'Enfant Plaza. The underground shops at L'Enfant Plaza are west of the subway stop. In this shopping area there is a drug store, a small grocery, several nice delis, a post office, a liquor store, a few boutiques, and Loew's L'Enfant Plaza Hotel. Scattered in a swath extending southeast from Maryland Avenue to north of the railroad tracks, you'll also find a few smaller shopping areas with a few restaurants and a Holiday Inn. See the appendix C sketch of Southwest Washington.

Several federal agencies are located in Southwest Washington. Some of the larger ones are the Department of Agriculture, the US Postal Service, the Department of Transportation, and the Department of Housing and Urban Development. The westernmost metrorail stop, Smithsonian, is at Independence Avenue and 12th Street, SW. This stop is on the Washington Mall and close to the Washington Monument and many of the museums of the Smithsonian Institution. The popular grassy Mall is bounded by Independence Avenue to the south and Constitution Avenue to the north. Nine of the 14 world-renown Smithsonian Museums (T 202 357-2700) can be found along the Mall. The National Air and Space Museum (T 202 357-1400), the National Museum of Natural History (T 202 357-2747) and the National Museum of American History (T 202 357-1481) are the three most visited.

The **Gangplank Marina** (T 202 554-5000) is a huge facility, having about 320 slips on 10 piers. Slip electrical service is up to 100 amps and the marina can accommodate up to 130-footers. All the docks are floating. In the summertime, the Gangplank outdoor bar is usually a lively place. Besides the *Odyssey III* and the *Nightingale II*, a few other large boats charter from the Gangplank Marina. Appendix B has a dock layout sketch of the Gangplank Marina.

The smaller **Capital Yacht Club** (T 202 488-8110) is northwest of the Gangplank. The yacht club has 89 slips on four piers. The largest slips are 65 feet, but you might see some real big and famous boats tied up at their last "T" pier at various times throughout the summer. The Yacht Club welcome transients. Both the Capital Yacht Club and the Gangplank have nice laundry rooms, showers, mail pickup, bag ice, dinghy docks, and a book-swapping library. Appendix B has a dock layout sketch of the Capital Yacht Club.

The **Washington Marina Company** sits on the other side of the 37-foot vertical clearance Case Bridge near the Tidal Basin. This fixed-pier marina is rather marginal (e.g., the bathrooms are closed and not all slips have utilities). However, the ship store has a good selection of marine hardware and chandlery. The personnel at the Washington Marina Company Ship Store, (T 202 554-0222) are knowledgeable about engine repairs, and they have a wide variety of engine parts available.

If you need boat work done while in Washington Channel, you can contact Stay-Side Systems (Don Waldecker) at T (202) 554-8690, Marine Systems (Will Whitehouse) at T (202) 488-4355, or Bailey Marine Services (Tony Bailey) at T (202) 488-0695.

The Washington **Tidal Basin** is at the head of Washington Channel. A very low-clearance bridge is between the Tidal Basin and Washington Channel. Even a small boat meeting the clearance requirement cannot enter the basin because of the weir gates. The Tidal Basin is restricted to rental paddleboats. You can rent two-seat or four-seat paddleboats (T 202-479-2426) and meander in the basin soaking in the Jefferson Memorial and other sites. The paddleboats are rented on the northeast side of the basin. The smaller ones rent for $7 per hour and the larger ones for $14 per hour.

The Tidal Basin is surrounded by Japanese cherry trees. The first cherry trees were presented as a gift from Tokyo in 1912. Their delicate pinkish-white blossoms peak about one flowery week some time in windy April. You can rest assure, that the annually scheduled Cherry Blossom Festival will miss this peak blossom time by about a week.

ANACOSTIA RIVER

At Greenleaf Point, Washington Channel forks to the north and the Anacostia River forks to the northeast. "Anacostia" an Indian name was bestowed on this body of water by Thomas Jefferson. There are eight marinas of varying size in the Anacostia River. **James Creek Marina** (T 202 554-8844), adjacent to Greenleaf Point, with 295 floating slips, is the largest facility in the area. Slips are serviced by 30-amp and 50-amp electric. The marina sells gas and diesel, 2-cycle oil, and block and bag ice. The marina also has a sewage pump-out. On the grounds, there are picnic tables and volleyball and horseshoe areas. Kas Lippa, the dockmaster, is trying to get a small snack bar in the marina.

The headquarters building of the US Coast Guard is northeast of James Creek Marina. **Buzzard Point Marina** (T 202 488-8400) is on the other side of the Coast Guard building. Buzzard Point has about 90 floating slips serviced by 30-amp and 20-amp electric. They sell bag ice, beer, and sodas. The marina also has a very steep concrete narrow boat ramp for cable launching. If you're thinking about using this launch ramp, call Buzzard Point Marina beforehand.

Appendix B has dock layout sketches of both Buzzard Point and James Creek Marinas. Both Buzzard Point and James Creek have bathhouses and both cost about half the price of the two big marinas in nearby Washington Channel. Neither Buzzard Point nor James Creek is close to the metrorail subway. A one-mile walk to the Waterfront Subway stop would require you to go through some rough neighborhoods, and the walk is definitely not recommended after dark.

A small military marina, the **Anacostia Naval Station Marina** (T 202 433-2269), is across the river from Buzzard Point. This marina has about 20 slips serviced by 30-amp electric on a floating dock. The marina also has a small but nice picnic area and three covered slips on a fixed dock. The Naval Station Marina is the first of five military marinas on the tidal Potomac. The other four are at Bolling Air Force Base, Fort Belvoir, Quantico, and Dahlgren. To keep a boat at these marinas, or at any other military facility, you must be active duty or retired military, or a civilian employed with the Department of Defense.

Anacostia Riverfront Park extends northeast along the Anacostia River for about two miles northeast of the Anacostia Naval Station. The park is pleasant, and has a paved boat ramp at the very northern end before the railroad causeway.

Behind Buzzard Point Marina, you can observe a power plant with three stacks. For nearly a mile northeast of the power plant, the northwestern side of the Anacostia River is not very appealing because of sand and gravel piles, fuel storage tanks, and various gritty industrial complexes. The 40-foot vertical clearance South Capital Street bridge crosses the river about a mile northeast of Buzzard Point Marina. This swing bridge might open for a naval ship about three times a year. If an opening is needed, at least 24-hour advance notice is required (T 202 727-1012).

The industrial waterfront gives way to the Washington Naval Yard. The Yard extends along the waterfront for a half mile west to the 11th Street bridge. Anacostia Park continues on the opposite side of the river from the Naval Yard. The Naval Yard, established in 1799, is the oldest naval facility in the country. Today, the Naval Yard is headquarters to the Chief of Naval Operations and is a restricted base. Often you may see a naval ship tied-up at the yard. The 11th Street bridge is a fixed bridge with a 28-foot vertical clearance. The beige and black Corps of Engineer boats, barges, and cranes dock north of the 11th Street bridge.

Anacostia Marina and four small powerboat clubs are located between the 11th Street bridge and the five-foot-vertical clearance railroad causeway. See NOAA chart excerpt 6-2. The railroad bridge does have a "lift section," but I've never seen it lifted, and trains frequently cross the bridge, so we'll end our Anacostia River tour at the railway bridge.

The **Eastern Powerboat Club** is the first facility past the Corps of Engineer docks. This unassuming facility has one extending floating pier, some riverfront dockage, and a small marine railway. The **District Yacht Club** is next to the Eastern Powerboat Club. The District Yacht Club has three floating piers and a small railway. The two outside piers of the District Yacht Club are covered. The **Washington Yacht Club** is less than a quarter mile northeast of the District Yacht Club. The Washington Yacht Club has two floating piers and about 30 slips. The 32-foot-vertical clearance Pennsylvania Avenue bridge is less than a quarter mile past the District Yacht Club.

The largest haul-out facility in the area is Anacostia Marina. The facility is colloquially known as "Tommy Long's" marina. The **Anacostia Marina** (T 202 544-5191) has about 100 wet slips on about five piers (four floating) and can easily accept up to 80-footers. Many slips are serviced by 30-amp electric. Anacostia Marina has three lifts with the largest being a 50-ton open-end travel lift. The marina also has a large boat shed and an extremely packed haul-out yard. If you're looking for a used boat part -- from an engine part to a steering part, to cables, to stanchions, to whatever -- you may find it at Tommy Long's. The marina is somewhat of "a last resting place," for many boats, and salvage parts abound. Anacostia Marina's repair yard has been the choice place for many Washington boaters to haul, especially if in need of major repairs.

The **Seafarers Yacht Club** is next to and upriver from Anacostia Marina. The Seafarers Yacht Club has three conspicuous piers (two float) and a marine railway. The marine railways at the Seafarers Yacht Club, District Yacht Club, and Eastern Powerboat Club appear to be infrequently used. The very-low clearance railway causeway is adjacent to Seafarers Yacht Club. The double concrete boat ramp is across the Anacostia River from Seafarers Yacht Club and at the north end of Anacostia Park. The ramp is often times cluttered with floating debris. Unfortunately, a lot of garbage finds its way into the Anacostia River.

WASHINGTON CHANNEL TO GEORGETOWN

Columbia Island Powerboat Marina (T 202 347-0173) is two miles northwest of Hains Point and just north of the 14th Street bridge on the Virginia side of the Potomac. The facility is across Pentagon lagoon and about one quarter mile from the massive Pentagon building. The vertical clearance beneath the George Washington Parkway bridge into the lagoon is only 18 feet, thus limiting this large marina to powerboats. The mean low-water depth (MLW) at the gas dock is about five feet. They do not sell diesel. This large marina has 384 slips on 12 piers, serviced by 30-amp and 50-amp electric. Columbia Island can accommodate up to 50-footers. The first three piers are fixed, including the third pier, "C" dock -- the fuel dock. The next eight piers are longer and have floating docks. Appendix B has a dock layout of Columbia Island Powerboat Marina.

Columbia Island is run as a National Park Service Concession operated by Guest Services. Kathy DeGroot is the manager. The marina has a friendly little snack bar and sells bag ice. They have 24-hour security, locked dock gates, and a small repair yard for trailerable boats. But there is no place to shower.

Being less than one mile north of National Airport's runways under the flight path, this area can get rather noisy. A paved boat ramp is located between "G" and "I" docks.

About three-quarters of a mile southeast of Columbia Island is another boat ramp at Gravelly Point VA. Four paved concrete ramps, with three piers, bulge into a shallow lagoon just north of the Reagan Washington National Airport runways.

The old port of Georgetown is less than two miles northwest of Colombia Island Marina. See NOAA chart excerpt 6-2. You'll go under the Arlington Memorial bridge (30-foot vertical clearance) and the Theodore Roosevelt bridge (24-foot vertical clearance). After the Roosevelt bridge, you'll pass the massive Kennedy Center, the Watergate Complex, and then the confluence of Rock Creek. Theodore Roosevelt Island is on the western side of the Potomac River.

Theodore Roosevelt Island (☏ 703 285-2598) has had many names -- Analostan (Native American), My Lord's Island (in the Lord Baltimores' days), Barbadoes (named by a Caribbean captain), and Mason's Island (from the famous Virginia family). In 1932, it took its present name. In 1967, a 17-foot bronze statue of our 26th president, surrounded by some of his thought-provoking quotes, was dedicated. Theodore Roosevelt was a man well ahead of his time in matters related to conservation and public land. There are several trails on the island and some are marshy. Many of the trees on the island are faring poorly. There is no place to dock a boat. Access to the island is via a footbridge from the western side.

Thompson's Boat Center (☏ 202-333-4861) is located just past the confluence of Rock Creek at the base of Georgetown. Thompson's has a large floating platform, but it is not a marina. Thompson's rents small sailboats, windsurfers, rowboats, and 16-foot canoes, and has rowing programs. You can also rent a bicycle from Thompson's and explore the Chesapeake and Ohio Canal, the Rock Creek Park bicycle path, or the Washington Mall.

Washington Harbour is a modern office-restaurant-condominium complex less than a quarter mile northwest of Thompson's. A seawall, with tie-up rings spaced about every 10 feet, stretches for almost two blocks along the waterfront. There should be no less than five feet of water at the seawall, and it's much deeper just a few feet further out. Washington Harbour is home to more than a half dozen elegant restaurants. You can tie your boat up to the seawall for a couple of hours, but not after midnight. During the summer, many boats anchor out for the night. The northwestern most part of the seawall is reserved for tour boats such as the *Nightingale II* which provides service between Washington Harbour and Washington Channel (at the Gangplank Marina) and police boats. On the river's bank, the Washington Harbour complex is protected from the often-rising river by flood gates. These gates rise between the white posts, and compressed air makes the seal watertight. The gates are necessary and have been deployed many times since 1985.

The old port of **Georgetown** is beyond Washington Harbour. Today, there are no places to tie-up between Washington Harbour and the Francis Scott Key bridge. Georgetown, higher than Washington Harbour, is protected from flooding by a 10-foot high concrete wall or high banks. Steep streets, many restaurants, boutiques, and a wide assortment of bars are located behind the Georgetown river bank. If there is any area along the entire Potomac that has that old dank port flavor, like that found in New Orleans' French Quarter or Saint Louis' Lacledes Landing, it is Georgetown. Georgetown was also once a strategic transfer point for the noble underground railroad.

The arched **Key Bridge** with it's 61-foot vertical clearance connects timeworn Georgetown to the modern high-rises of Rosslyn VA. The free-admission **Newseum** (T 703 284-3544) is an interesting indoor-outdoor news museum in Rosslyn. Past the base of the Key Bridge, in Georgetown, you'll find Jack's Canoe and Boat Rental. The Washington Canoe Club's bright green and somewhat dilapidated building is upriver from the Key Bridge. The **Three Sisters** (exposed rocks) sit near the middle of the Potomac less than a half mile west of the Key Bridge. Although there are many deep patches in this part of the river, navigating a boat northwest of the Key Bridge can be hazardous. Navigation aids have already ended, and there are many rocks in the river past Key Bridge. Still, I have heard of boats as big as 32-feet plying all of the way to Chain Bridge. Despite the many exposed rocks in this part of the river, it is reported that in many places there is deep enough water not far from those treacherous exposed rocks.

Chapter 7
HAINS POINT TO OLD TOWN ALEXANDRIA

South of Hains Point
Old Town Alexandria

SOUTH OF HAINS POINT

There is much boating traffic in this part of the river. This is not the place to be fooling with your automatic pilot, GPS, or any other gizmo. All of the larger boats and most of the mid-sized vessels are constrained by their draft to the narrow channel. See NOAA chart excerpt 7-1. Stay alert for approaching traffic from either direction.

The **Washington Sailing Marina** ($_T$ 703-548-9027) is Guest Services' sailing counterpart to Columbia Island's Powerboat Marina. This facility is less than a mile southwest of the National Airport runways and the overhead air traffic can be thunderous. The MLW depth is four and a half feet; there is talk about dredging the area deeper. The marina has 150 wet slips, from 15 feet to 34 feet in length. The electric service is 15-amp and 30-amp. About halfway out on the piers, the docks go from fixed pier to floating dock. The dock gates, like Columbia Island's, are locked. Appendix B has a dock layout of Washington Sailing Marina. The marina also has land to store more than 400 small trailerable sailboats and catamarans in 12 separate rows. On the grounds, they can store up to 24-footers on trailers, and small cartop boats can be stored on racks. Besides a launching ramp, the marina has four cranes which are used to deploy land-stored boats. Three are one-ton cranes and the other crane is four-ton crane with a webbed cradle.

The Washington Sailing Marina is the home base to a sailing school, the Sailing Club of Washington (SCOW) and many other sailing organizations and activities. The sailing school has Hobie Cats, 14-foot Sunfish, 19-foot Flying Scots, and a Catalina 25-footer. The marina also rents boats and bicycles. The bicycle path to Mount Vernon runs through the area. The marina sells a wide assortment of sailing hardware, bag and block ice, and has showers for slipholders. There are two restaurants on the premises. The After Deck Cafe is an informal light-fare grill. The Potowmack Landing Restaurant ($_T$ 703-548-0001) is for upscale and fine dining.

The **Bolling Air Force Base Marina** ($_T$ 202 767-9137) is across the river from the Washington Sailing Marina. The inconspicuous entry is not marked. A gas pump is just inside the entry on your port side (i.e., north). The manmade harbor has 88 floating slips with about 10 slip for larger boats. Many slips have 30-amp electrical service, but some slips have no electrical service. The marina has a paved boat ramp and a large secure yard for trailerable boats. The Slip Inn Cafe is on the premises. The marina office is not open on weekends during the winter months, nor is it open after 5:00 PM at other times.

OLD TOWN ALEXANDRIA

There are three power plants on the Potomac, south of Washington's Buzzard Point power plant. The five stacks of the coal-fired PEPCO plant mark the northern end of the city of Alexandria. The US Naval Research Lab is the spread of buildings across the Potomac. About a mile and a quarter of the Potomac channel, from "R6" to the Woodrow Wilson Bridge, is a no-wake zone. Boats traveling past Alexandria should not exceed 6 MPH.

Alexandria was founded in 1749 by a Scottish merchant, and it soon became a major tobacco port on the

Potomac. Alexandria hosts the Alexandria Red Cross Waterfront Festival during the second weekend of June. No city along the entire Potomac has done a better job at creating a string of appealing waterfront parks than Alexandria. Running intermittently for almost two miles from the power plant to past the Wilson bridge, there's Canal Center, Tide Lock Park, Oronoco Bay Park, Founder's Park, Waterfront Park, Lumley Park, Harborside Shipyard Park, and Jones Point Park. All are delightful and well-maintained. See appendix C for a street sketch of Alexandria.

The Canal Center complex is the first series of tall glass building south of the PEPCO plant. The Alexandria Canal Lock is to the south. Today the short canal doesn't go anywhere. The Alexandria High School's rowing facility building sits south of the canal. This bright blue-roofed building on the waterfront is unmistakable with its floating docks on the river. Oronoco Bay Park is south of the rowing facility. The Robinson Terminal is south of the small park. Much of the *Washington Post* newsprint comes from Sweden, and you may see a Swedish newsprint ship tied-up at the Robinson Terminal docks. Years ago, Alexandria was a bustling commercial seaport. Today the only facility handling water-borne commerce is this Robinson Terminal. Another Robinson Terminal facility, about a half of a mile south, has closed down.

Founder's Park is a relatively wide buffer area south of Robinson Terminal. The two piers near the south end of Founder's Park are part of the **Alexandria City Marina** (τ 703 838-4265). You'll likely see the *Cherry Blossom* tied-up north of the main Alexandria City Marina dock. This yellow and white classic is a rare TRUE paddlewheeler. The *Cherry Blossom* (τ 703 548-9000) doesn't go out on a schedule; the whole boat must be chartered. behind the *Cherry Blossom*, sits the Chart House Restaurant, and behind that, a large food pavilion. South of the Chart House is the main portion of the Alexandria City Marina. The **Torpedo Factory**, with a brew of more than 160 assorted artisans, is the large indoor art center behind the main Alexandria City Marina.

Alexandria City Marina has 61 slips, with 30-amp and 50-amp electric, and a bathhouse. The marina has slips up to 40 feet but can accommodate much bigger boats -- even 80-footers. Deac Heath has been the dockmaster for many years. Although the marina is exposed to the river for nearly 180 degrees, from the north, to the east, to the south, Deac says that usually only the winter months produce worrisome conditions in the marina.

Three charter boats also embark from the Alexandria City Marina docks. In season, the *Matthew Hayes* makes five 90-minute daily trips to Georgetown. The *Miss Christin* takes two 5½-hour trips to Mount Vernon. The smaller *Admiral Tilp* can make several 40-minute narrated cruises right off the Alexandria waterfront. Phone τ (703) 548-9000 for more information on these three vessels.

The **Old Dominion Yacht Club** (τ 703 836-1900), the oldest boating club in the country, sits south of the Alexandria City Marina. The club has about 50 slips on two piers with 30-amp and 50-amp electric. Having a multiyear waiting list for slips and being relatively small, the club doesn't cater to transient boaters. However, the Old Dominion Yacht Club will try to accommodate boaters from reciprocating yacht clubs.

The low-clearance *Dandy* (τ 703 683-6076) is docked south of the Old Dominion Yacht Club. The *Dandy* specializes in dinner and luncheon cruises but offers other types of tours as well. *Dandy* dinner cruises start boarding at 6 PM.

There are three decrepit wooden piers south of the *Dandy* dock where a couple of boats might be tied-up. The infamous Interarms complex is behind these piers. Interarms has been on television's *60 Minutes* and is in the business of selling guns and munitions to clients all over the world. South of Interarms is the closed-down Robinson South Terminal facility.

The Harborside condominium complex is south of closed-down Robinson Terminal. This waterfront complex has a floating dock with about eight slips for condominium owners. There was once a marina south of this complex, but today all that remains are some dangerous exposed pilings. The old Ford plant was once south of here. Today, Ford Landing Waterfront Condominiums are being erected on the site. *Backyard Boats*, a *Catalina* dealer and boating supply store, is across Union Street.

A concrete bulkhead, with a few steel bollards, is underneath and just to the north of the Wilson Bridge. The water off the bulkhead appears reasonably deep. However the seawall is falling apart and metal rebar protrudes from the concrete in many places. It appears too dangerous for tieing-up.

The **Alexandria Seaport Foundation** (т 703 549-7078) has their small building on Lee Street, 100 yards from the Potomac and under the Wilson Bridge. The volunteer seaport foundation is dedicated to preserving and promoting Alexandria's maritime heritage. The foundation offers maritime programs and runs the Craddock Boat Building School, as well as the sailing dory, *Potomac*. Shallow-draft dories of the type built by the Foundation's Craddock Boat Building School, were the Potomac workhorses for oystering, fishing, and cargo transport nearly a century ago. The 42-foot *Potomac* sails from the dock at the end of Prince Street and operates as a floating classroom. In 1998, the Alexandria Seaport Foundation hopes to have a new facility, a Maritime Heritage Center, closer to the center of Alexandria's waterfront activity.

Jones Point is about 300 yards south of the Wilson Bridge. The Jones Point Light operated from 1836 until 1925. The historic lighthouse building stands west of the point. Besides the lighthouse building, this spacious park contains two soccer fields and is very popular with dog lovers.

Smoots Cove and the Wilson Bridge
Belle Haven Area
Swan Creek
Fort Washington and Piscataway Creek
Mount Vernon Area
Dogue Creek
Gunston Cove
Craney Island

SMOOTS COVE AND THE WILSON BRIDGE

Smoots Cove is a popular anchorage close to Washington, as well as a good place on the south side of the Woodrow Wilson Bridge to await an opening if you need a draw. See NOAA chart excerpt 8-1. Two interstate highways aren't far from the cove. Previously, the traffic noise was somewhat veiled by trees. Plans for developing this prime spot have fallen apart in the past. However in early 1998, trees were cleared, and commercial development appears imminent. The latest plan would designate the site The National Harbor and would include hotels, offices, retail stores, and restaurants. To enter Smoots Cove, go to buoy "R90" which is three-quarters of a mile south of the Wilson Bridge. A shallow spoil area is north-northeast of "R90". From "R90" head northeast, passing the spoil area on your port and go for about one half mile into the Smoots Cove anchorage.

The mean high-water (MHW) clearance under the center span of the Wilson Bridge is about 50 feet. If you're not exactly sure where the tide stands, there is help. On each side of the center span, a white "clearance measuring stick" is attached to the massive concrete vertical supports. This on-the-water measuring stick provides the overhead clearance under the center span. Before there were the stringent opening restrictions, I always tried to get under the bridge without requesting an opening, knowing the disturbance I was inflicting on the vehicular traffic above. I have a 48-foot mast with more than 3 feet of accoutrements atop (i.e., I need about 51 feet of clearance not to break anything). I'm not recommending this, but I have been able to squeeze through with my 51 feet of height when I have read only 49 feet at the waterline measuring stick. There may be a slight amount of additional clearance at the very center of the double span. Before you even think of attempting this, I'd suggest talking to the Wilson Bridge tender over the VHF.

To get the latest Wilson Bridge opening restrictions, call T (202) 727-5522. You can also reach the bridge tender on VHF 13. Recreational boats are required to make an appointment for an opening at least 12 hours in advance. Furthermore, the double-bascule drawbridge will only open between midnight and 5 AM during the week, and between 10 PM and 7 AM on the weekends. Commercial and military vessels are also subject to opening restrictions, but the restrictions are less stringent than those imposed on recreational boaters. The bridge WILL NOT OPEN FOR ANYBODY from 5 AM to 10 AM (i.e., morning rush hour) and from 2 PM to 8 PM (i.e., afternoon rush hour) during the week. However, it will open at other times for large commercial and military vessels. If the bridge opens for one of these vessels, you could get lucky and fall in behind it. If it's a foggy day, this may help -- the draw span is located at 38°47.60'N/77°02.25'W. Beware, the winds can sometimes become mischievous underneath the bridge.

The Wilson Bridge was built in 1961 and was designed for carrying 75,000 vehicles per day. In 1998 the bridge was carrying 190,000 vehicles per day. One estimate indicates that at its current rate of deterioration, the bridge will be structurally unsafe for traffic in about six years. The three-state jurisdiction has had a difficult time agreeing on a replacement plan for this aging bridge. The city of Alexandria has been ardently opposed to anything lowering the aesthetics of its waterfront. A renovation plan drawn up in September 1996 calls for a twin-drawspan, 12-lane bridge with 70-foot vertical clearance. This 20-foot increase in the vertical clearance should reduce the draw openings by 70 percent. Nearly all pleasure craft should be able to go under a 70-foot bridge, versus the current 50-foot bridge. The latest plan has the new bridge being constructed just south of the existing six-lane bridge.

BELLE HAVEN AREA

Belle Haven Marina ($_T$ 703-768-0018), on the Virginia shore, is the first marina south of the Wilson Bridge. They have about 60 slips, and most slips are serviced by 30-amp electric. Belle Haven has a launching ramp but no fuel. They sell bag ice, soda, and bait worms. Belle Haven also rents sailboats, kayaks, canoes, and jon boats up to 19 feet. The Mariner Sailing School is also here. The sailing school has 14-foot Sunfish, 19-foot Flying Scots, and one C&C 34-footer.

There is very shallow water north and east of Belle Haven Marina. If you require deep water, enter from the southeast. At "C87" break out of the Potomac channel in a northwesterly direction, about 320°M, toward the marina, three-quarters of a mile away. Belle Haven monitors VHF 16 and 78, and should be able to inform you of where to find the deeper water on approach (i.e., on which side to leave the various floats and pilings). Once you arrive at the marina, you can find 7 feet of water in the lagoon south of the marina where their small boats are moored, or you can find 4 or 5 feet off of the marina docks.

Fort Foote is across the river from Belle Haven and sits on the south edge of Rosier Bluff. At the beginning of the Civil War, only Fort Washington, three and a half miles downriver, guarded the Union capital from a Confederate river assault. In the early years of the Civil War, 68 more forts and 93 batteries were constructed around Washington. Today nearly all of these small forts have been swallowed by urban sprawl. However, two 15-inch Rodman cannons sitting on the bluff silently guard the Potomac at Fort Foote. You'll also see the old bermwork at Fort Foote.

SWAN CREEK

The entrance to Swan Creek is located at 38°43.16'N/77°01.99'W. The entire creek is a no-wake zone. See NOAA chart excerpt 8-2. The small creek houses **Tantallon Marina** ($_T$ 202-554-5446), and the Tantallon Yacht Club. The marina docks are floating wooden docks, and many require refurbishment. The marina has recently come under new management, Marina Management Services, and conditions should likely improve. Tantallon Marina has about 100 slips. The slips on a few docks have 30-amp and 50-amp electrical service. The Tantallon Yacht Club occupies the large floating structure east of the old fuel dock. There is about eight feet of water off the floating fuel dock platform, but the gas and diesel pumps were not working in 1998. Appendix B has a dock layout of Tantallon Marina. The marina is situated in a very well-protected cove in Swan Creek.

FORT WASHINGTON AND PISCATAWAY CREEK

Fort Washington is on the point of land north of the creek and commands a broad vista of the downriver Potomac. In 1809, Fort Warburton was built on this site to protect Washington from the British. In 1814, the British still sacked and burned Washington. They took a few warships up the Patuxent River to the east and reached Washington via a short overland leg. The following day, another contingent of British warships

70

traveled up the Potomac and approached Fort Warburton. The American defenders, fearing sure defeat, blew up the fort and fled. Soon afterward, present-day Fort Washington was built in its place.

At the start of the Civil War, Fort Washington was the only "Union river defense" of Washington. The fort loomed vitally. After the Civil War, the threat of foreign invaders seemed real and the nation believed in sound inland coastal fortifications. After the Spanish American War, the importance of inland river coastal fortifications waned, and Fort Washington became a military garrison. After World War II, the fort was handed over to The National Park Service, who still manages it today. For more on Fort Washington's history and current programs, you can call the visitor center at ☏ (301) 763-4600.

The entrance to Piscataway Creek is located at 38°42.52'N/77°02.45'W. **Fort Washington Marina** (☏ 301 292-7700) is about a mile southeast of Fort Washington on Piscataway Creek. Appendix B has a dock layout of Fort Washington Marina. The marina is a modern state-run facility with 296 slips and seven docks. Six of the docks float, and the marina can handle up to 50-footers. The controlling depth is six feet. They have 30-amp and 50-amp electric. The marina has a laundromat, two grooved-concrete launch ramps, and a 35-ton open-end travel lift. The Maryland Marine Police are also located here. The marina sells gas and "bio-diesel" -- a diesel fuel that is purported to be less offensive to the environment. The all-purpose Galley Cafe serves breakfast, lunch, and dinner and has a liquor license.

A couple of questionable launching ramps are further in Piscataway Creek and on the south shore. The Farmington Landing ramp is the westernmost. It's gravel, it has no pier, and trailer parking is sparse. Furthermore, a gate across the road could be locked. Less than a half mile east is the Calvert Manor Park's private ramp. A patch of concrete gives way to gravel on this ramp. The bottom off both of these ramps is very shallow with not much sloping for a quite a distance. The Marshall Hall ramp, four miles downriver, is much preferred and is a good ramp for any level in the tidal range.

MOUNT VERNON AREA

Mount Vernon VA was the home of George and Martha Washington. This beautiful estate has more than 30 acres of gardens and woodlands. The grounds contain the mansion, gardens, a museum, and the tombs of George and many of his family. Many claim that the best view of Mount Vernon is from the Potomac River. The channel to Mount Vernon off the main Potomac channel begins near 38°41.81'N/77°05.24'W in about 20 feet of water. This channel leads to the private Mount Vernon dock. The *Spirit* ships have docking priority here. However, on a case-by-case basis, recreational boaters can use the pier. Phone ☏ (703) 799-8678 for more details and to make an arrangement. You will be charged the normal admission fees to the grounds, which is around $8. You may wish to consider dining at the elegant Mount Vernon Inn (☏ 703 780-0011).

The **Marina House Yacht Club** (☏ 703-360-3832) is north of Dogue Creek and about a mile southwest of Mount Vernon. This private club is only for trailerable boats and not much else. They have a launch ramp and a substantial pier into the Potomac on the north side of the ramp. Dozens of trailerable boats are stored in the private yard just ashore.

Marshall Hall is across and slightly down the river from Mount Vernon. The area was home to the Marshall family, friends of George Washington. For almost a hundred years a large amusement park was located at the landing. Excursion ships from Washington would visit Marshall Hall. Passengers could disembark at the Marshall Hall Landing or visit Mount Vernon. The brick walls of the old Marshall mansion still stand. Today, the landing has a very nice boat ramp. The double ramp is wide grooved-concrete with a pier in between the ramps. There is adequate parking for boat trailers.

DOGUE CREEK

Dogue Creek, about a mile and a half southwest of Mount Vernon and across from Marshall Hall, is a wide shallow cove housing two private facilities, the Mount Vernon Yacht Club and Fort Belvoir Marina. See NOAA chart excerpt 8-3. The western shore of Dogue Creek houses Fort Belvoir and the eastern shore is residentially developed. George Washington bequeathed Fort Belvoir to the US Army to be used as their Engineer School. For close to two centuries, Fort Belvoir was the Army Engineer School. However, in the 1980s the last of the school moved to Missouri. Today, Fort Belvoir is home to a loose array of military activities. The Fort Belvoir Officer's Club is the large building on the hillside with a choice vista on the Potomac.

The **Mount Vernon Yacht Club** (T 703 780-8850) is a nice private facility with about 130 slips. About one-third of the slips, the smaller ones, are on floating docks. Most of the slips and a gas dock are in a small protected creek off of Dogue Creek. The gas is for members only. The club has a clubhouse, pool, a nice picnic area, and a boat ramp. The Mount Vernon Yacht Club is staffed by volunteers two hours a day and only during the weekends. Transients are welcome, but transient arrangements must be made well in advance.

Fort Belvoir Marina (T 703 805-3745) is at the head of Dogue Creek (i.e., where the bay really does become a creek). The marina has 105 wet slips from 24 feet to 36 feet in length. All of the slips are on floating docks serviced by 30-amp electric. The haul-out yard is impressive. The yard can store about 500 boats and has two 20-ton travel lifts. One lift is open-end. The marina has twin launch ramps and rents jet skis and boats up to 26 feet in length. Fort Belvoir Marina has a bathhouse and sells a good selection of boating supplies, bag ice, and bait worms. The MLW depth in the channel is only two and a half feet, but you'll see a handful of five-foot-plus draft boats hauled in the yard. They get in here on the high tide, which is about three feet above MLW. If you go past the third pier, beware of the overhead powerline. For more on navigational nuances in the Fort Belvoir Marina area, talk to dockmaster Harold Burrows. He has been here for more than 20 years.

GUNSTON COVE

Pohick Bay and Pohick Bay Regional Park are near the western edge of Gunston Cove. In the summer, you can rent reasonably priced small sailboats, jon boats, and pedal boats at the park's floating dock. A large paved quadruple boat ramp with three piers is west of the facility building. The outside piers are "L" shaped. The park has seasonal ramp passes for $196; individual ramp launches costs $8. Pohick Bay Regional Park also has a trailered-boat storage yard. One drawback to boating from the park is that all trailerable boats that require storage have to be out of the water before sunset when the park shuts down. The park's phone number is T (703) 339-6104.

CRANEY ISLAND

Craney Island is a very small island with a clump of trees and a duck blind in a shallow part of the river. The island is located south of Gunston Cove and south of a line between Hallowing Point VA and Chapman Point MD. The main river channel passes to the east of Craney Island, close to Chapman Point. The river channel makes almost a 90-degree gradual turn east of Craney Island. In my slow moving boats, I almost always take a shortcut, passing on the western side of Craney Island, closer to Hallowing Point. This shortcut

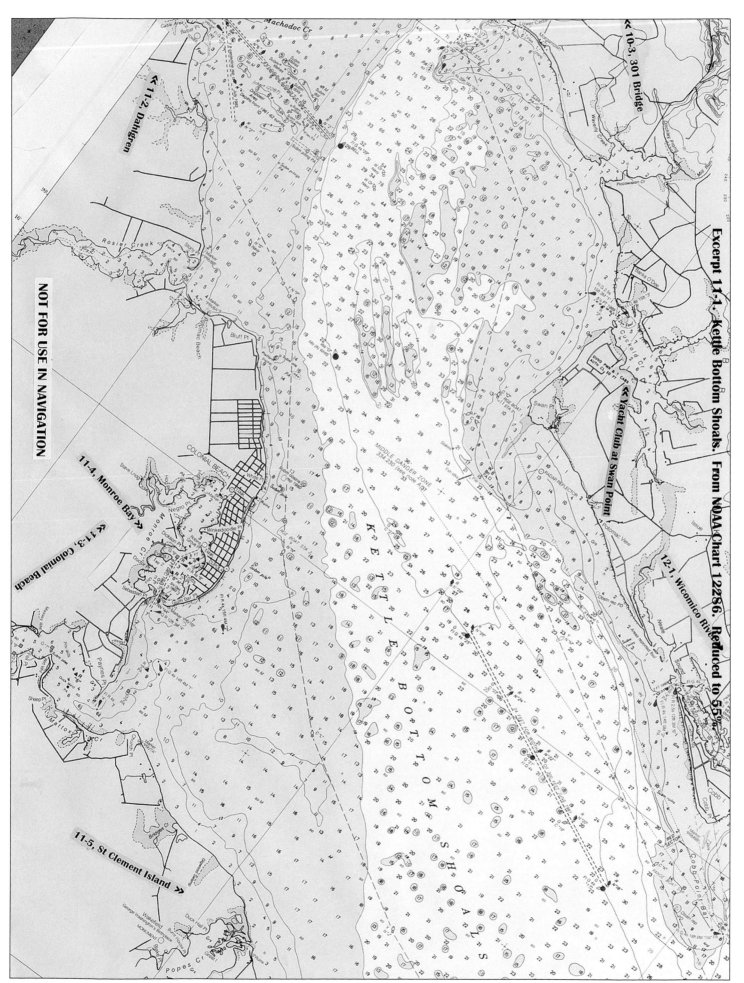

Excerpt 11-1. Kettle Bottom Shoals. From NOAA Chart 12286. Reduced to 55%.

NOT FOR USE IN NAVIGATION

<< 10-3, 301 Bridge

<< 11-2, Dahlgren

<< Yacht Club at Swan Point

12-1, Wicomico River >>

11-4, Monroe Bay >>

<< 11-3, Colonial Beach

11-5, St Clement Island >>

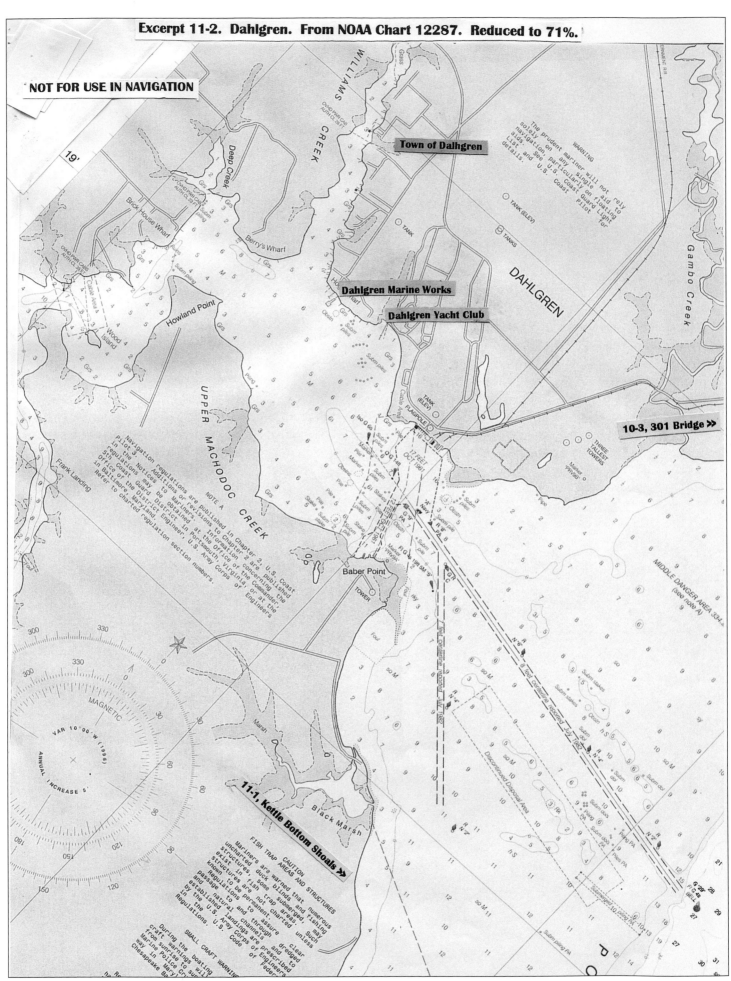

NOT FOR USE IN NAVIGATION

19'

Brick House Wharf

Deep Creek

WILLIAMS CREEK

Grass

Town of Dahlgren

Berry's Wharf

TANK

TANK (ELEV)

TANKS

Howland Point

Wood Island

Cable Area

Dahlgren Marine Works

Dahlgren Yacht Club

DAHLGREN

UPPER MACHODOC CREEK

Gambo Creek

TANK (ELEV)

FLAGPOLE

Cable Area

17 FEET OCT 1967

10-3, 301 Bridge »

THREE TALLEST TOWERS

Frank Landing

NOTE A

Navigation regulations are published in Chapter 2, U.S. Coast Pilot 3. Notices to Mariners, or revisions to Chapter 2 are published in the Notices to Mariners. Additions or revisions to the regulations may be obtained at the Office of the Commander, 5th Coast Guard District in Portsmouth, Virginia, or at the Office of the Maryland Engineer, U.S. Army Corps of Engineers in Baltimore. Refer to charted regulation section numbers.

Baber Point

TOWER

MIDDLE DANGER AREA 334
(see note A)

300   330

330

MAGNETIC

VAR 10°00'W (1996)

ANNUAL INCREASE 5'

300

330

150   120

180   150   120

11-1, Kettle Bottom Shoals »

Black Marsh

Marsh

FISH TRAP CAUTION AREAS AND STRUCTURES
Mariners are warned that numerous uncharted structures, duck blinds and fishing structures exist in fish trap areas. Such structures are not charted unless known to be permanent. Regulations and through dredged passage natural channels and to assure clear established landings are prescribed by the U.S. Army Corps of Engineers in the U.S. Code of Federal Regulations.

SMALL CRAFT WARNING
During the boating season, small craft warnings will be displayed from sunrise to sunset by the Marine Police in suitable places on navigable way in Maryland and Chesapeake Bay.

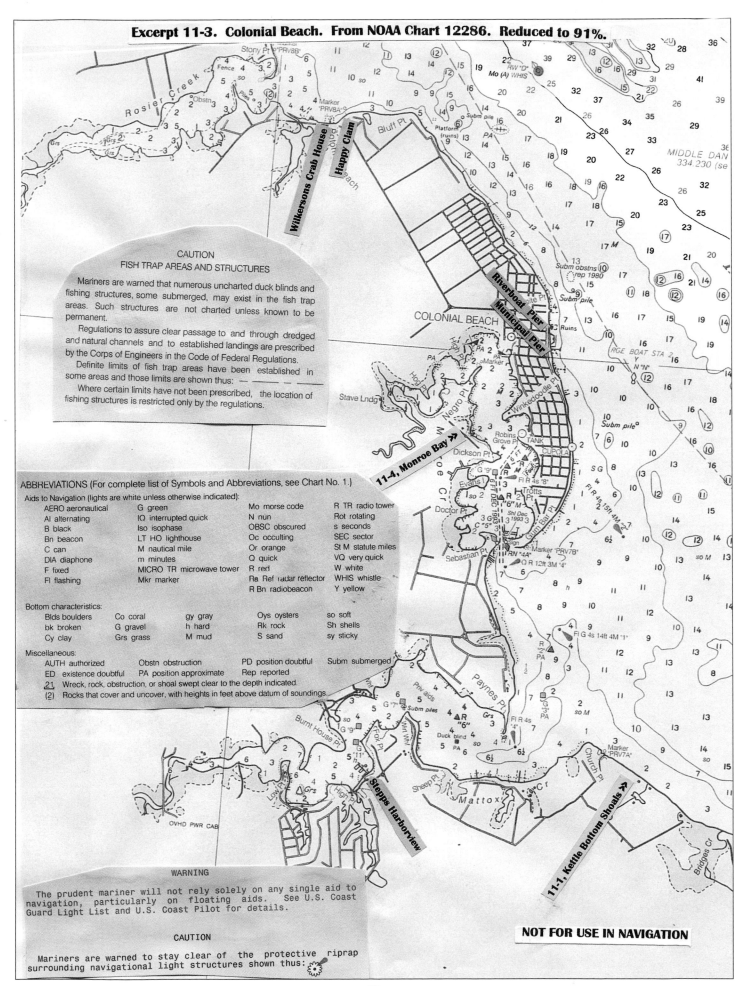

CAUTION
FISH TRAP AREAS AND STRUCTURES

Mariners are warned that numerous uncharted duck blinds and fishing structures, some submerged, may exist in the fish trap areas. Such structures are not charted unless known to be permanent.

Regulations to assure clear passage to and through dredged and natural channels and to established landings are prescribed by the Corps of Engineers in the Code of Federal Regulations.

Definite limits of fish trap areas have been established in some areas and those limits are shown thus: ————

Where certain limits have not been prescribed, the location of fishing structures is restricted only by the regulations.

ABBREVIATIONS (For complete list of Symbols and Abbreviations, see Chart No. 1.)

Aids to Navigation (lights are white unless otherwise indicated):

AERO aeronautical	G green	Mo morse code	R TR radio tower
Al alternating	IQ interrupted quick	N nun	Rot rotating
B black	Iso isophase	OBSC obscured	s seconds
Bn beacon	LT HO lighthouse	Oc occulting	SEC sector
C can	M nautical mile	Or orange	St M statute miles
DIA diaphone	m minutes	Q quick	VQ very quick
F fixed	MICRO TR microwave tower	R red	W white
Fl flashing	Mkr marker	Ra Ref radar reflector	WHIS whistle
		R Bn radiobeacon	Y yellow

Bottom characteristics:

Blds boulders	Co coral	gy gray	Oys oysters	so soft
bk broken	G gravel	h hard	Rk rock	Sh shells
Cy clay	Grs grass	M mud	S sand	sy sticky

Miscellaneous:

AUTH authorized	Obstn obstruction	PD position doubtful	Subm submerged
ED existence doubtful	PA position approximate	Rep reported	

21 Wreck, rock, obstruction, or shoal swept clear to the depth indicated.
(2) Rocks that cover and uncover, with heights in feet above datum of soundings.

WARNING

The prudent mariner will not rely solely on any single aid to navigation, particularly on floating aids. See U.S. Coast Guard Light List and U.S. Coast Pilot for details.

CAUTION

Mariners are warned to stay clear of the protective riprap surrounding navigational light structures shown thus:

NOT FOR USE IN NAVIGATION

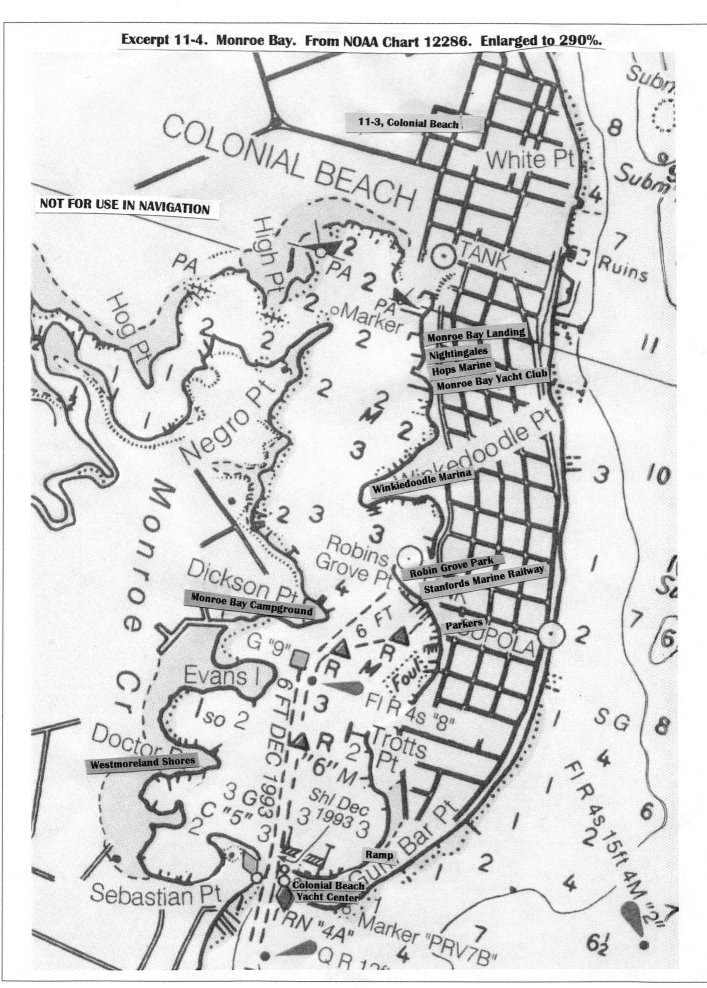

Excerpt 11-4. Monroe Bay. From NOAA Chart 12286. Enlarged to 290%.

11-3, Colonial Beach

NOT FOR USE IN NAVIGATION

Monroe Bay Landing
Nightingales
Hops Marine
Monroe Bay Yacht Club

Winkiedoodle Marina

Robin Grove Park
Stanfords Marine Railway

Monroe Bay Campground

Parkers

Westmoreland Shores

Ramp

Colonial Beach Yacht Center

Excerpt 11-5. St. Clement Island. From NOAA Chart 12286. Reduced to 56%.

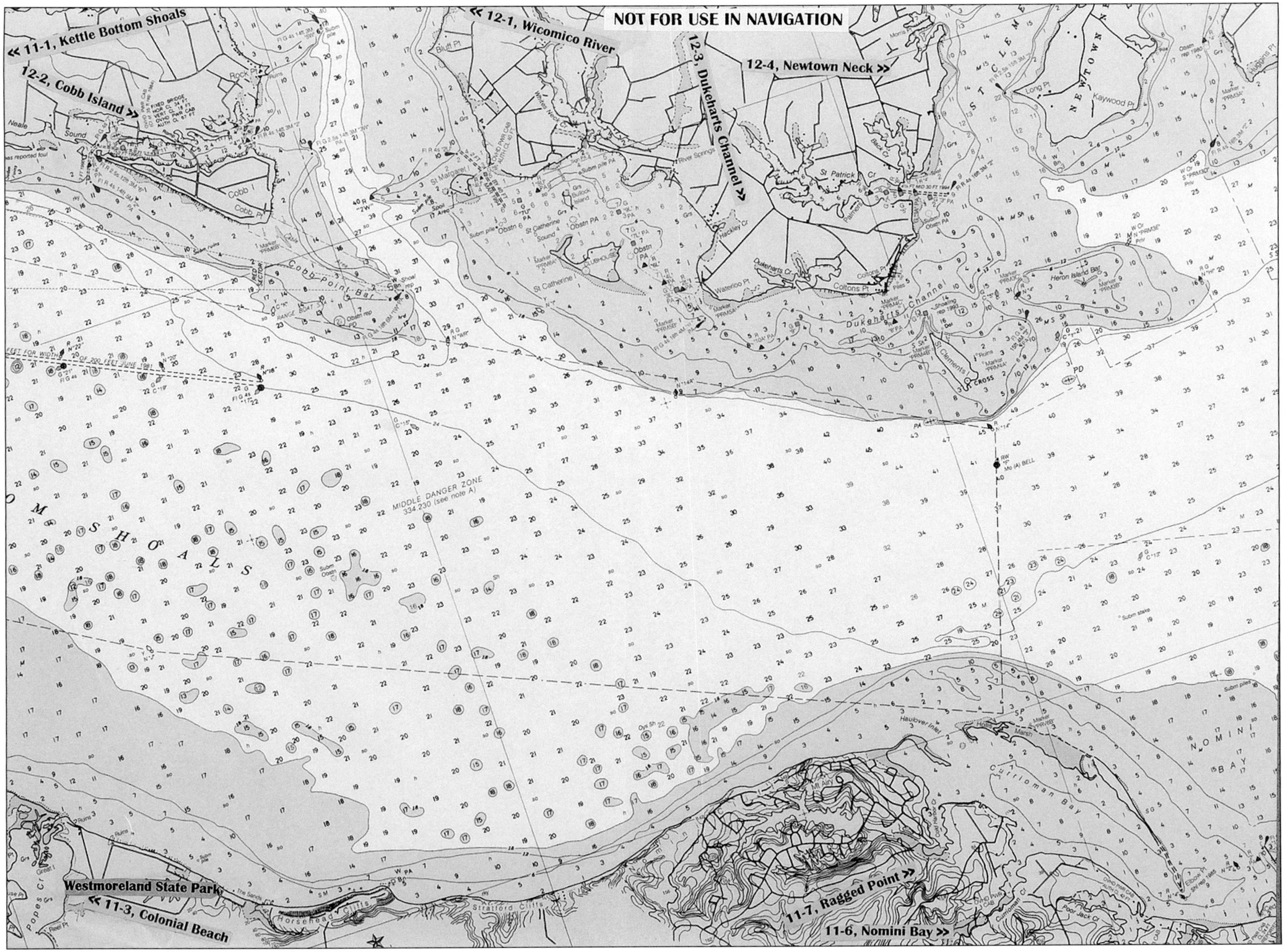

NOT FOR USE IN NAVIGATION
« 11-1, Kettle Bottom Shoals
12-2, Cobb Island »
« 12-1, Wicomico River
12-3, Dukeharts Channel »
12-4, Newtown Neck »
Westmoreland State Park
« 11-3, Colonial Beach
11-7, Ragged Point »
11-6, Nomini Bay »
MIDDLE DANGER ZONE
334.230 (see note A)
Cobb Point Bar
Dukeharts Channel
St Clements I
Heron Island Bar
Currioman Bay
Nomini Bay
Stratford Cliffs
Horsehead Cliffs

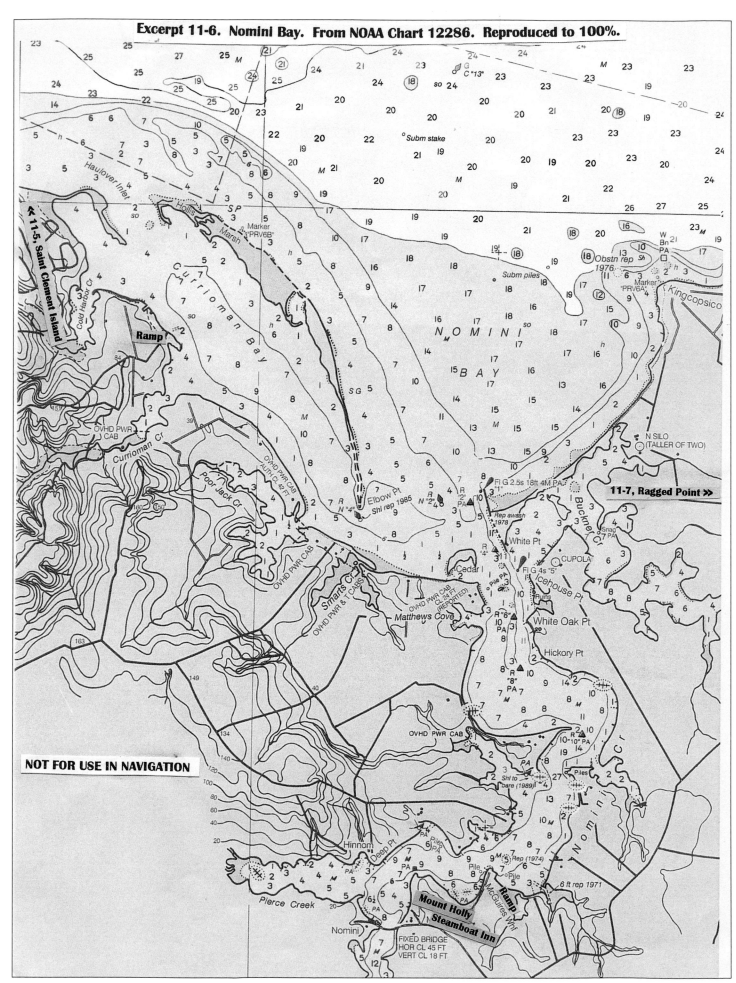

Excerpt 11-6. Nomini Bay. From NOAA Chart 12286. Reproduced to 100%.

NOT FOR USE IN NAVIGATION

78

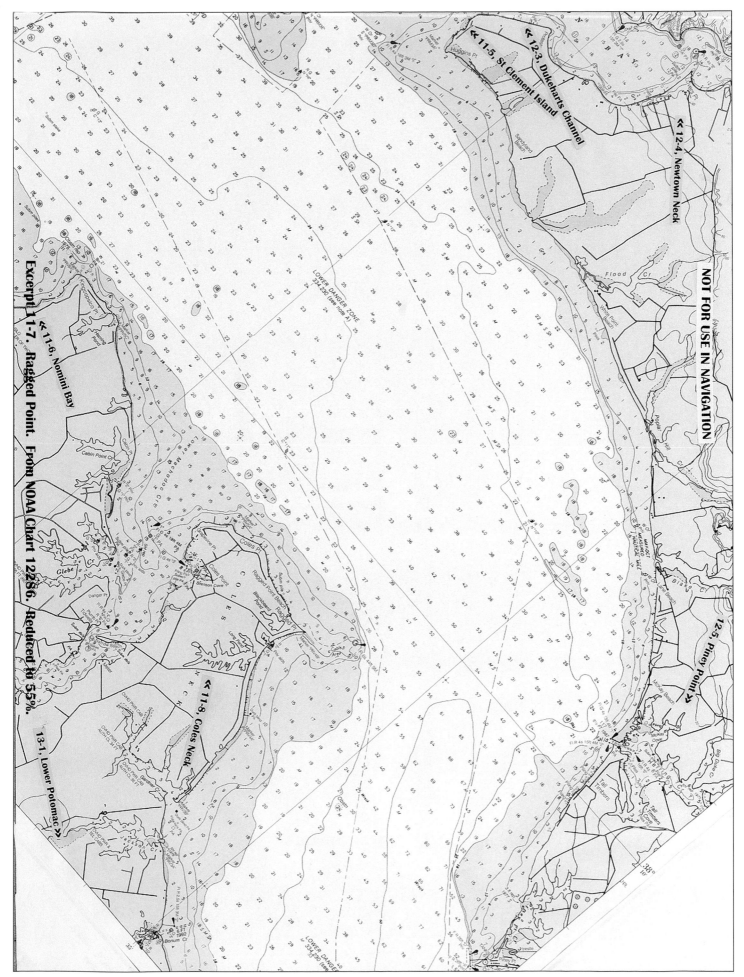

NOT FOR USE IN NAVIGATION

≪ 12-3, Dukeharts Channel

≪ 11-5, St Clement Island

≪ 12-4, Newtown Neck

12-5, Piney Point ≫

Excerpt 11-7. Ragged Point. From NOAA Chart 12286. Reduced to 55%.

≪ 11-6, Nomini Bay

≪ 11-8, Coles Neck

13-1, Lower Potomac ≫

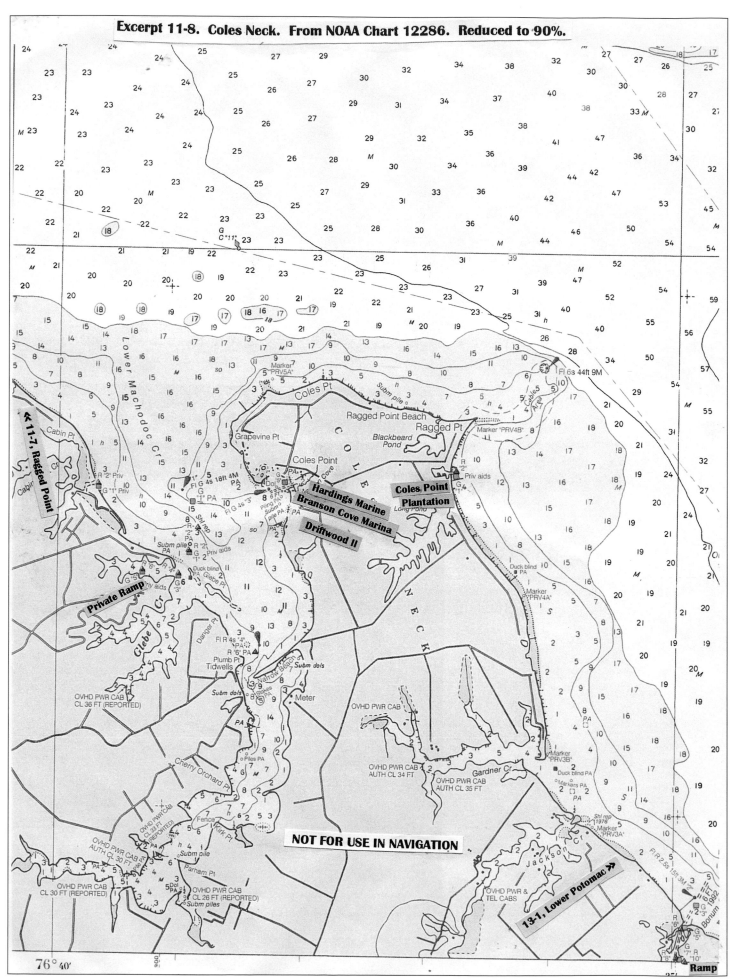

Excerpt 11-8. Coles Neck. From NOAA Chart 12286. Reduced to 90%.

NOT FOR USE IN NAVIGATION

76° 40'

is not for deep-draft vessels. If you draw less than five feet, you're probably OK. When heading south, depart the main channel at "G59" and position yourself at 38°37.75'N/77°08.00'W in about seven feet of water. Head 257°M for about one and a quarter miles. You should also be keeping an equal distance (i.e., about a quarter mile on each side) between the island to your east and the Virginia shore to the west. Hopefully, you'll read no less than five feet at MLW in this shortcut. Near 38°37.35'N/77°09.25'W and in about seven feet of water, you'll be through the passage. If you wish to go from south to north, position yourself at that western waypoint and head 77°M for about one and a quarter miles to "G59" and back to the center of the Potomac channel.

Occoquan Bay and River
Old Town Occoquan
Neabsco Creek and South
Mattawoman Creek
Quantico Area
Wades Bay
Aquia Creek
Potomac Creek
Fairview Beach

OCCOQUAN BAY AND RIVER

The Potomac River significantly widens around Occoquan Bay. See NOAA chart excerpt 9-1. If you're in a deep-draft sailboat, this may be the first place south of Washington where there is ample room for multidirectional sailing. From Cornwallis Neck MD to Freestone Point VA, the Potomac is more than two miles wide. The mouth of Occoquan Bay, from Freestone Point to High Point VA is also more than two miles wide. Much of the outer part of Occoquan Bay is five feet or deeper. After Captain John Smith established Jamestown VA in 1607, he explored much of the tidal Potomac. When Smith reached Occoquan Bay, he found the river churning with fish. During the Civil War, the Confederates successfully blockaded the Potomac with artillery positioned at Freestone Point.

The **Tyme n' Tyde Boatel** is in Occoquan Bay south of Deephole Point. There's no "deep hole" around here. Tyme n' Tyde is a huge boatel with two massive boatel buildings and three modern forklift trucks. The entry channel to Tyme n' Tyde is well marked by six buoys, three red and three green. The channel leads to a small harbor with capacity for about a dozen wet slips. Tyme n' Tyde also has a bathhouse and a sewage pump-out. The Boatel sells gas, and has a fireboat in the small harbor.

Less than one-mile southwest of High Point and near 38°36.44'N/77°12.44'W, in more than 10 feet of water, is the beginning of the channel leading to the Occoquan River. A sand barge and tug plying the river, and drawing about 12 feet, regularly "cuts" this channel. The tug and barge have limited maneuverability and must make wide turns around the buoys. The deepest channel, cut by the barge, is likely to be found in wide turns around some of the buoys.

Belmont Bay is the shallow body extending north from Sandy Point. The first facility after Belmont Bay is the **Fairfax Yacht Club,** which is on the northeast side of the channel. All the slips are like condominiums. They are not rented but bought and sold for between $10K to $40K. The Fairfax Yacht Club has five floating modern docks, and the easternmost dock is covered. The slips range from 30 feet to 50 feet in length. There is no fuel or other services; nor are there slips available for transient boaters at this yacht club. They even redirect disabled vessels, under tow, away from their facility. A no-wake zone starts on the Occoquan River before the Fairfax Yacht Club.

Captain Johns Beach Marina (T 703 339-6726) is the next facility, on the northeast side of the river and just before the 65-foot-clearance railroad bridge. This facility has about seven short docks, 94 wet slips, and a trailerable storage area for 108 boats (30 covered). Electrical service on the docks is 30-amp and 15-amp. They sell bag ice, sodas, and gas and have a ship store with some boating supplies. The facility also has a sewage pump-out and shower facilities. The marina is in a fenced-in secured area, limiting access to slipholders with keys. Their boat ramp is only for slipholders and they generally don't cater to transients because of this security arrangement.

Occoquan Harbour Marina (T 703 494-3600) is after the 65-foot railroad and highway bridges and on the southwest side of the channel. If you need more than a 44-foot vertical clearance, this is as far as you go. But Occoquan Harbour offers much. The marina has 216 slips, ranging in size from 15 feet to 65 feet. They have seven floating docks, a large yard, boat sales, and 24-hour security. Appendix B has a dock layout of Occoquan Harbour Marina. A tiki bar and Geckos restaurant are on the premises. Geckos has a southwestern motif and is packed on weekends. Most of the electric is 30-amp, but they do have 50-amp service on two docks. Occoquan Harbour sells gas on two docks and has diesel. The grounds are exceptionally well maintained and manicured. The marina has a launch ramp, a 25-ton open-end lift, and a near-spotless boatyard. They also have mechanics, a marine store, a bathhouse, laundry, and barbecue pits.

There are more facilities on the other side of that 44-foot-vertical clearance interstate highway bridge, all on the southwestern shore. **Hoffmasters** (T 703-494-7161) is the first marina on the other side of the bridge. Hoffmasters has four fixed docks and 135 slips (59 covered slips) with 30-amp and 50-amp electrical service. They can accommodate up to 50-footers. Hoffmasters also has a ramp, gas (no diesel), a 30-ton open-end travel lift and limited yard space. Their personnel are capable of doing engine repairs, and a few locals speak very highly of them. Hoffmasters is a major Cris Craft dealer.

Prince William Marine Sales (T 703-494-6611) is next to Hoffmasters. Prince William Marine Sales is a large dealer for SeaRays. A boat showroom and sales office are located behind the boatel and up the hill on the main highway. Prince William Marine Sales is a large facility with 300 wet slips and a boatel capable of storing 270 boats. Wet slips have 30-amp and 50-amp electrical service. Despite the size of the facility, the docks are primarily reserved for customers who purchase boats from Prince William Marine Sales. They generally don't cater to transient boaters. The first "T" dock has three gas pumps (one for high octane gasoline) and one diesel pump. A bay beyond the third pier is for a 25-ton open-end travel lift. In 1997, Prince William Marina Sales had another set of docks in Old Town Occoquan and an adjacent facility, called the Riverview Marina. In 1998, all of that was consolidated into one large integrated facility.

Prince William Marine Sales, Hoffmasters, and Occoquan Harbor Marina all have paved launch ramps, bathhouses, and sewage pump-outs. All sell bag ice and marine supplies. Hoffmasters sells some fishing supplies and Occoquan Harbor offers telephone hookups through GTE.

The Occoquan River is the border between well-established Fairfax County and still-developing Prince William County VA. **Occoquan Regional Park** is in Fairfax County on the northeast side of the Occoquan River and just before the 25-foot-clearance VA Route 123 bridge. The park has a ramp area wide enough to launch four boats abreast. The ramp is grooved concrete with a pier to the southeast and a long bulkhead for tieing-up on the northwest. There is ample trailer parking, but the entire park closes at dark. The spacious Fairfax County Park also has a fairly large fenced-in area for storing trailerable boats. Baseball and soccer fields, a batting cage, volleyball courts, picnic shelters, and a snack bar are also located in the park. Some nice vistas of Occoquan are near the northwestern edge of the park. You'll see a few private docks across the river and before the low-clearance 25-foot highway bridge.

OLD TOWN OCCOQUAN

The charming little town of Occoquan is just beyond the Route 123 bridge. Occoquan was established as a Potomac port, and it has quite a history of Potomac commerce. At the turn of the century, there were grist mills, saw mills, and forges. Today, Old Town Occoquan has successfully resisted being bowled over by the nearby developments in suburban Prince William County. The main street, Mill Street, is nearest to and parallels the Occoquan River. Mill Street and the small plazas off of Mill Street are loaded with antique stores, boutiques, and other "tique" shops. Along Mill Street, and on the river, are three restaurants, Sea & Sea Company, Occoquan Inn, and Virginia Grill. The Mill House Museum (T 703 491-7525), a footbridge over the river, and the Fairfax County Water Authority treatment plant are at the head of Mill Street. A tourist information office on Mill Street is across from the Sea & Sea Restaurant. A small municipal park is northwest of the restaurant.

Facilities for boaters are limited in Occoquan. Ladys Landing Marina (T 703-385-9433), behind Sea & Sea Restaurant, has a few slips and a tour boat that works the narrow river. Other than that at Ladys Landing, there may be room to tie-up near the vacated Prince William Marine Sales area. The channel around Occoquan is very narrow. There are many rocks in the river which built up over the years because a hundred years ago and earlier, sailboats dumped out their "rock ballast" in the Occoquan River at the end of a long journey. The tidal range is less than a foot near the town of Occoquan.

NEABSCO CREEK AND SOUTH

Neabsco Creek is north of Freestone Point and houses three nice marinas and a nice restaurant. All of the facilities are on the southwestern shore of Neabsco Creek. The Neabsco Creek channel may be marked with a few flagged stakes and possibly some buoys. The channel makes a small dogleg from a northwesterly to more westerly direction before the railroad bridge. **E-Z Cruz Marina** (T 703-221-1010) is the first facility past the 33-foot-vertical clearance railroad bridge. E-Z Cruz sells gas and has four docks, a 12-ton closed-end travel lift, and a small boatyard. E-Z Cruz has about 190 slips and can accommodate up to 40-footers. Electric service is 15-amp, 30-amp, and limited 50-amp.

The **Pilot House Marina** (T 703-221-1010) is the next marina, and the largest facility on Neabsco Creek. The Pilot House has two large piers with about nine branch docks off the two piers. The marina has 250 slips and can accommodate up to 40-footers. Most slips are serviced by 30-amp electric. A few slips are under cover and a few have lifts to haul boats out of the water. The Pilot House has gas and diesel pumps shoreside and in between the two main piers. They also rent jet skis, repair engines, do canvas work, and fabricate aluminum on the premises. The marina has a 10-ton closed-end truck-pulled lift.

The Pilot House Restaurant is renowned. This boat-shaped restaurant has been around for more than 27 years. It was built by dragging out a large barge and building a restaurant atop. A paddle wheel was placed at the stern. The first floor is an upscale restaurant, closed on Mondays. The second level, or upper deck, is open on weekends and is home to a tasteful bar.

Hampton's Landing Marina (T 703-221-4915) is the third facility on Neabsco Creek. Hampton's Landing has two piers and 93 slips, and sells gas. Their slips can handle up to 40-footers, and the electrical service is 30-amp. Terry Hill, the proprietor at Hampton's Landing, also coordinates all Boat/US towboat activities on the upper Potomac. Hampton's Landing usually harbors more than one of the six Boat/US towboats operating on the upper Potomac.

Hampton's Landing, the Pilot House, and E-Z Cruz Marina all have sewage pump-outs and bathhouses, sell bag ice and some boating supplies. All three facilities have launch ramps. The Hampton's Landing launch ramp is open 24 hours. The water depth off all three marinas is reportedly between three feet and five feet. The Corps of Engineers is supposed to ensure that everything is dredged to five feet on a regular basis. Appendix B has a dock layout sketch of these three Neabsco Creek Marinas.

Next to Hampton's Landing is Neabsco Harbor Marina, which advertises slips for $100 per month. Last year this facility was neglected. There were a few boats floating in the marina, but there were also eight sunken derelicts semi-attached to the docks.

Leesylvania State Park was once the home of Henry "Light Horse Harry" Lee III, a Revolutionary War hero and Robert E. Lee's father. The 508-acre park is south of Neabsco Creek on the Potomac. The park has multiple paved boat ramps, which are in excellent condition. These ramps are sheltered by four breakwaters with three cuts in between the breakwaters. There is a massive parking area for boat trailers as well as some nice piers into the protected breakwater area for temporary boat tie-ups.

Tim's RiverShore Restaurant and CrabHouse ($_T$ 703-441-1375) is south of Leesylvania Park, and south of Powells Creek. Tim's has a long 400-foot "T"-shaped dock with about a seven-foot depth at the end. There's a shallow mud flat about 300 yards straight off the dock. Bobby Sharpe, who's been boating the area for 20 years, stated that at a rare extremely low tide, at some distance away from the pier, he has noticed exposed heaps of broken concrete both north and south of the pier but much closer to the shoreline than that mud flat. Tim's has a taxi boat service for anchored boats. The restaurant is open year around and crowded in the summer. Dining can be either inside or outside. Besides a good restaurant, Tim's RiverShore has jetski rentals. Tim's is a lively colorful place.

MATTAWOMAN CREEK

Mattawoman Creek is across from Tim's on the Maryland side of the River. See NOAA chart excerpt 9-2. You'll often see a large steel mooring ball on the Potomac, slightly north of Mattawoman Creek and south of Occoquan Bay. Barges sometimes moor here. Be careful in this area, especially in times of reduced visibility. The barge mooring area is about one quarter mile northwest of the main Potomac River channel.

Cornwallis Neck is the peninsula between Mattawoman Creek and the Potomac. The Naval Surface Warfare Center and naval ordnance storage facility is situated on Cornwallis Neck. The facility is sometimes called Indian Head. The actual town of Indian Head is about three miles northeast of Deep Point, the tip of Cornwallis Neck. This naval facility was once a depot for storing explosives removed from naval ships and called the "powder plant." Ships stopped here and unloaded their explosive cargo before proceeding upriver to the Washington Naval Yard. Today, it remains an explosive storage facility, and some ordnance training takes place at the base.

Mattawoman Creek, in a lovely area, is arguably the first "rural" creek south of suburban Washington. East of "G45" and "R46" in about 12 feet of water, position yourself at 38°33.60'N/77°13.50'W. From here head about 120°M to "G1" the first mark on Mattawoman Creek. When entering, stay close to both "G3" and "G5"; the latter mark almost has to be extracted from the shoreline. Once nearly atop "G5" turn southeast to "R6" the last mark in the creek. **General Smallwood State Park** is southeast of "R6". The park is home to Sweden Point Marina. The entrance to the marina is well marked by three small red and three small green buoys. The channel and marina area should be dredged to about six feet. A large floating breakwater is at the end and east of the channel. Two piers and a ramp leading to the marina services building are within the breakwater.

Sweden Point Marina (ᴛ 301 743-7613) contains 50 slips and can accommodate up to 32-footers. The slips have 30-amp electric and water, and harbor the marine police. The marina services building has showers, free laundry services, and a meeting room popular with the boat club flotillas who arrive here throughout the summer. If you're coming with your flotilla, reservations are recommended. Appendix B has a dock layout of Sweden Point Marina.

The gas pump (no diesel), a sewage pump-out, six paved launch ramps, and the concession building are southwest of the floating breakwater. The seasonal concession sells sandwiches, snacks, and ice. They don't sell any boating supplies, but they do sell some fishing supplies and fishing licenses. The grounds of Smallwood State Park are well maintained and the park offers many pleasing sites and tables for picnicking. A secured and paved trailerable boat storage area can house about 50 boats on trailers. A footbridge over a small marshy lagoon to a day-use area and museum begins south of the boat launch ramp area. A small museum about Governor Smallwood is also in the state park. Major General William Smallwood was Maryland's Revolutionary War leader. He later served as governor from 1785 to 1788.

By boat, you can travel further up Mattawoman Creek than Sweden Point Marina. Much of the creek is shallow, but there is a deep sinewy channel. Follow either NOAA chart 12289 or 12288 carefully. There are three abandoned wooden footbridges about two miles past Sweden Point Marina. The best gaps between the old footbridge pilings are found near the northwestern shore. The entire river north of the three abandoned footbridges is a no-wake zone.

The boat ramp at E F Mattingly Park is less than a mile past the footbridges. The concrete on the ramp is broken and there is a precarious drop-off at the end of the ramp. Also, the ramp has a short pier, and the trailer parking area is small. Two fishing piers, parallel to the shore, are east of the ramp.

The sand dunes area is about one and a half miles past the three footbridges and past a large area of lily pads. The sand dunes are popular in the summer. Small powerboats can pull right onto the dunes. Mattawoman Creek, a wooded and relatively unspoiled creek -- and a far cry from the hustle and bustle of Washington -- is only 20 nautical miles outside the Washington beltway.

QUANTICO AREA

Stump Neck and Chicamuxen Creek lie about two miles southwest of the entrance to Mattawoman Creek on the Maryland shore. Chicamuxen Creek is very shallow. Stump Neck houses the Naval Explosive Ordnance Disposal Technology Division. The powerlines, with an authorized 70-foot vertical clearance (170 feet over the main channel), cross the river from the mouth of Chicamuxen Creek in Maryland to north of the Possum Point power plant in Virginia. The six tall towers across the river are unmistakable. About half the towers have strobe lights. Don't get too close to any of them at night. I think of the powerlines as one quarter of the distance to the mouth of the Potomac River and the US Route 301 bridge, another 25 miles downriver, as about one half of the distance out of the river.

Quantico Marina (ᴛ 703 784-2359) is about four miles southwest of Mattawoman Creek, on the Virginia shore, and one and a half mile southwest of the powerlines. See NOAA chart excerpt 9-3. The marina is a small manmade harbor that was created by building three solid concrete walls into the Potomac (see picture). If you position yourself at 38°31.12'N/77°17.09'W, you'll be about 40 yards off the entry between the two breakwaters. Quantico Marina has 125 slips on two floating docks and one fixed bulkhead.

Electrical service is 15-amp and 30-amp. The marina has a bathhouse and a limited ship store. Quantico Marina doesn't have a travel lift, but a crane visits the marina twice a year. For about a week in the fall, boats are hauled, and for about a week in the spring, boats are splashed. The marina also has a sailing school with instruction aboard 14-footers and 19-footers. To rent a slip or haulout at Quantico, you must be connected with the Department of Defense. However, anybody can buy gas, and block and bag ice, or take advantage of the sailing school. The marine police and the marina's own rescue boat also harbor at the marina. The marina is closed on Sundays and Mondays.

A short walk from the marina is the town of Quantico or "Q Town." The civilian town is actually an enclave of the US Marine Corps base. In the town, you'll find a some restaurants, a sandwich shop, a post office, and even an AMTRAK train station.

A reliable source informed me that after World War I, several ships were deliberately scuttled in the Potomac, after their useful life. Starting a few miles south of Quantico, in **Mallows Bay** on the Virginia shore, you might see a few of these partially submerged derelicts. A tree or two will be sprouting out of them. It's also possible that other parts of the Potomac bottom from Sandy Point MD to Brent Point VA hold a graveyard for sunken vessels.

WADES BAY

Wades Bay, about five miles south of Quantico Marina, is on the Maryland side. Wades Bay is between Douglas Point and Smith Point, and a tall radio tower sits about a half mile southeast of Douglas Point. Purse State Park, also accessible by about a quarter mile hike from the road, is in the center of Wades Bay. The bay with its long sandy beach lined with scattered sycamore trees, is popular in the summertime with boaters. There are small cliffs both north and south of Wades Bay, which are a favorite of fossil collectors. Many boaters anchor in shallow water or beach their boats about one-third of a mile south of the park, near 38°25.54'N/77°15.63'W. The best sandy beach is in this area south of Purse State Park. In recent years during the summer, hydrilla has been filling in Wades Bay. The hydrilla is worse nearer the north end of Wades Bay. In this part of the Potomac shore, you'll find more than a few shallow creeks that have become tidal pools, thanks to beavers. Along the shore, there are many fallen trees gnawed down by beavers, as well as beaver dams.

AQUIA CREEK

From about 1676 to 1686, the northern frontier of Potomac Virginia was Aquia Creek. A renowned sandstone quarry was situated near Aquia Creek. Rock from this quarry was used for the US Capitol, the White House, and many of the lighthouses on the Potomac and Chesapeake Bay. The Potomac's Piney Point Lighthouse, about 60 miles downriver, still stands and is made from Aquia Creek sandstone. In 1862, during the Civil War, the Union's Army of the Potomac landed in Aquia Creek, and the creek served as a supply line for Union troops.

The entrance to Aquia Creek is about four miles south-southwest of Wades Bay, on the Virginia shore. Aquia Creek is a big wide creek with a broad section that goes back nearly five miles. The southwest shore of the creek has higher topography than surrounding areas. The bottom of the entire creek is fairly uniform with no sharp ridges or drop-offs, holding about a five-foot depth. The bottom is soft mud. A railroad bridge, with 26-foot overhead clearance and about four miles into the creek channel, limits most sailboats. Behind the broad section of the creek, there is a narrow channel that goes back almost another two miles to Aquia Harbour Marina. This last part of Aquia Creek is a no-wake zone.

To get into Aquia Creek, position yourself at 38°22.91'N/77°18.15'W in about seven feet of water just off "R2." See NOAA chart excerpt 9-5. Usually there are no crab pots near the mouth of Aquia Creek. The trickiest part of Aquia Creek channel is immediately after the first daymark, "R2" and still in the Potomac River. After you reach "R2" you have a long stretch to the next mark. You can easily find yourself drifting out of the shallow seven-foot channel before arriving at "G3". After "G3" things are well marked as far as "R12". At "R12" you'll be near the center of the broad creek in about five feet of water. Southwest of "G5" on shore, is a county beach and park, Aquia Landing Beach Park. In the summer, the park sells ice.

In Aquia Creek the marked channel seems to end at "R12". A lot of speeding boats, even at night, make a rhumbline from somewhere near "R12" to the railroad bridge. It isn't advisable to anchor in this path. Because there are a few sandbars on the northeast side of the rhumbline, Scott Willis, at Aquia Bay Marina, recommends anchoring northeast of Aquia Bay Marina, on the southwest side of this rhumbline. If you don't want to go this far into Aquia Creek, I've liked my anchorage about 400 yards due north of "R12" in about four and a half feet of water.

No marina in Aquia Creek has diesel pumps but Jimmy Franklin, at Hope Springs Marina, can have a diesel tanker truck at his marina with a 24-hour notice. The only marina before the railroad bridge is **Aquia Bay Marina** (T 540 720-7437). Aquia Bay Marina has 87 slips on two solid fixed piers. Electrical service is 15-amp and 30-amp, with a few 50-amp outlets at their spaces for 50-footers. Aquia Bay sells gas, bag ice, and some boating supplies. A clubhouse, bathhouse, laundry machines, and a sewage pump-out are on the grounds. They have a 15-ton closed-end travel lift and a large hydraulic trailer capable of pulling out 10 tons and 33 feet, providing the vessel has no more than a four-foot draft. The marina has a ramp but it is not available to the public. East Coast Marine Works (T 540 720-6196) also operates on the premises. East Coast has a boat shed and can perform a wide array of marine repairs.

Underneath the 26-foot railroad bridge, there is about 10 feet of water in the center channel. Beyond the railroad bridge and on the same side of the creek as Aquia Bay Marina (i.e., the southwestern shore), there are three more marinas. The first marina, almost abutting the railroad bridge, is **Hope Springs Marina** (T 540 659-1128) which has 130 slips on three fixed piers. The marina sells gas, bag ice, some boating supplies, and bait, and has a sewage pump-out. The shaded grounds house a clubhouse, a picnic area, a sandy beach, and concrete twin boat ramps. Like Aquia Bay, Hope Springs can haul boats on a large hydraulic trailer. Their trailer can handle up to 34-foot powerboats. Hope Springs Marina has a good-size yard for storing boats. Ken's Marine, in nearby Stafford, can do a variety of boat work on the premises.

Holiday Harbor RV Park and Marina (T 540 659-9935) is on the same side of the creek as Hope Springs. Holiday Harbor has one set of large docks in a shallow water-lilied part of the creek with minimal facilities and services for transients. Most, if not all, of the boat slips at Holiday Harbor are retained for RV-park tenants.

Willow Landing Marina (T 540 659-2653) is about one mile past Holiday Harbor, around the broad point and on the same side of Aquia Creek. Willow Landing has 87 slips on two fixed piers and can handle up to 40-footers. Electrical service is up to twin 30-amp (i.e., 60-amp). The marina sells gas, bag ice, sodas, and some boating supplies. A launch ramp, a pump-out, and a bathhouse are on the premises. The local marine police also launch from Willow Landing. Like Aquia Bay and Hope Springs, Willow Landing Marina has a sizeable hydraulic trailer for pulling and launching bigger boats. Their yard personnel have been highly recommended for mechanical, fiberglass, and electrical work.

After the railroad bridge, the marked and numbered channel reappears. There are plenty of daymarks, starting with "G13" and going well past "G25." Beyond "G25" there is a long no-wake zone in a lily-padded creek that goes back to Aquia Harbour Marina another couple of miles. The trickiest place in the narrow creek is where it makes a bend to the right and across from where Austin Run dumps into the creek from the northwest. The deeper water can be found closer to the bend and on the opposite side from Austin Run.

Aquia Harbour Marina (T 540-659-4232) is at the head of Aquia Creek, and off NOAA chart 12288. Aquia Harbour Marina has 154 slips (20 covered), serviced by 30-amp and 15-amp electric. Appendix B has a dock layout of Aquia Harbour Marina. The area is extremely sheltered, and the slips are on floating concrete docks. The marina welcomes transients and sells gas, bag ice, and some boat supplies. On the premises, there's a bathhouse, pool, and launch ramp. The ramp fee is $5 for Aquia Harbour residents, but it is $40 for other users. There is about a three-foot depth off most of the docks.

POTOMAC CREEK

In 1613, Captain Samuel Argall kidnaped Pocahontas from her Indian village near the mouth of Potomac Creek. Two centuries later, a steamship landing was at the mouth of Potomac Creek. Passengers could catch a stage coach to Fredericksburg, and from there, the railroad. The creek, near its mouth, forms the border between Stafford and King George counties. King George county touts itself as being the gateway to the Northern Neck of Virginia. The Northern Neck is a relatively narrow neck of land, about 70 miles long, hemmed in by the Potomac River to the northeast and the Rappahannock River to the southwest.

On the Potomac, between Aquia Creek and Potomac Creek, you may notice some fish traps and a few crab pots during the summer months. To get to Potomac Creek's "R2" position yourself at 38°20.65'N/77°16.63'W. You'll be in about seven feet of water. See NOAA chart excerpt 9-4. Like Aquia Creek, Potomac Creek has higher topography on its southwestern shore. Halfway between the "G3" and "R4" the water depth comes up to five feet.

Waugh Point Marina (T 540 775-7121) is southwest of "G5" and has about three-foot water depths. Waugh Point Marina is in a small manmade harbor and has about 50 slips, but none are available to transient boaters. The marina does have a gas dock on a pier east of harbor and near Waugh Point. The marina has no ship store but can do engine and canvas work. Waugh Point Marina also has a launch ramp and a trailerable boat storage area.

FAIRVIEW BEACH

About two miles east-southeast of Potomac Creek is the riverfront community Fairview Beach. Near the western end of Fairview Beach and out on a pier is the Fairview Beach Crabhouse with an adjoining pier. The GPS waypoint, about 100 yards off the Crabhouse in six feet of water, is 38°19.99'N/77°14.83'W. The Crabhouse has been open seasonally and has changed ownership regularly in the past. A small general store selling light groceries and bag ice is less than a 100 yards up the hill from the Crabhouse. East of the Crabhouse, the beach is peppered with "Private Beach for Residents Only" signs.

A small channel leading to visible Fairview Beach Yacht Club, Inc. Marina is at the western edge of Fairview Beach. Position yourself at GPS coordinates 38°20.03'N/77°14.12'W in six feet of water and 60 yards offshore. The sluggish channel to the **Fairview Beach Marina** (T 540-775-5971) shoals up easily. Generally, the naturally occurring deeper channel will likely be found on a downriver angle to the jetties. This particular channel can be dredged beneath the reaching radius of the towering bucket crane. Where the bucket crane can reach over the jetty, the channel can be dredged.

Fairview Beach Marina has a paved double boat ramp, a 10-ton closed-end travel lift, a small boatyard, and a proprietor's abode. The marina also sells gas and bag ice. The colorful proprietor, Chuck Bowie, offered me a drink before I opened my mouth. It seems like Chuck has traveled the globe looking for the next party. He retired in the 1970s with a fistful of dollars and blew it all. Today, Chuck appears to live with gusto while finding a way to make ends meet.

Chapter 10
NANJEMOY CREEK TO CUCKOLD CREEK

Nanjemoy Creek
Port Tobacco
Goose Bay
Popes Creek, Maryland
Aqualand and Near the US Route 301 Bridge
Lower Cedar Point Cut
Cuckold Creek

The Potomac upriver from Nanjemoy Creek was often referred to as the Big Bend in earlier times. Looking at NOAA chart excerpt 9-4, you'll see the reason why. For perhaps six miles upriver and nine miles downriver from Nanjemoy Creek, the tidal Potomac currents flow strongly. Near maximum ebb and maximum flood tides, there can be a two-knot-plus current running through this part of the river. John Wilkes Booth found this out at an inopportune time. From Port Tobacco, Booth and David Herold tried to row south toward Dahlgren, but a flooding tide took the craft the wrong way -- west, beyond Nanjemoy Creek. The following night, this time on an ebbing tide, Booth and his companion landed in Virginia, downriver from Port Tobacco. In this area, the River's cross-sectional area is relatively small (i.e., the river is narrow and shallow). If you're in a slow-moving displacement hull boat, it may behoove you to plan your river trip factoring the tidal currents through this part of the Potomac River. That's what I try to do.

NANJEMOY CREEK

Nanjemoy Creek has a wide mouth and is the first Maryland Creek south of Mattawoman Creek, more than 20 nautical miles upriver. At one time Nanjemoy Creek had many fish stakes, but today, none can be found. The deepest entry to the creek is on the eastern side about 100 yards off Blossom Point. See NOAA chart excerpt 10-1. Another method of entering the creek is to leave the Potomac channel at buoy "G11". Northbound and looking backwards, keep "G11" slightly east of due south. I was able to get into Nanjemoy Creek as far as 38°25.00'N/77°06.75'W before I read only five feet of water and anchored. There is a beautiful launch ramp and an "L" pier at Friendship Landing (on the west side of creek). There is also a gravel ramp at Tayloe Landing but not much of a turn around space for vehicles. The Charles County Public School System has an education center with cabins, a dock, a nature center, and trails east of the Tayloe Landing ramp.

Caledon Natural Area is on the Virginia side across the Potomac from the mouth of Nanjemoy Creek. Most of the natural area is southwest of Metomkin Point. Caledon is a Virginia State Park noted for bald eagles, nature trails, and a visitor center. Boating near Caledon is restricted to 1,000 feet from the Virginia shore. During the Civil War, a prisoner of war camp for Union soldiers was located to the east and near Mathias Point VA.

PORT TOBACCO

Before the colonists renamed many areas, the Indian village of "Potopaco" lay in this creek. Around 1638, Father Andrew White settled in the village and composed a catechism in the native Indian language. Later, much tobacco heading for Europe also departed from this port. Until the end of the Revolutionary War, Port Tobacco was the second largest Potomac port after Saint Marys City. Years of clearing and cultivating the surrounding valley caused the creek to seriously silt. A railroad to nearby La Plata further foiled the future of Port Tobacco. Today, on the east side of the creek, stand only a reconstructed historical courthouse, a museum and a couple of old homes.

The first channel mark to Port Tobacco Creek, "G1" is near 38°26.54'N/77°01.85'W and is in eight feet of water. See NOAA chart excerpt 10-2. Halfway between "R4" and "R6" I found only five feet of water at high tide. Historic 200-year-old Saint Ignatius Catholic Church graces the scene over Chapel Point. A few palatial estates on the bluffs dot the shoreline between Saint Ignatius Church and Popes Creek. There is a gravel boat ramp between Deep Point and Fourth Point at Chapel Point State Park.

Port Tobacco Marina (T 301 932-1407) has three peninsulas, three seaward entries, and three separate vehicle entries onto each of the three peninsulas. The southernmost peninsula contains a large boatel capable of storing more than a 100 boats, a small yard, forklift and travel lift bays, a boat ramp, and the marina office. This southernmost peninsula also has a few wet slips behind the marina office. The cut between the southernmost and middle peninsula has the gas dock (no diesel). A high footbridge connects the two peninsulas near the gas dock. The main attraction at Port Tobacco is off-track betting near the Turf Club Restaurant. Both are on the second peninsula. A tiki bar is next to the restaurant. The second peninsula also has more than a 100 boat slips on its eastern side. The western side of the peninsula, under and beyond the footbridge, has an area for side tieing. There is also a long spur peninsula on the east side of the second peninsula. The third peninsula holds the campground, the Chaparral and Caravelle boat sales office, and another boat ramp. The side-tieing on the third peninsula is reserved for the campground users' boats. Appendix B has a large-scale dock layout of expansive Port Tobacco Marina.

GOOSE BAY

The broad mouth of Goose Bay, a westward arm in Port Tobacco Creek, is about halfway between "G1" and "G3" on Port Tobacco Creek. Once in Port Tobacco Creek, you can position yourself at 38°27.15'N/77°02.62'W in about five feet of water. This large shallow bay has several duck blinds along the south shore. Wherever you see a duck blind, even if there is a lot of water all around it, you can assume the blind is planted in shallow water. Generally, to minimize your chances of running aground, turn away from any duck blind before getting too close.

Goose Bay Marina (T 301 934-3812) has four piers with 250 slips, and this marina can handle up to 40-footers. A good portion of the electric service is metered 30-amp, especially on the third dock. There is about four feet of water near the end of most docks. The gas pump (no diesel) is shoreside between the second and third docks. The marina has a travel lift bay and a boat ramp. The "end of the boat ramp" is well marked. The travel lift is a 25-ton closed-end lift, and the boat storage yard is very large. Appendix B has a dock layout of Goose Bay Marina. The quaint marina store sells bag ice, snacks, fishing supplies and some light boating supplies. Two bathhouses and a large shady campground are on the premises. Goose Bay Marina has limited accessibility during the winter months, and the gates are usually locked. Maple Bowie (no relation to Chuck Bowie at Fairview Beach) is the engaging "hands-on" proprietor. Goose Bay Marina was selected to host three of the Red Man bass tournaments in 1998.

POPES CREEK, MARYLAND

There are three restaurants and three sets of docks in this area. From north to south, they are Robertson's, Captain Billy's, and the Pier III Beach Club and Restaurant. To arrive at Captain Billy's, the middle restaurant, position yourself at 38°23.87'N/76°59.60'W. You'll be in about five feet of water, 30 yards from Captain Billy's dock. There are colorful, two-toned cliffs both north and south of Popes Creek which attract fossil hunters. Across the river, during the summer and fall months, there are many crab pots south of Mathias Point.

Robertson's is built on the shore and has a dock with three western-facing finger piers. The outermost finger pier has two large dolphin pilings on each end. This is helpful for tieing-up. Near the beginning of the main dock is an interesting signpost indicating the distances to various locales in the Bahamas, the Caribbean, and even Hawaii.

Captain Billy's (т 301 932-4323) is actually built over the water and has one long pier extending to the west. There is also a wooden dock apron around the seaside edge of the restaurant. Captain Billy's has been around for a long time. It is an established favorite for some locals. Naturally, their specialty is crabs.

The Pier III Crab House and Beach Club is the southeasternmost facility in the immediate area. It attracts a young crowd with its "beachy atmosphere," tiki bar, volleyball court, imported sand, and palm sprouts. The dock is solid, with finger piers starting about two-thirds of the way out.

AQUALAND AND NEAR THE US ROUTE 301 BRIDGE

Aqualand Marina (т 301 259-0572) is just west of the Maryland base of the US Route 301 bridge. See NOAA chart excerpt 10-3. Appendix B has a dock layout of Aqualand Marina. The marina exudes a friendly working-class atmosphere and several watermen harbor their boats here. There is no buoy at the entrance; nor is there a lot of water in here. The entry may shoal up a bit each year, but is usually dredged back to six feet every spring. The entry channel may be difficult to pinpoint at night. To arrive here, position yourself at 38°21.98'N/76°59.10'W. You should be in no less than 15 feet of water off Aqualand's entry channel.

Aqualand Marina has about 160 slips (about 30 covered). Most of the slips have 30-amp electrical service, but some have 50-amp. The marina has a launch ramp, a 20-ton closed-end lift pulled by a tractor, and a large fenced-in boatyard. Aqualand sells gas and diesel, block and bag ice, and some boating and fishing supplies. The marina has a bathhouse and a sewage pump-out. They also rent 16-foot fishing boats. There is a truck stop diner up the road and an affiliated campground with a laundry. Aqualand Marina is also on a straight shot on Route 301 to La Plata MD, the seat of Charles County. La Plata has shopping centers, grocery stores, a selection of restaurants and Physicians Memorial Hospital (т 301 609-4000).

The Governor Harry W. Nice Bridge, or **US Route 301 bridge**, is the last bridge over the Potomac. When the bridge was built in 1940, it was the longest continuous steel truss bridge in the United States. The bridge has two lanes and carries much truck traffic. In order to avoid the crowded Washington DC beltway, many truckers traveling from points on Interstate 95 south of Washington to points in the northeastern corridor take Route 301, bypassing east of Washington, and cross this bridge. The bridge is one and a half miles long and has a clearance of 135 feet at the center span. The deep channel just beneath the center span is at 38°21.77'N/76°59.44'W. Two very large unlit can buoys are on the west side of the channel and on each side of bridge -- "G35" on the south and "G1" on the north side of the bridge. Be careful in this area at night because striking one of these unlit buoys could inflict serious damage to any pleasure boat.

The fourth and last power plant on the tidal Potomac, with its two towering red and white stacks, is the coal-fired PEPCO plant just south of the Route 301 bridge in Morgantown MD. Coal is railroaded directly to the plant.

Across the river in Virginia, there is a nice wayside park on the north side of the bridge. The King George Wayside Park, at the base of the bridge, has picnic tables, grills, a sandy beach, and a sandy landing, but no place to leave a boat trailer. Boats can anchor in the shallow water while the crew comes ashore to picnic.

LOWER CEDAR POINT CUT

There is a steep underwater ledge going from only a few feet of water to more than 50 feet of water. Surface water roils over the ledge. You may observe many drifting (or anchored) fishing boats working the ledge. Coming from (or going to) the Maryland shore southeast of here (i.e., to and from Cuckold Creek), it may be more expeditious to take a shortcut if you can get by with less than five feet of water. With no groundings, I've successfully done it twice. Coming from the northern side (i.e., the deep side) of this ledge, my GPS waypoint, in 50 feet of water, is 38°20.34'N/76°59.03'W. From this waypoint, I head south looking for the comfortable water depth on the shallow side of the ledge. You should find about eight feet of water about one quarter of a mile south of that waypoint. If you want to go from south to north, plug in the waypoint, skirt about a quarter mile offshore, and when you are able to head due north or slightly east of due north, aim for the waypoint. Be ready to take evasive action if the depth becomes uncomfortably shallow.

CUCKOLD CREEK

Three marks -- "G1" "R2" and "G3" -- lead to Cuckold Creek. Outside the channel marks, position yourself at 38°18.77'N/76°55.87'W in about 12 feet of water. See NOAA chart excerpts 11-1 or 12-1. Once in the channel, I barely registered six feet at high tide (i.e., four feet at low tide). When I started reading only five feet of water, I turned around just before "G3". Later I was told the shallowest spot is between "R2" and "G3". Wayne Kuster, the friendly commodore of the **Yacht Club at Swan Point,** said that if you really know what you're doing, you can get into Cuckold Creek with four feet. After you're in the creek, hug the south shore, head back to the north shore, and then swerve back to the yacht club dock on the south shore. I suggest following "a local knowledge boat" on this one.

If you are interested in joining the yacht club, it is likely that you'll be cordially accommodated at the Yacht and Country Club. The club has one dock with 20 to 40 slips serviced mostly by 30-amp electric. The biggest slips are only about 20-feet long. This yacht club has a small but nice gravel boatyard, a launch ramp, a bathhouse, and a pool. A golf course and tennis courts are also in the community. A security detail patrols the well-manicured grounds.

Chapter 11
DAHLGREN TO RAGGED POINT, INCLUDING COLONIAL BEACH, VIRGINIA

Dahlgren and Upper Machodoc Creek
Potomac Beach
Colonial Beach and Monroe Bay
Mattox Creek
Popes Creek and Westmoreland State Park
The Cliffs
Nomini Bay and Creek
Lower Machodoc Creek
Ragged Point Area

DAHLGREN AND UPPER MACHODOC CREEK

Nine days after he assassinated Abraham Lincoln, John Wilkes Booth fled across the Potomac, hoping to find sympathy in Virginia. Right after the end of Civil War hostilities, Virginians were less than enthusiastic about helping Booth. After fleeing Washington with a fractured leg, Booth crossed into Maryland over the Naval Yard Bridge. In southern Charles County, Booth and fellow conspirator David Herold hid in a pine tree stand for six days while Union search parties often passed close by. They first departed Maryland in a rowboat near Port Tobacco, but the tide took them the wrong way and they had to spend another night in Maryland. The following night, on an ebbing tide, the two landed far to the south at Gambo Creek, near Dahlgren VA. Booth didn't make it much farther. In Port Royal, about 20 miles southwest of Dahlgren, and nearly 12 days after Lincoln was assassinated, Union soldiers caught up with the assassin. Most historians agree that Booth's days ended at Garrett's tobacco barn in Port Royal, but others speculate he ended his final days elsewhere.

Upper Machodoc Creek is about three miles south of the US Route 301 bridge, on the Virginia shore. The Dahlgren Naval Weapons Station and the town of Dahlgren are on the north side and on the mouth of Upper Machodoc Creek. See NOAA chart excerpt 11-2. The Naval Weapons Station was located at Dahlgren because for almost 20 miles downriver, there is "a clear shot." From the head of land on the naval base, naval guns, most five inches or less, are test-fired southeast across the Potomac. Naturally, when the Navy is test-firing, the main part of the river is closed to boating. This seldom happens during the weekends, and more often occurs during hostile times (e.g., during the Persian Gulf War).

Naval firing range boats and Dahlgren Range Control monitor VHF radio channels 16 and 14. The naval range control boats should escort you off the firing range. On close inspection, you can find the boundary of the firing range on NOAA chart 12286 (i.e., the boundary of MIDDLE DANGER AREA). Yellow buoys also mark the boundary of the range. A prudent boater should consider contacting Dahlgren Range Control on the VHF radio before reaching the area (i.e., near the Route 301 bridge southbound or near Saint Clements Island northbound). During times of test-firing, some pleasure boats have traveled up and down the river by closely skirting the Maryland shore and outside of the MIDDLE DANGER AREA boundary.

Upper Machodoc Creek is a long entry with lots of hazards and is not recommended for a night approach -- at least not for a first timer. Three tall towers are first observed. Along the shore, you can notice a wide array of naval station hardware. The conspicuous blue gantry that was once here has been removed.

From out in the Potomac at "G29" turn westward and follow the three red buoys -- "R2" "R4" and "R6" -- until arriving at channel junction buoy "BP". Don't stray too far from these three red nun buoys because about a dozen or more pilings are south and close to this channel. NOAA charts 12286 and 12287 also indicate some submerged pilings on the north side of this channel. Furthermore, in the summer and fall months, the north side of the channel is strewn with crab pots.

A pair of tall **range lights** is also very helpful when entering Upper Machodoc Creek. The two range light platforms are less than a quarter mile apart and well into the creek. As you approach them from a mile or two out, keep them lined up. The forward range light is usually lower than the rear light platform. If you keep the range lights lined up, you should be able to stay in the channel. The lights atop these range platforms are green.

At junction mark "BP" a secondary channel joins from the southeast (see NOAA chart excerpt 11-2). This junction buoy is painted "green over red" signifying that green is the preferred channel (i.e., the top band color). After the "BP" buoy, hold the primary channel course past "R8" "G9" and the two range light platforms. Near "G9" you'll see an attractive beach off of Baber Point. The gravel boat ramp off Baber Point is inaccessible and only for naval use. After the two range light platforms, the water maintains a consistent five-foot depth.

The first dock after the range marks is the military base's **Dahlgren Yacht Club** (T 540 653-5449). The fixed wooden pier has about 30 slips and can handle up to about 32-footers. The club also has a launch ramp. You have to be affiliated with the Department of Defense to use this facility.

Dahlgren Marine Works (T 540 663-2741) is a quarter mile west of the military base's dock and is open for civilian business. Dahlgren Marine Works has 58 slips (12 covered) serviced by 30-amp and 15-amp electric. The marina also sells gas, diesel, and bag ice, as well as a good assortment of boating supplies. Dahlgren Marine Works has a 6-ton closed-end tractor-pulled travel lift, a paved launch ramp, and a sewage pump-out. The boatyard is packed in the winter, and they have a large work shed. Don Paul and his team will do just about any kind of boat job (e.g., engine, electrical, etc.) except fiberglass work. About a mile walk from the Dahlgren Marine Works is the little town of Dahlgren, which has about four restaurants.

POTOMAC BEACH

Less than three miles southeast of the Dahlgren channel is Potomac Beach and two nice restaurants on the river. See NOAA chart excerpt 11-3. Both restaurants are highly touted by locals and have a dock for their boating customers. **Wilkerson's,** the westernmost restaurant, has two docks. The **Happy Clam,** the easternmost restaurant, has one "L"-shaped dock. Staff at both restaurants indicated that the MLW at the end of the docks is four and a half feet. There is a small scrubby beach between the restaurants. Off Wilkerson's dock in six feet of water, the position is 38°16.56'N/76°59.76'W. At only 100 yards off the dock, my depthfinder was registering only six feet at low tide. Beware of the many old pilings in the area. This shore of the Potomac is also exposed to waves coming from the north and east.

COLONIAL BEACH AND MONROE BAY

Colonial Beach, the largest river town south of the Washington beltway, is steeped in history. Three of our nation's first five presidents, including George Washington, and 14 signers of the Declaration of Independence, were born nearby. Robert E. Lee, the great Confederate general, and much of his lineage had a plantation a few miles to the south. Alexander Graham Bell, inventor of the telephone, once resided in town.

Colonial Beach was the "Oyster Capital of the Potomac" and was a hotbed of conflict during the bloody Maryland-Virginia waterman wars of the 1940s. In the late 1940s and early 1950s, it was a rip-roaring river town with gambling around the clock. The town attracted many, by car and by boat, from upriver Washington. After the Chesapeake Bay Bridge was built in 1952, Washingtonians had another way to access the beaches -- by easily crossing the Delmarva peninsula and reaching the beaches on the Atlantic Ocean. Thus Colonial Beach retrenched.

Today Colonial Beach has about 3,100 year-around residents but the population swells to 10,000 in the summer. You'll discover the Victorian homes and homey streets named after colonial era persona. But you'll also find off-track betting, a new McDonald's, a Food Lion grocery store and a Days Inn Motel. Despite its anomalies, Colonial Beach remains one of my favorite places on the Potomac. It's always a refreshing change of pace from Washington.

Approaching Monroe Bay and Colonial Beach from the northwest, you should round "R2" before bending around in deep enough water and arriving close to the bay entry. If you are coming from the southeast, you can head straight for "R4" and GPS waypoint 38°13.62'N/76°57.72'W before negotiating the Monroe Bay cut. You'll be in seven feet of water about 100 yards southeast off "R4". Navigation aid "R4" is almost a full mile west-southwest of aid "R2".

Coming from the northwest, if you're close enough to the beach, you'll see the **Riverboat "Gaming Center"** perched on pilings over the water. Like a few other "over-the-water" places on the Virginia shore, this place is actually in Maryland. Maryland gaming laws, not the generally more conservative Virginia laws, apply here. The main draw of the Riverboat is off-track betting on 51 television screens. At one time, in calm conditions, you could tie-up to a pier and visit the Riverboat. You can't today. Many dangerous pilings extend a good ways into the river east of the Riverboat and, to a lesser degree, from the south side of the Riverboat. There's no connecting pier from any of the pilings to the gaming center. By boat, your safest way to reach the Riverboat is to enter Monroe Bay, land somewhere in the bay, and then walk back to the Riverboat.

The Colonial Beach Municipal Pier is also on the Potomac about a couple hundred yards south of the Riverboat. This handsome pier is popular with locals fishing. The GPS waypoint, in about 10 feet of water and about 50 yards off of the municipal pier, is 38°15.08'N/76°57.50'W. The much-shorter Fisherman's Pier is north and right next to the municipal pier. The Fisherman's Pier, unlike the municipal pier, has a locked gate and is used by local charter fishing vessels. These Potomac piers are very exposed from the northwest all of the way to the southeast.

A concrete boardwalk stretches from the Days Inn (north of the Riverboat) to the municipal pier. Many of the boardwalk's more rumpled hotels have been torn down, and the once unrefined image of 20-50 years ago has been cleansed. I recollect having a few foot-stomping nights here 20 years ago. A swimming area, protected by a jellyfish net, lies between the municipal pier and the Riverboat. South of the boardwalk and municipal pier, a series of rock groins thwart beach erosion. Where there are no rock groins, there is no sandy beach. The intermittently constructed groins and a rock seawall stretch all of the way to the tip of Gum Bar Point.

Back on the water, navigation aid "R4" sits a couple hundred yards south of Gum Bar Point. After "R4" line up as many aids as you can and stay in the center of the narrow channel as you enter Monroe Bay. At maximum ebb or flood tide, there can be a slight current through the entry. See NOAA excerpt 11-4, for an enlargement of Monroe Bay. The **Colonial Beach Yacht Center** (☏ 804 224-7230) is on Gum Bar Point just inside the Monroe Bay entry. The Yacht Center is the premier marina in Colonial Beach, with a 160 slips serviced by 50-amp, 30-amp, and 15-amp electric. Many of the larger slips are covered. The Yacht Center can accommodate 18-footers to 150-footers. The marina sells gas and diesel, block and bag ice, and boating and fishing supplies. They have a bathhouse, a sewage pump-out, a paved launch ramp, and a sandy beach. The marina has a 17-ton closed-end lift pulled by a tractor as well as a forklift. Their haul-out yard is of modest size. Appendix B has a dock layout of Colonial Beach Yacht Center. Their service personnel can handle a wide array of boat repairs. The premises is home to the **Dockside Restaurant**, touted for seafood and steaks, and Martin's Tavern. The Virginia Marine Police harbor a couple of vessels at the marina.

A public launch ramp is about 200 yards northeast of the Yacht Center in Monroe Bay. The area has dual ramps and two short piers. The ramp closest to Gum Bar Point is concrete, giving way to gravel, while the ramp further away from the point is sandy. Boat trailer parking space is ample. A beefy but abandoned and inaccessible, "T" pier is about 500 yards north of the boat ramp on Trotts Point. I registered about seven feet of water right off of this "T" pier.

There is not much room to anchor in Monroe Bay. At all times, day and night, small powerboats zoom in and out of the bay. Hence, if you wish to anchor in this tight bay, make every attempt, factoring in your draft, to anchor out of "harms way" leaving an unobstructed path for these small speeding powerboats. I've found in more than a few places that there is usually more water outside of the channel than depicted on NOAA chart 12286. Near Stanford's and closer to the eastern side of the bay, I've been able to anchor in six to seven feet of water.

Parker's Restaurant is in between Trotts Point and Stanford's. For restaurant boating patrons, Parker's has a nice dock with no utilities. At the end of this dock, there is about five feet of water. Parker's seafood restaurant is very popular with locals. Parker's also has a modest marina, with utilities, just north of the restaurant dock.

Stanford's Marine Railway (T 804 224-7644) has a well-stocked ship store. The marina has a couple dozen slips and a good place to get yard work done. The 25-ton open-end travel lift is the biggest in Colonial Beach. However, Stanford's yard is pretty tight, with limited space to dry-store a boat for any length of time. Stanford's has eight feet of water near the end of his docks. Clarence Stanford has a well-deserved and respected reputation on this river.

Pleasantly shaded Robin Grove Wayside park is on the small peninsula next to Stanford's. A water tower sits near the north end of the park. Winkiedoodle Point is the next point north in Monroe Bay. **Winkiedoodle Marina** is near the end of the point and on the southeast side. Near the tip of Winkiedoodle Point, a sloping bed of oyster shells looks like it has been used as a boat launch ramp before. The water near Winkiedoodle Point is shallow at three to four feet.

The **Monroe Bay Yacht Club** (T 804 224-8278) is the next commercial pier north of Winkiedoodle Marina. The yacht club has some covered and some open slips. **Hop's Motor and Marine Supplies** (T 804 224-3123) is the pier just north of the Yacht Club. Hop's has a solid pier and sells gasoline. **Nightingale's Hotel and Marina** (T 804 224-7956) is just north of Hop's. Nightingale's grounds are well kept and they're doubling the length of their one pier. The water depth of Nightingale's pier was purported deeper than shown on NOAA chart 12286. The **Monroe Bay Landing** Restaurant and Lounge is the next commercial dock north. With the Riverboat Lounge having succumbed to gaming, the Monroe Bay Landing Lounge seems to have filled the void for those desiring late night entertainment. This can include live bands.

As you continue counterclockwise along the shore through Monroe Bay, you'll come to more pilings, an elegant Baptist Church with a water tower behind it, and a new dock for the recently built condominiums. If you follow the creek southwest, past the marshy area, you will arrive at a waterfront trailer park southwest of Negro Point. You'll likely see lots of heron in this part of Monroe Bay. Between Negro Point and Dickson Point, you'll find many private docks with nice homes gracing the shoreline.

Monroe Bay Campground (T 804 224-7418) extends to Dickson Point. The campground is about 200 yards north of "G9" and across the Monroe Bay from Stanford's. The campground store sells beer, bait, and ice. The well-furbished campground has a wide sandy bathing beach with a floating swimming platform, basketball courts, and a children's playground. The big white building extending two-thirds over the water is an amusement center. The campground has a wide concrete boat ramp with a short pier southeast of the amusement center. A large wide wooden platform pier with two cranes is about 40 yards southeast of the ramp.

Doctor Point is a couple of points south of Dickson Point. **Westmoreland Shores** community dock and a paved ramp are on Doctor Point. Both the ramp and pier are private and are owned by the residents of Westmoreland Shores. The Colonial Beach Yacht Center is on the opposite side of Monroe Bay.

If you desire to walk around Colonial Beach, land at any of the marina docks between the Colonial Beach Yacht Center and Monroe Bay Landing Restaurant. By far, the Colonial Beach Yacht Center has the most amenities. However, if your draft permits, landing at one of those smaller facilities further up the bay puts you closer to the town's "commercial district." See appendix C, for a detailed street sketch of Colonial Beach.

The town of Colonial Beach has six motels and more than a dozen restaurants. Four of the motels, including Nightingale's and the new Days Inn are a short walk from the head of Monroe Bay. Five of the restaurants, including Monroe Bay Landing, Flanagan's, Hunan Diner, the Riverboat's and Lenny's are also within walking distance. Lenny's is a great place for breakfast, with excellent service. The Hunan Diner has good Chinese food.

If you are willing to walk a little further, on the main street away from the beach, you'll come to a pizzeria. A ways past the pizzeria, there's a shopping center with a McDonald's, Hardee's, Subway, and Domino's Pizza. You'll also find a Food Lion grocery store, Rite-Aid Pharmacy, Rankin's True Value Hardware, and an automatic bank teller machine in or near this modern shopping center.

Colonial Beach has many scheduled varied events throughout the year -- festivals, fireworks, fishing tournaments, and more. The Potomac River Festival is usually in early June. The Rockfish Tournament is held over Columbus Day weekend. The entry fee for the Rockfish Tournament is $125, and the prize for the largest rockfish is $5,000. For more information on the Rockfish Tournament and other activities in Colonial Beach, call the Colonial Beach Chamber of Commerce at (T 804 224-8145).

MATTOX CREEK

By land, Mattox Creek is more than eight miles from Monroe Bay. See NOAA chart excerpt 11-3. But by water, the entrance to Mattox Creek is about a half mile away from the entrance to Monroe Bay. To enter Mattox Creek, position yourself at 38°13.35'N/76°57.40'W. You should be in about eight feet of water off "G1". Don't cheat the first three marks in this creek (i.e., "G1" "R2" and "G3"). There is a duck blind off Church Point near "G3". The approach is straight until a 90-degree right turn is needed at "R4". Before "R4" there is a pleasing isolated beach going out on a spit on the western side of the creek. You should encounter no less than nine feet of water before "R4". The duck blind is further west than shown on NOAA chart 12286. There is a large pier south of "R6" and the Ebb Tide Beach is east of this pier. The Ebb Tide Beach is a private community beach and pier. You'll see a few private docks in the area.

Stepp's HarborView Marina (☏ 804 224-9265) is behind Fox Point and south of "G11". This full-service marina has a lot of amenities. Appendix B depicts a dock layout. Stepp's has 145 slips (80 covered) and can handle up to 60-footers. Slip electric service is 30-amp and 50-amp. At the fuel dock, you'll find three gas pumps. They sell block and bag ice and some boating and fishing supplies. The grounds contain a swimming pool, picnic tables, and a bathhouse. Stepp's has a wide concrete ramp giving way to sand on a gradual slope. Stepp's doesn't have a travel lift, but they are able to haul very heavy powerboats, up to 55 feet long, with a large hydraulic trailer pulled by a tractor at their ramp. Their staff can do engine, electrical, and fiberglass work. Stepp's is a dealer for Rinker and Silverton boats as well as MercCruiser.

POPES CREEK AND WESTMORELAND STATE PARK

Popes Creek VIRGINIA (distinguished from Popes Creek in Maryland, about 14 miles to the north-northwest), is about three miles east of Mattox Creek. The entrance may be totally blocked at low tide. Even at high tide, it is often too shallow for all but the shallowest draft vessels. Then why even mention it? Because on February 22, 1732, George Washington was born about a quarter mile from this creek entrance. A visitor center and a small "Washington Monument" are on the grounds. Boats are not allowed to tie up near the estate. In George's day, a mercantile dock was just northwest of the creek's entrance. Today, there is an attractive beach here.

Westmoreland State Park (☏ 804 493-8821) is about a mile southeast of Popes Creek. See NOAA chart excerpt 11-5. This pretty park offers a lot. A boat ramp and a gasoline dock are near the northwest end of the park. The park also rents rowboats and paddleboats. A very nice bathing beach is southeast of the piers. Behind the beach is a freshwater swimming pool. The park also has cabins and camping. If you can't get to Horsehead Cliffs by boat, you can drive to the park and walk along the beach to the base of the cliffs. It's best to make this walk at low tide.

THE CLIFFS

Undoubtedly, these three sets of Potomac River cliffs are the most spectacular. Many of their bluffs rise more than 150 feet above the Potomac. There are other cliffs along the 100-mile tidal river that attract shell, fossil, shark-teeth and whale bone hunters too. Some nice cliffs are found upriver both to the north and to the south of Popes Creek MD. Further upriver on the Maryland side, scattered and smaller bluffs can be found between Liverpool Point and Maryland Point. At low tide, you'll see "fossil hounds" scrounging the beaches, looking for elusive sharks teeth and whatever else.

Horsehead Cliffs are about one mile to the east of Westmoreland State Park. These cliffs have more of a "Badlands" type formation (i.e., the cliffs are more cut back) than the other two sets of cliffs to the south. There is a small bay and a little beach to the east of Horsehead Cliffs. To get to Horsehead Cliffs by water, position yourself near 38°10.38'N/76°51.80'W. You'll be in about eight feet of water and about 80 yards off the cliffs.

Stratford Cliffs are about a mile east of Horsehead Cliffs. Beyond the bluff at Stratford Cliffs, the rolling terrain goes back to Robert E. Lee's estate, Stratford Hall. Private property signs, facing the water, pepper the beach at the base of Stratford Cliffs. It's therefore obvious you shouldn't land here. Nonetheless, if you just want to enjoy the scenery and anchor at the base of the cliffs, position yourself at 38°10.10'N/76°50.95'W. You'll be about 80 yards off the cliffs in about six feet of water. A dirt road coming down to the beach from Lee's estate is near the east end of Stratford Cliffs.

Nomini Cliffs are the largest and possibly the prettiest of the three sets of cliffs. The bluffs stretch for more than two miles along the Potomac. The center of the cliff area is near 38°10.16'N/76°48.09'W. A "cliff front" private community is atop and just behind the cliffs. There used to be a beach at the base of many of these bluffs, but the bluffs have eroded significantly and what was once a beach is now littered with fallen trees and other debris dropped from the cliffs. Nor'easters, winter storms with strong northwest to east-northeast winds, incessantly pound the shoreline and re-cut these cliffs.

NOMINI BAY AND CREEK

Nomini Creek may be one of the most working-class creeks on the Virginia side of the Potomac. There are a couple of seafood packing houses, including the largest eel-packing house in the country, Robberecht's. There are more workboats and fewer affluent homes seen on Nomini Creek than in most other nearby Virginia creeks. There's also an abandoned fishing shack over the water near the mouth of the creek (see front cover picture). I like the scene here.

Before entering Nomini Creek, you'll need to be in Nomini Bay. See NOAA chart excerpt 11-6. At a comfortable depth near the center of Nomini Bay head, for the entrance to Nomini Creek. The waypoint just outside Nomini Creek is 38°08.50'N/76°43.52'W. This waypoint, being at the head of Nomini Bay, should be approached from a relatively narrow seaward cone bounded by Hollis Marsh Island to the northwest and the tip of Kingcopsico Point to the northeast. Near the creek waypoint, the seaward tip of Hollis Marsh Island should have a bearing of 325°M and the tip to Kingcopsico Point should have a bearing of 60°M. Upon arriving outside the creek, you'll be in 10 feet of water, about 100 yards off the channel entry to Nomini Creek.

A rock jetty, which may be partially submerged, is southeast of "G1". Give this area east of the entry plenty of room. However, there is an enticing unoccupied beach just east of the jetty. The shallowest water in the entire creek channel is right after the entry, just past "R2". I registered only six feet near "R2" but more than 12 feet at "R4" lighted "G5" and "R6". Furthermore, the channel narrows between "R2" and "R4". On the west side, give the abandoned fishing shack and the duck blind south of it plenty of room. Except close to the shore, most of the creek has more than seven feet of water and many places have 10 to 12 feet of water.

Currioman Bay extends between the Hollis Marsh Island and the mainland. A curious narrow wooden boat ramp at Currioman Landing is about two and a half miles northwest of the Nomini Creek entrance and well into Currioman Bay. The docks around the ramp will likely be harboring a few well-used workboats (see picture).

Back in Nomini Creek and southbound, don't cheat on "R10". Near the western shore, there is a pleasant little cove to anchor before "R10". After "R10" go back to the western side, giving the point with the first packing house plenty of room. There are many wide places in the creek to anchor after "R10". George Robberecht's eel-packing house is on the point at McGuires Wharf. Robberecht's also has a boat ramp on the east side of its packing house. If you continue to the next point west of McGuires Wharf on the same side of the creek, leave the stakes near that point (what is remaining from an old duck blind) to your port (i.e., to your south). You can still find five or six feet of water in most of this wide basin just before the 18-foot-clearance highway bridge. The **Mount Holly Steamboat Inn** is a restored colonial mansion converted to an upscale restaurant on the east side of this basin. Down the hill from the restaurant is a rickety dock that may be tricky for a large boat, but is probably OK for a dinghy.

LOWER MACHODOC CREEK

To enter Lower Machodoc Creek, favor the center of the creek. There is shallow water extending about one half mile southwest of Coles Neck on the eastern shore. See NOAA chart excerpts 11-7 or 11-8. In deep enough water, work your way to 38°08.65'N/76°39.25'W, and you should find a 14-foot depth. At this point the two green channel markers should be in a line and on a heading of 140°M. Coles Point should be on a heading of 65°M and less than a mile away, and the tip of land east of Kingcopsico Point should be on a heading of 315°M.

After the first lighted "G1" there is a second unlighted "G1". The second "G1" begins marking a second channel -- the channel into Branson Cove. If you turn left into Branson Cove, you will encounter two more green marks, "G3" and "G5" before you enter protected little Branson Cove. Most of the channel into Branson Cove has about an eight-foot depth. I sounded eight feet near "G3" but only six feet near "G5". **Branson Cove Marina** (₸ 804 472-3866) is the first facility on your starboard side (i.e., south) just past "G5". Branson Cove Marina has 38 slips (23 covered slips), serviced with 30-amp electric. They have a ramp and sell gas and diesel, and block and bag ice. You'll usually find the owner, Mike Bigelow, working in the quaint little country store. The store sells some groceries and a few boat supplies. The lunch counter at the store is one of my favorites for breakfast. There's also a pool table in the back of the store. About one quarter of a mile walk up the road from Branson Cove Marina is the **Driftwood II** restaurant. The food is high quality, and on weekends the place is packed. It seems a significant portion of Westmoreland county comes here for dinner every weekend.

Harding's Marine Railway (₸ 804-472-2698) is next to Branson Cove Marina and further in the cove. Harding's has a 40-ton railway and can simultaneously work on two boats pulled out on the tracks. **North Point Marine** (₸ 804-472-2164) is next to Harding's. This small marina has about a dozen and a half slips and a small yard for trailerable boats. But it has no boat ramp, nor electric, nor water service. About six feet of water depth was sounded near the western edge of North Point Marine. The eastern edge of North Point Marine is nearly at the head of the cove. **Lower Machodoc Marina** (₸ 804-472-4038) is across and on the north side of Branson Cove. Lower Machodoc Marina has about two dozen slips. Some are covered, and some have 15-amp electrical service. A fair number of slips harbor workboats. Lower Machodoc Marina has a ramp and a modest size yard for storing trailerable boats. **Allen's Oyster House** is next to Lower Machodoc Marina and across from Branson Cove Marina. Allen's has a commercial pier and a few booms for unloading the oyster boats. The Coles Point Post Office is west of Allen's Oyster House, and about halfway between "G3" and "G5". In Virginia, this is likely the closest post office to the water. On Maryland's Potomac, there are at least four post offices on the water -- at Piney Point, Coltons Point, Saint Marys City, and Cobb Island.

If you didn't turn east into Branson Cove but continued south in Lower Machodoc Creek, you'll pass three red navigation aids, "R2" "R4" (a lighted aid), and "R6". Not far past Lower Machodoc "R2" is another shallow channel off to the west into Glebe Creek. A wide, paved boat ramp with two piers is in the north branch of Glebe Creek, near the end of the channel. However, this ramp has a locked gate and is for the exclusive use of Glebe Harbor residents.

Southbound on Lower Machodoc Creek, stay close to "R4" and "R6" and you should find no less than eight feet of water. On Plum Point, you'll see a large white seafood-packing house. After the narrow opening past "R6" the creek will widen out again. To the east, on a narrow spit of land are some nice homes. The front lawns of these homes face northward toward the Potomac. The back of these homes also face the water -- the headwaters of Lower Machodoc Creek. On the side opposite the Potomac, you'll also see the road leading to these homes as well as many private docks and a few private boat ramps. You'll find many stakes in the water past this "residential spit." They must mean something? I stayed away from areas where the stakes were plentiful, and gravitated to areas more devoid of stakes, and I never read less than eight feet of water. In this part of the creek, there will be a handful of nice homes with some substantial boats, even some large sailboats at some of the private docks. Nosing as close as 30 yards from shore, I still read no less than six feet of water depth.

RAGGED POINT AREA

The shoals off of Ragged Point are very popular with local fisherman. In the summer this area is teeming with fish and fishermen. Unless you want to fish the lucrative shallows off Ragged Point, give the Ragged Point spider tower a comfortable berth. See NOAA chart excerpt 11-7. A sometimes-open bar built out over the water under the jurisdiction of the state of Maryland (i.e., the more liberal liquor and gambling laws) is on the western side of Ragged Point near the northern tip of Coles Neck.

South of Ragged Point is a small channel, about seven feet deep, leading to the lavish harbor of **Coles Point Plantation** ($_T$ 804 472-3955). To arrive at the Coles Point Plantation entry, work your way to 38°08.60'N/76°36.70'W, but keep a safe distance from the shallows to your north. Coles Point Plantation has something for everyone. Besides the full-service marina, the resort is home to the **Pilot's Wharf Restaurant**, sandy beaches, a 500-foot fishing pier, pool, campground, cottages, picnic area and grills, hiking and biking trails, and canoe and paddleboat rentals on an 80-acre freshwater pond. The resort has 130 slips (62 covered), from 25 feet to 60 feet in length. They also have plans for a major expansion. The slips have 30-amp and 50-amp electrical service. The Virginia Natural Resources Police harbor two boats here. The marina sells propane, block and bag ice, gas and diesel, and fishing and boat supplies. You can also do your laundry here. Their boatyard isn't enormous, but they do have a 30-ton open-end travel lift. Appendix B has a dock layout of Coles Point Plantation.

Bonum Creek is about four miles south-southeast of Ragged Point and Coles Point Plantation. About a half mile past the first Bonum Creek mark, "R2" is "R10". A paved boat ramp is near "R10" on the east side of Bonum Creek. There's no dock, but there is a bulkhead to the north where you could temporarily tie your launched boat. An oyster-packing house is also north of this ramp.

Chapter 12

COBB ISLAND TO PINEY POINT, INCLUDING SAINT CLEMENTS ISLAND, MARYLAND

Wicomico River
Cobb Island and Neale Sound
Saint Clements Island and Coltons Point
Dukeharts Channel Area
Saint Clements Bay
Saint Patrick Creek
Breton Bay and Leonardtown
Herring Creek
Piney Point Area

WICOMICO RIVER

The Wicomico River is the largest tidal river on the Potomac. It is wide, with more shoreline than the Saint Marys River. This expansive, peaceful river is sparsely inhabited. There is less development here than on the Virginia bays and creeks across the Potomac. You'll find farms, barns, and pastoral scenes as you travel along the river. There are many duck blinds in the shallower parts of the Wicomico.

The Wicomico River marks all have a "W" suffix. To enter the Wicomico River, position yourself near 38°14.39'N/76°49.34'W, and you'll be in 35 feet of water close to the center of the river's mouth. The lighted two-and-a-half-second "R6W" may not be shown on some charts off of White Point Bar. On the Wicomico River, there are three paved launching ramps in Saint Marys County. See NOAA chart excerpt 12-1.

The Bushwood Wharf ramp is a paved narrow ramp, southeast of White Point Bar. During the Civil War, Union troops occupied the area. Until 1930, Bushwood Wharf was a steamboat wharf and known as Port Wicomico. Next to the wharf is **Quade's Country Store** (☏ 301 769-3903). Alice Quade and son, George, sell ice, some groceries, and beer. Quade's Store also has a meal counter. At the end of their pier, Quade's sells gas and rents boats. They have 18 boats -- 16-footers and 20-footers.

The Chaptico Wharf Landing paved boat ramp is on the eastern shore of the Wicomico, about halfway between Manahowic Creek and Mills Point. The Chaptico Wharf ramp is slightly wider than Bushwood's. The ramp has a sturdy "T" pier and an ample-size parking area. The town of Chaptico, about three miles north, was a shipping center as recent as the early twentieth century.

The Wicomico Shores Waterfront Park also has a concrete ramp. The accompanying pier is short and high but the trailer parking area is ample. The park also has bathrooms, a playground, a pavilion, and a long "L" pier.

In these reaches, the Wicomico River is the border between Saint Marys County and Charles County. Back in Charles County, Camp Saint Charles (☏ 301 858-7119) is located in Charleston Creek on the Wicomico's western shore. This Catholic-run camp has cabins, a pool, basketball courts, rifle and archery ranges, and a private pier. Canoes, jon boats, and paddleboats launch off the pier during the summer.

COBB ISLAND AND NEALE SOUND

Cobb Island is the most lively place on the Wicomico River and is at the southernmost tip of Charles County. Since 1994, the annual Cobb Island Day Celebration, held on a Saturday in June, comprises such local events as a pig roast, wagers on crab races, and other river-related fare.

After you enter the Wicomico and leave "G3W" on your port, work your way to 38°15.95'N/76°50.38'W. You'll be in about 11 feet of water near the eastern end of Neale Sound. On entering Neale Sound, leave the two red marks, "R2" and "R4" to your starboard and the unmarked aid to your port. See NOAA chart excerpt 12-2. The anchorage in Neale Sound is northeast of the Cobb Island Marina. It is a tight anchorage; two boats at anchor make it crowded. There are a few boats at the two-piered **Cobb Island Marina**, but not much else. This marina is in receivership. Cobb Island Marina has had a restaurant, a bathhouse, and an open-end travel lift pulled by a tractor. Although its location and facilities seem to supply potential, it has changed ownership about three times in the past 10 years. A small supermarket, post office, and the Cobb Island Inn bar, also on Cobb Island, are just west of the marina. Appendix B depicts a layout of this area and the two marinas across Neale Sound.

Shymansky's Marina and Restaurant (☏ 301 259-2221) is across Neale Sound from Cobb Island Marina. They have about 75 slips and can handle up to 50-footers. The docks are serviced by 30-amp and 15-amp electric. Shymansky's has three docks east of the Neale Sound bridge, a 15-ton open-end travel lift, and a concrete ramp. They have a large fenced-in boatyard, but the water at the travel lift bay can be shallow. Some boats can only be hauled at high tide. The marina also has a well-stocked ship store and sells gas and diesel, bait and fishing supplies, and block and bag ice. Shymansky's also rents 16-footers, and has a sewage pump-out and a bathhouse. Shymansky's also has two docks on the west side of the Neale Sound bridge and two marine police boats tie-up here. The restaurant and enclosed deck bar are popular with locals.

The Neale Sound bridge has only 18 feet of vertical clearance. The navigation aid logic reverses itself at the bridge. Eastbound or westbound, you're returning until you reach the bridge. Once beneath the bridge, you're going back out to sea.

You can also enter Neale Sound from the west side of Cobb Island and right from the Potomac River. Position yourself at 38°15.98'N/76°52.02'W in about 11 feet of water. You'll come to "R2" "R4" and "R6". Make a bend to the east between "R6" and "G7". Three marshy islands west of Cobb Island are in the vicinity of "R6". Soon you'll be leaving "G9" and "G11" to the north (or your port). Between "G7" and "G11" there is another privately maintained channel with two green and two red marks. **Saunder's Marina** is at the end of this short shallow channel. Saunder's has more than a dozen slips, electrical service, a closed-end lift with a fair-sized yard, and a wide boat ramp. This marina doesn't sell any supplies nor have a bathhouse.

On the west side of the Cobb Island bridge, there are many private docks with boats (see back cover picture). There is even one large sailboat. I read five-foot depths near "R6" but also read nine-foot depths in a few other parts of western Neale Sound. **Captain John's Marina and Restaurant** (☏ 301 259-2315) is on this western side of Neale Sound adjacent to the Shymansky's docks just west of the bridge. There is only about four feet of water off Captain John's docks. Captain John's has a boat ramp next to the Shymansky's piers. The marina has 52 slips, and a part of their dock makes two left turns (see appendix B). The marina also has a side tie-area in front of the restaurant and 30-amp and 15-amp electrical service. Captain John's Marina sells block and bag ice, boat and fishing supplies, and gas (no diesel) and has a sewage pump-out. They also rent 17-footers. Like Shymansky's, Captain John's Restaurant is very popular.

SAINT CLEMENTS ISLAND AND COLTONS POINT

Saint Clements Island is a half mile southeast of Coltons Point. The island is also a half mile north of the Potomac River's third, and last, Morse Code buoy, Mo(A)"F". See NOAA chart excerpt 12-3. Saint Clements Island is regarded as the birthplace of Maryland. Saint Clement, an early pope, is the patron saint of fishermen who were the only boaters in his days. An annual **blessing of the fleet** takes place off of Saint Clements Island during the first weekend of October. The blessing of the fleet was started by the Seventh District Optimist Club in 1968. It's a jolly time -- a beer-gulping fair atmosphere fused with spirituality. The local bishop is usually there blessing the boats and offering a Catholic mass.

In November 1633, dispatched by Lord Baltimore Cecil Calvert, the *Ark* and the *Dove* set sail from England with a party of more than 200 persecuted English Papists (i.e., Catholics) seeking a haven in the New World. Leonard Calvert, younger brother to Cecil, commanded the expedition. On March 25, 1634, after sailing up the Potomac, the ships made landfall on 400-acre Saint Clements Island. Father Andrew White said the first English Catholic mass in the Americas, and a large wooden cross was erected. Father White also called [the Potomac is] "the most delightful water I ever saw." Heeding the local knowledge of the Native Americans, two days later the colonists transplanted themselves back downriver to what became Saint Marys City. Saint Marys City was the first capital of Maryland and the third oldest continuously inhabited English settlement in the New World. The Maryland colony was established as a place where "religious toleration first took root in America."

During the Revolutionary War, the War of 1812, and the Civil War, Saint Clements Island had a strategic importance. Any force that could occupy the island was able to exert much control along this relatively narrow part of the Potomac. In the 1880s, the reduced-in-size 100-acre island experienced its heyday. A hotel, brewery, tomato cannery, and orchards graced the island near the end of the 19th century. For more than 200 years the island was owned by the Blackistone family and known as Blackistone Island. The 40-foot concrete commemorative cross was erected and dedicated in 1934 by the governor of Maryland. Today, that unmistakable white cross is often the first thing a boater sees when approaching Saint Clements Island, especially from the south (see picture). In 1962, 43 years of federal ownership, the island reverted back to the state of Maryland. The eroding island, with only 40 acres remaining, was stabilized by adding riprap stone to the most vulnerable shores.

There are two piers by which boaters can reach the island. On the south side of the island, close to the commemorative cross, is the shorter pier, but the water here is very shallow. Deeper draft boats needing more water should use the longer pier, just east of the northern tip of the island. If you approach this northern pier, beware of the long shoal extending about 200 yards from the north tip of the island to northwest of the pier. When the Potomac has been calm, I have reached Saint Clements Island by anchoring about a one-third of a mile north-northwest of "R14" and have either swum or taken a dinghy to visit the island. It's a great place to picnic and also be in the shadow of history.

The **Potomac River Museum** (☏ 301 769-2222) is on nearby Coltons Point and is worthy of a visit. The museum contains 17th and 18th century ceramics, artifacts, and tools from Maryland's rich past. Outside, you'll find life-size models of early historical characters as well as a few working boats. Inside, there are smaller models of the *Ark* and the *Dove* as well as a library and a gift shop. The dock off the museum is also the ferryboat departure point for throngs of nonboaters who visit Saint Clements Island during the annual blessing of the fleet every October.

DUKEHARTS CHANNEL AREA

Dukeharts Channel runs from the mouth of Saint Clements Bay, inside Saint Clements Island, to east of Coltons Point. Coming from the west, if you draw less than five feet, you can slip over the shallows south of Dukeharts Channel and into the channel in order to take a shortcut to Saint Clements Bay. See NOAA chart excerpt 12-3.

Near the western end of Dukeharts Channel and north of Saint Catherine Island, a cut leads to a small backwater area called Whites Neck Creek. On both sides of the cut, there are unimproved places to launch a small boat. The western launch area is broken concrete next to a few piers and a closed-down restaurant. The eastern launch area has a gravel slope and is on the private property of the Jefferson Islands Club. The eastern side of the cut also has three piers harboring a few workboats. Several mud flats were observed in the area at low tide.

SAINT CLEMENTS BAY

Saint Clements Bay is about a mile northeast of Saint Clements Island. The bay extends northward for about five miles, and there is deep water and few obstructions in most parts of the bay. See NOAA chart excerpt 12-4. **Heron Island Bar** sits outside the mouth of the bay, about a mile east of Saint Clements Island. Heron Island Bar is a shallow area sometimes visible at low tide. The bar was once an island. To enter Saint Clements Bay, you must either wriggle your way through the channel on the west side of Heron Island Bar (i.e., the beginning of Dukeharts Channel) or pass the bar in the wider gap to the east and near the mouth of Breton Bay. If you follow NOAA chart 12286, you should have no problem entering Saint Clements Bay.

Along the shore of the bay, there are farms and a few pockets of residential development. Two creeks, each slightly more than a mile in length, extend westward from the Saint Clements Bay. Saint Patrick Creek has two full-service marinas; Canoe Neck Creek has many residential homes and some private docks. Immediately after entering Canoe Neck Creek, the first smaller creek to the port houses a comely little crab house. Once in Canoe Neck Creek, take your first left and on the right (north) shore you'll see a short pier, with a gas pump and picnic tables. **Frank Morris Carryout Restaurant** (☏ 301 769-2990) is at the base of this pier. There is plenty of deep water off the pier. Should you eat dinner here, you are welcome to tie-up overnight at their four-slip pier. Frank Morris plans to refurbish another nearby pier.

SAINT PATRICK CREEK

If you reached Saint Clement Bay by wriggling your way through the channel on the western side of Heron Island Bar (i.e., the beginning of Dukeharts Channel), you are less than a mile from the entrance to Saint Patrick Creek. See NOAA chart excerpt 12-3. The entrance to Saint Patrick Creek is actually on Saint Clements Bay. **Cather Marina** (☏ 301-769-3335) is the first marina in Saint Patrick Creek about a mile into the creek on the left side (i.e., south) after "R8". Don Cather has about 70 slips (11 covered) and the electric service is 30-amp and 15-amp. Cather harbors a few Boat/US towboats and sells gas and fishing and boating supplies. Cather is also a factory-authorized dealer for six different popular engine manufactures, and stocks many engine parts. They have a modest-size boatyard which can store many trailerable boats. Cather has a 30-ton open-end travel lift.

Kopel's Marina (☏ 301-769-3121) is the second facility in Saint Patrick Creek. This facility has 125 slips (94 covered) and electric service is 50-amp and 30-amp. Appendix B has a dock layout of Kopel's marina. Kopel's has a large shop building and a fairly large boat storage yard. Besides a 30-ton open-end travel lift, they have a railway, forklift trucks and a forklift bay. Kopel's sells gas and diesel, a reasonable selection of marine hardware, and fishing supplies. Kopel's offers winter haul-out specials and has a maintenance staff who specialize in wooden boat restoration projects. Their docks are well maintained, and their overall operations are pretty ship-shape. Both Kopel's and Cather sell block and bag ice, and have sewage pump-outs, bathhouses, and launch ramps.

BRETON BAY AND LEONARDTOWN

Newtown Neck is a narrow peninsula between Saint Clements Bay and Breton Bay. See NOAA chart excerpt 12-4. The isthmus of Newtown Neck accommodates Saint Francis Xavier-Newtown Manor, on a serene open knoll. The church was built in 1731, and it is the oldest continuously used English-speaking Catholic Church in America. The entrance to Breton Bay is less than one and a half miles northeast of Heron Island Bar. The wide bay weaves its way about six miles into Saint Marys County. Many tugboat barges carry sand from the large sand pit in Breton Bay to various industrial sites upriver.

Leonardtown is at the head of the bay. Combs Creek is about one-third of the way into the bay, near the base of Newtown Neck. On the western shore of Breton Bay, about a quarter of a mile outside Combs Creek, you'll encounter **Fitzies**, a marina and restaurant. Fitzies has a couple dozen slips, some with electric service. They also have a long pier into the bay and a gas dock. The next facility north, and in Combs Creek, is the Harbor View Inn -- a crab house. The Harbor View has about a half-dozen slips behind the restaurant. However, several times when I have visited both Fitzies and the Harbor View Inn, there was nobody around.

Beyond the Harbor View and further into Combs Creek is the reasonably priced **Comb's Creek Marina** (T 301 475-2017). Combs Creek Marina has 36 slips (6 covered) with a fair proportion of sailboats. Electrical service is 20-amp and is being upgraded to 30-amp. Comb's Creek Marina, a Honda Marine dealer, has a launch ramp, a few boat supplies, a 30-ton railway, and a modest-size yard. The proprietors, Kevin and Linda Barnes, run a friendly family operation. Kevin does engine repairs, and Linda can do upholstery and sail cloth repairs using a zigzag sewing machine. This couple permits boaters to use the bathroom of their private home. The Barnes will also drive boaters to nearby Leonardtown for errands. There's five and a half to six feet of water off their dock, and the tricky Combs Creek channel has five to six feet of water in some places. Near the narrow entry, the Combs Creek channel makes two 90-degree turns. Kevin recommends obtaining some "local knowledge," before negotiating tricky Combs Creek.

You could reach **Leonardtown** by going to almost the end of Breton Bay. However, once at the head of the bay, there is no place to tie-up and no good place to land a dinghy. At one time there was a large tavern out over the water, but it burned down long ago. Dangerous pilings are all that remain today. Saint Marys ice house is east of those burnt pilings. A county public boat ramp is west of the ice house. This paved ramp looks marginally maintained and has a sharp drop-off.

Interesting Leonardtown, the county seat of Saint Marys County, sits behind this uninviting waterfront, less than a half a mile up the hill. See appendix C for a street sketch. Leonardtown is home to the Relax Inn Motel, Virnelli's Pizza, Penrod's Tap and Grill, and the Ye Olde Restaurant. Ye Olde Restaurant is a converted movie theater and a great place for breakfast. The Leonardtown Supermarket, a pharmacy, a bank, and a small visitor center are just off the town square. But, perhaps the most prudent way to visit Leonardtown is to stay at Comb's Creek Marina and ask Kevin or Linda Barnes to drive you here.

Outside the city center of Leonardtown, there are a few nearby establishments worth visiting. If you prefer gourmet dinning, try the Willows, east of Leonardtown. If you desire great and reasonably priced Chinese food, try the Happy Dragon in the shopping center west of Leonardtown. A Food Lion grocery store is also in that shopping center. Mattingly's grocery store is located about a mile east of the Leonardtown Shopping center. Mattingly's also has a hardware store next to their grocery store with a good inventory. You'll come to the Saint Marys County Hospital ($_T$ 301 475-8981) in between the Food Lion shopping center and the Mattingly stores. The Saint Marys County Fairgrounds are past the Willows, and a couple of miles east of Leonardtown. The fairgrounds hosts a wide array of outdoor events (Fourth of July fireworks, oyster festivals, church fairs, and a lot more). Call the Saint Marys Chamber of Commerce for an annual schedule of events, ($_T$ 301 884-5555).

HERRING CREEK

The entrance to Herring Creek is about 10 miles southeast of Breton Bay. Herring Creek is a very protected creek with some reasonably deep water (i.e., eight feet) but it also has some shallow water. See NOAA chart excerpt 12-5. The channel is also regularly dredged to eight feet. Two full-service marinas are on the creek, and access to the Potomac is quick. To get into the creek, position yourself near 38°10.56'N/76°33.01'W and then head for the jetty entrance. Both the outside marks at the end of each jetty -- a red and a green -- are four-second flashers. After these two marks, you'll find "R4" "G5" and lighted "R6".

Tall Timbers Marina ($_T$ 301 994-1508) is inside and to the right (i.e., south) after the jetty entrance. Make sure you go past "R6" and then backtrack to Tall Timbers Marina. There is a submerged oyster bar between the south jetty and "R6". The marina has 170 slips (40 covered) with 20 slips set aside for transients. Electric service is mostly 30-amp. Most of the slips are in a basin behind the jetty and shoal. A fuel dock which sells gas and diesel, extends into Herring Creek. The marina has a 20-ton closed-end lift pulled by a tractor. They sell block and bag ice and some fishing and boating supplies. The Reluctant Navigator Restaurant is opened seasonally. The marina has some nice features like a sandy beach on the Potomac and picnic areas.

Cedar Cove Marina ($_T$ 301 994-1155) is about a mile due east of Tall Timbers Marina on the south side of the creek. Even though you cannot see this marina from "R6" just head due east at the daymark. Cedar Cove has three piers and 70 slips, and can accommodate 18-to-56 footers. The water off the gas dock (no diesel) is pretty shallow at 4 feet (MLW). Slips are serviced by 30-amp electric. Dan and Kathleen sell bag ice and some boating supplies and are also dealers for Sea Hawk and Pursuit boats. They're also in the charter business with three Holiday Mansion (38-foot-plus) houseboats for rent. You can get these bareboat or hire your own captain. The marina has a 25-ton open-end travel lift and a good-size boatyard. On the premises, there is a little neighborhood bar and restaurant serving tasty dinner specials. Patrick, the head cook, is first rate.

Cedar Cove Marina and Tall Timber Marina have launch ramps, sewage pump-outs, and bathhouses. Both marinas have contract personnel on hand who can do fiberglass, electrical, and mechanical work. Tall Timbers likes undertaking wooden boat projects. Appendix B has a dock layout of both Cedar Cove and Tall Timbers Marinas.

PINEY POINT AREA

There is a private harbor, the Landings at Piney Point, about a mile south of Herring Creek and north of Piney Point. The entrance to this harbor is marked by two unlighted private aids on short jetties. There is no room to anchor in the basin, which contains one dock extending northwest into the basin with slips all around the edge of the basin. When I visited, only about a dozen of the 80 slips were occupied. Nonetheless, the slips are designated for community homeowners. There are no services nearby.

Piney Point protrudes into the Potomac between Herring Creek and Saint George Island. See NOAA chart excerpt 12-5. The second Potomac Morse Code A buoy, Mo(A)"B" is slightly more than one mile south of Piney Point. Stuart Petroleum has a dock on the southwest side of Piney Point, and you may see a small tanker (i.e., 668 feet in length) tied-up there. If you want to park your boat nearby and the weather is rough, you can see the terra firma side of Piney Point by harboring somewhere in Saint George Creek (see the next chapter).

During World War II, German submarines terrorized the Eastern Seaboard. During the first half of 1942, hundreds of US cargo ships with thousands of men perished along the Eastern Seaboard, victim of German U-boat attacks. But one German U-boat made it to the bottom of the Potomac! A US war prize, the rubber-skinned (an early stealth feature) *Black Panther* was deliberately sunk one mile west of Piney Point after the Navy was through experimenting with it in 1949. It landed upright in more than 90 feet of water. Her conning tower rises to within 68 feet of the surface. The *Black Panther* was forgotten for the next 36 years. In 1985, the wreck was rediscovered by a team of SCUBA divers. In 1994 the *Black Panther* became Maryland's first Historic Shipwreck diving preserve. If you consider diving here, this is an "advanced dive" in a low-visibility environment. There are a handful of diving and boating protocols that should be observed, including no anchoring within 500 feet of the blue and white mooring buoy, which usually floats from April to December.

The Piney Point Lighthouse and the lighthouse keeper's residence were constructed in 1836. The lighthouse is thus the oldest on the Potomac (see picture). Its beacon lit the way for more than 125 years. From 1820 to 1910, the area around Piney Point was a resort and the Summer White House to many presidents, from James Madison to Abraham Lincoln. Hence, the lighthouse was nicknamed "the lighthouse of presidents." A hurricane in 1933 demolished the resort hotel. Today, nothing remains of the hotel, but still standing are the lighthouse, the lighthouse keeper's residence, and a small interesting museum. In 1964, like almost all inland lighthouses, the Piney Point Lighthouse ceased operations.

There is a small pier in the river off the lighthouse and a nice beach arcing northeast towards Saint George Island. Private docks and residences dot this beach area. **The Oakwood Lodge and Restaurant** (T 301 994-2377) is also on the beach about three quarters of a mile east of the Piney Point Lighthouse. The Oakwood has a 100-foot pier into the Potomac and serves upscale dinners.

Chapter 13
SAINT MARYS RIVER, MARYLAND

Saint George Island
Saint George Creek
Carthagena Creek
Saint Inigoes Creek
Saint Marys City
Upper Saint Marys River

SAINT GEORGE ISLAND

Saint George Island, like the State of Maryland, was founded in 1634. In July 1776, the island was the site of Maryland's first Revolutionary War engagement.

If you are coming from the mouth of the Potomac, heading northwest, the tip of Saint George Island is prominent and usually the first land feature seen once inside the Potomac. The boating-accessible parts of the island are on the northeastern side in Saint George Creek. If you can't squeeze under the 29-foot-vertical clearance bridge on the northwestern side of the Saint George Island, you need to clear the bar on the southeastern side of the island. Saint George Bar extends southeast from the island and you may barely find 10 feet of water a mile southeast of the tip of the island. See NOAA chart excerpt 13-2. Be aware of the many fish traps on this bar area. If you have a deep-draft vessel, I don't recommend cutting inside any of the fish traps. The water can be shallow.

Near the eastern end of the island, there's a shallow channel leading to a protected lagoon called Island Creek. The Island Creek channel runs southwest off the Saint Marys River and has a jetty on the southeast side. After passing the jetty, turn right (i.e., northwest) into Island Creek. Once in the shallow creek, you will see more navigation aids than shown on NOAA chart 12233. Near the end of the navigation aids, you'll find about five piers on the southwest side and about three piers on the northeast side of Island Creek. Shallow-draft workboats dominate the piers (see front cover picture). On the middle pier on the northeast side of the creek you'll see the Sea Fruit pier. The **Sea Fruit** (☎ 301 994-2245) advertises crabs, "arsters" (Maryland oysters), and skipjack tours (☎ 301 994-0897). You'll see the skipjack docked at the end of their pier. Shallow-draft skipjacks were sailing workboats on the Chesapeake Bay. Today a few of these classic boats still sail as workboats, the last commercial Sailing fleet in the United States. Some skipjacks have gone into the "tourist trade," like this one. There's even an annual gathering of skipjacks not far from here. Every Labor Day weekend, across the Chesapeake on Tangier Sound, there's the Deal Island skipjack race.

Camp Merrylande Vacation Cottages (☎ 301-994-1772) are northeast of Deep Point and right on the beach inside Saint George Bar. The area has campsites, showers, and brightly colored cottages with one to five bedrooms.

Evan's Seafood restaurant is on the opposite end of Saint George Island from Camp Merrylande and about a half mile southeast of the low-clearance bridge. Evan's is located just northwest of the narrowest point on Saint George Island. At this point, the island is barely wide enough for a two-lane roadway, and there is rock riprap on both sides of the road. Evan's has a 350-foot "T" pier for boaters. The deepest approach to the "T" pier is from the east (versus the north). In the summer, Evan's opens the upper deck. Evan's has been around for about 35 years.

111

SAINT GEORGE CREEK

If you're coming from Piney Point and need less than 29 feet of overhead clearance, you can enter Saint George Creek from under the bridge about a mile and a half east of Piney Point. Otherwise you need to go to the Saint Marys River, around Saint George Island and Saint George Bar, to get into this creek. A county boat ramp is in Saint George Creek, on the "mainland" side and just north of the bridge. This whole area -- all four corners at the base of the bridge -- is popular with night fishermen during the summer. In the winter, at low tide, you might see someone shoveling deep into the sandy spits looking for manoes (soft-shelled clams). On the Saint George Creek side of the bridge, there are sandy spits on both sides. The longer shallow sand spit is on the eastern side of the bridge channel.

Swann's Hotel and General Store (T 301 994-0774) is in Saint George Creek about a quarter mile northwest of the bridge. Swann's has a restaurant, a gas dock, a tiki bar, cottages, and hotel rooms. At the store you can purchase groceries, ice, beer, bait, fishing supplies, and fishing licenses. The Piney Point Post Office is across the street from Swann's on the Potomac. The **OCI Pub** is about a half mile northwest, on the road, from the post office. OCI stands for "Old Country Inn" and is a favorite of seaman who are taking courses at the school, as well as long-time locals. You can get a pizza at the OCI too. Proprietor Sheila Holmes, although coming from England, has a good pulse on Saint Marys County. Both her sons, Glen and Mark, have traveled the world as merchant seamen. Glen, one of the best pool players in the county, grew up on the pool tables at the OCI.

The **Paul Hall Center for Maritime Training** (T 301 994-0010) is on Saint George Creek, about a half mile northwest of Swann's. The Center encompasses the **Harry Lunderberg School of Seamanship** which offers a variety of courses, from "Able Bodied Seaman" to "Chief Engineer" to "Chief Steward," to "First-Class Pilot." The school is funded by US shipping companies and operated by the Seafarers International Union. Seafarers graduating from the school serve worldwide on US-flagged merchant ships. A large dormitory building and a huge crane are clearly visible from Saint George Creek. The fenced-off campus-like grounds are only open to the public during the first Sunday of the month. The *Paul Hall Maritime Library and Museum* is worth a visit. You'll find splendid replicas of sailing, steam, cargo, and military ships. Many model ships are more than three feet long.

Curley's Marina (T 301 994-1212) is in the first cove after the seamanship school. Curley's has 30 slips, a couple wooden piers, a muddy concrete boat ramp, and an ice machine, and harbors many workboats. Less than a mile northwest of Curley's, on the same side of the creek is another cove harboring Deagle's Boat Yard and Lumpkin's Seafood. Deagle's has two railways and specializes in building custom wooden workboats. Deagle's, Lumpkin's, and Curley's docks primarily cater to local watermen and workboats. There is not much development on the northeast shore of Saint George Creek.

CARTHAGENA CREEK

In the Saint Marys River, there are three navigation aids near the entrance to Saint George Creek. See NOAA chart excerpt 13-2. The first NUMBERED Saint Marys River navigation aid is about four miles into the wide river and about a mile and a half beyond Saint George Creek. This Saint Marys River aid, "G1" flashes at two and a half seconds. Another *unlighted* "G1" daymark is less than a half mile past the first *lighted* "G1" daymark. This second "G1" is the first mark for the Carthagena Creek channel. After clearing Carthagena Creek "G3" lighted "R4" (off Josh Point), and "G5" you are in the well-protected creek. See NOAA chart excerpt 13-3.

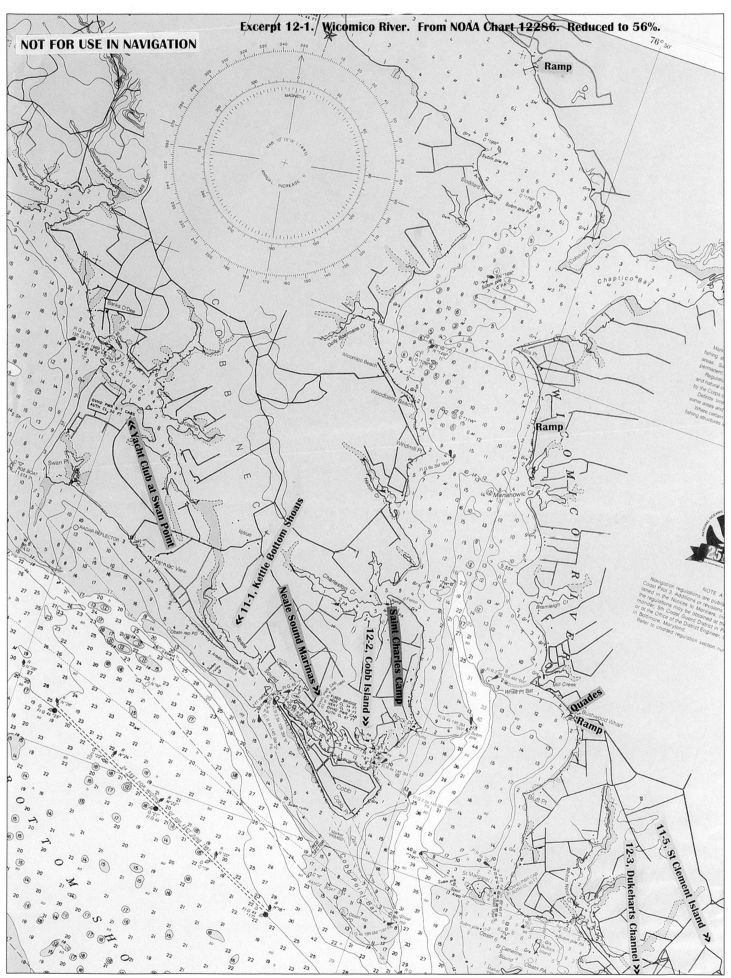

Excerpt 12-1. Wicomico River. From NOAA Chart 12286. Reduced to 56%.

NOT FOR USE IN NAVIGATION

Ramp

Ramp

Quades
Ramp

Yacht Club at Swan Point

11-1, Kettle Bottom Shoals

Neale Sound Marinas

12-2, Cobb Island

Saint Charles Camp

11-5, St Clement Island

12-3, Dukeharts Channel

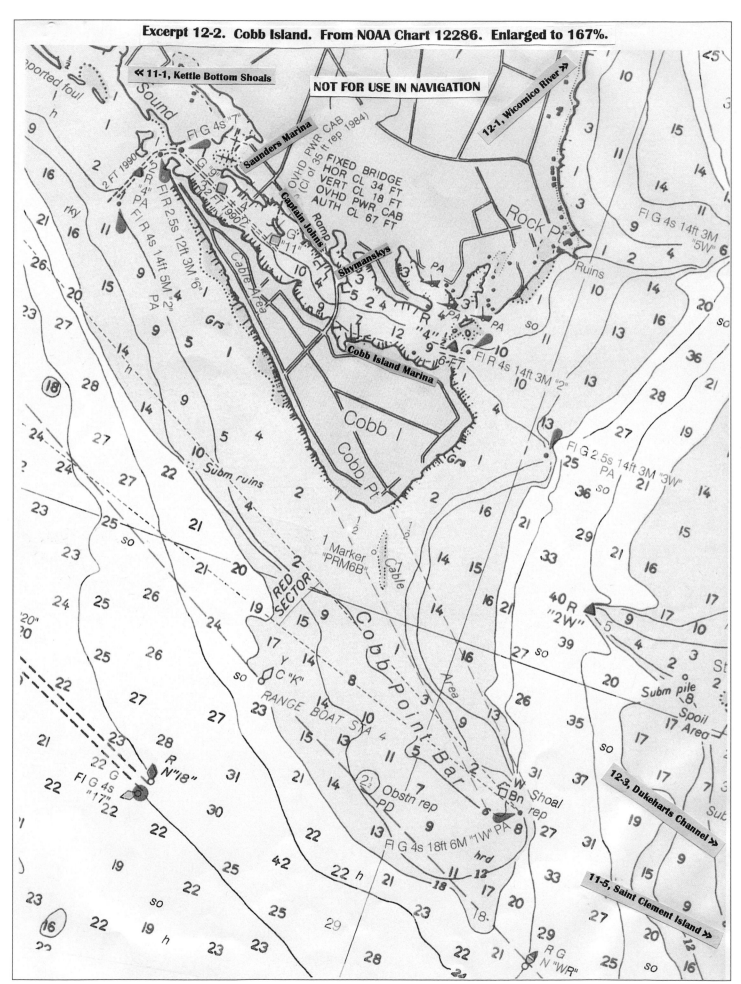

Excerpt 12-2. Cobb Island. From NOAA Chart 12286. Enlarged to 167%.

NOT FOR USE IN NAVIGATION

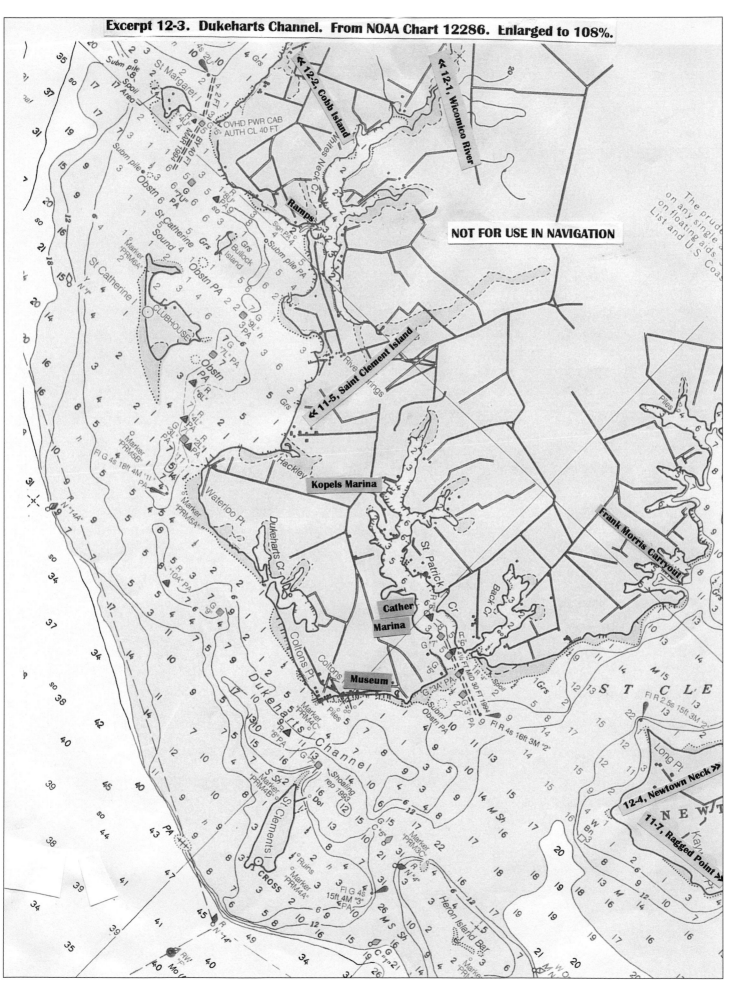

Excerpt 12-3. Dukeharts Channel. From NOAA Chart 12286. Enlarged to 108%.

NOT FOR USE IN NAVIGATION

12-2, Cobb Island

12-1, Wicomico River

Ramps

11-5, Saint Clement Island

Kopels Marina

Frank Morris Carryout

Cather Marina

Museum

12-4, Newtown Neck

11-7, Ragged Point

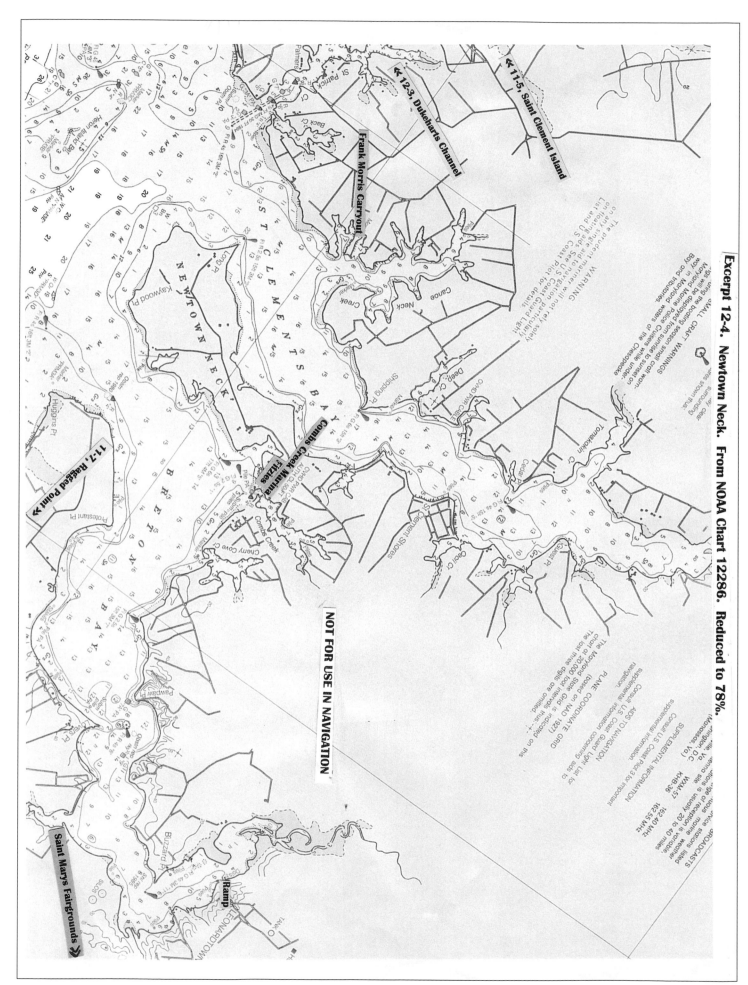

Excerpt 12-4. Newtown Neck. From NOAA Chart 12286. Reduced to 78%.

11-5, Saint Clement Island

12-3, Dukeharts Channel

Frank Morris Carryout

Combs Creek Marina Tizzies

11-7, Ragged Point

Saint Marys Fairgrounds

Ramp

NOT FOR USE IN NAVIGATION

116

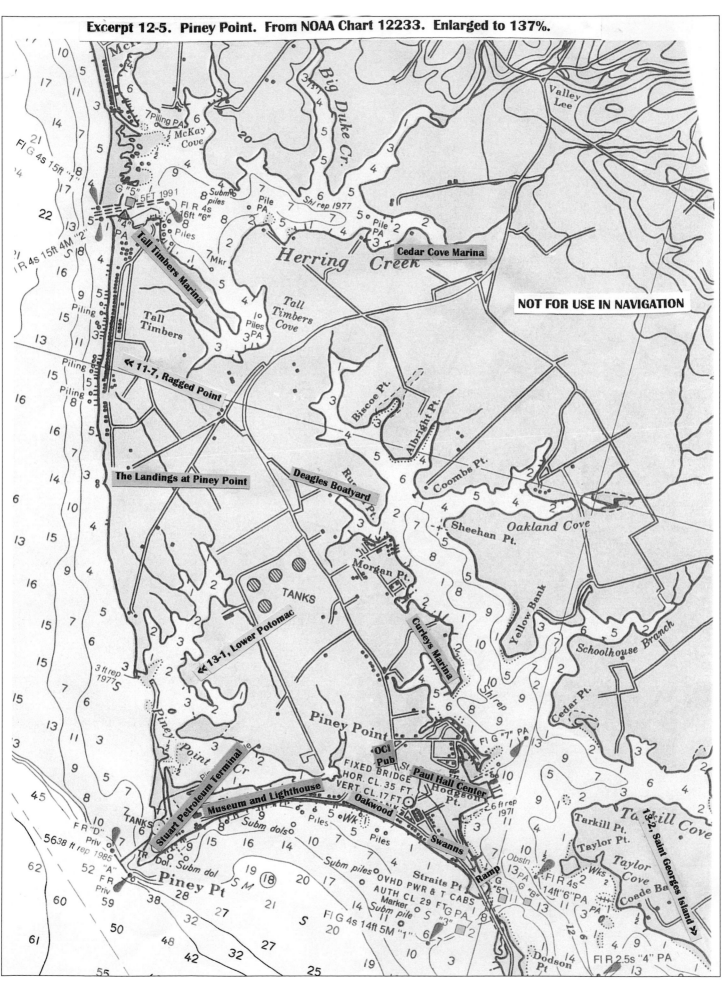

Excerpt 12-5. Piney Point. From NOAA Chart 12233. Enlarged to 137%.

NOT FOR USE IN NAVIGATION

Tall Timbers Marina

Cedar Cove Marina

11-7, Ragged Point

The Landings at Piney Point

Deagles Boatyard

13-1, Lower Potomac

Curleys Marina

Stuart Petroleum Terminal

Museum and Lighthouse

OCI Pub

Paul Hall Center

Ramp

13-2, Saint Georges Island

Nanjemoy Creek

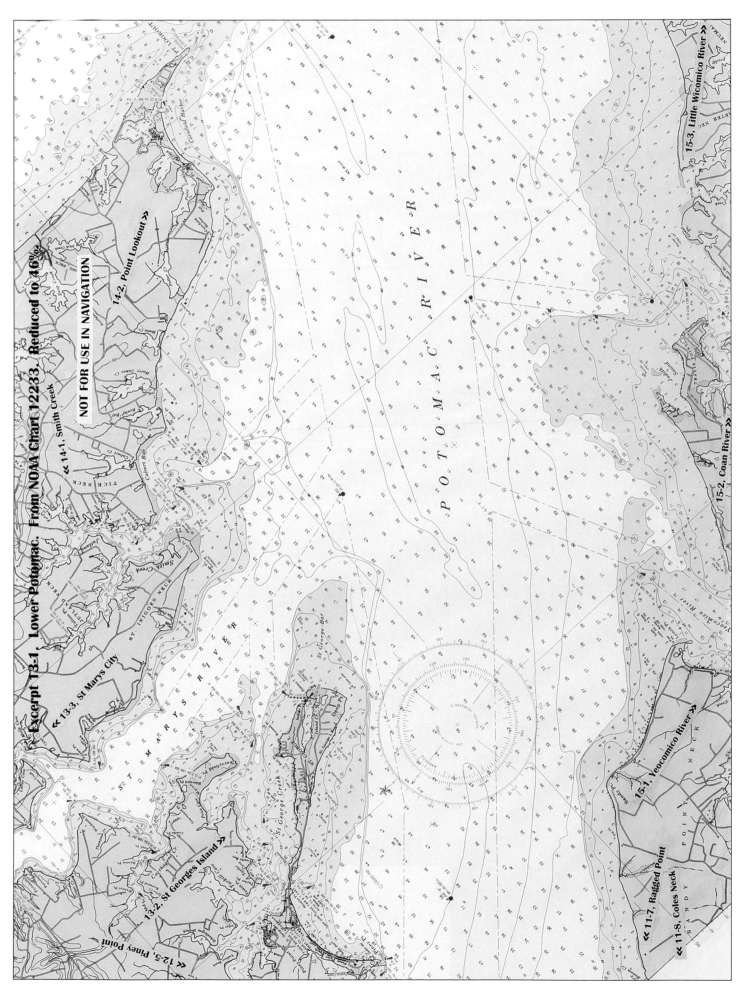

Excerpt 13-1, Lower Potomac. From NOAA Chart 12233. Reduced to 46%.

NOT FOR USE IN NAVIGATION

<< 14-1, Smith Creek

14-2, Point Lookout >>

<< 13-3, St Marys City

13-2, St Georges Island >>

<< 12-5, Piney Point

15-3, Little Wicomico River >>

15-2, Coan River >>

15-1, Yeocomico River >>

<< 11-7, Ragged Point

<< 11-8, Coles Neck

POTOMAC RIVER

ST. MARYS RIVER

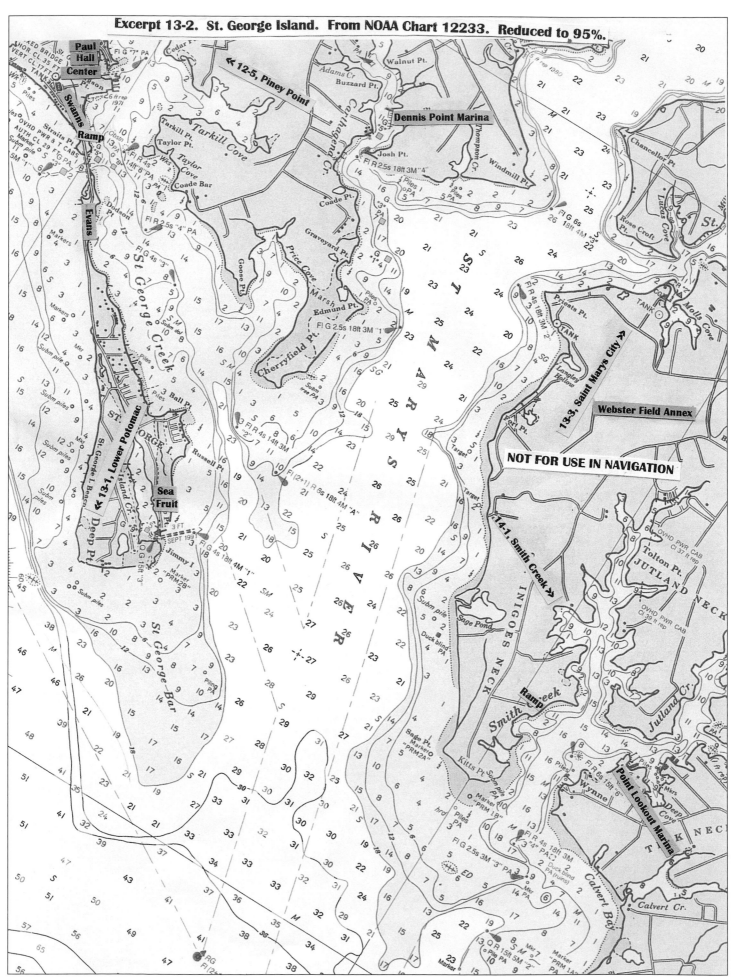

Excerpt 13-2. St. George Island. From NOAA Chart 12233. Reduced to 95%.

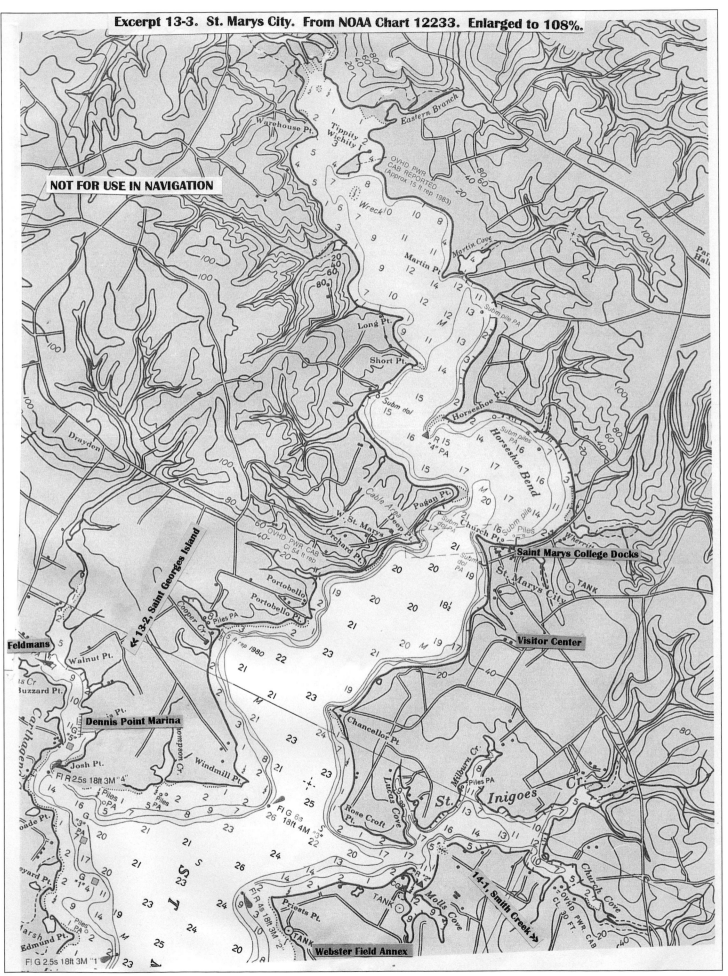

Excerpt 13-3. St. Marys City. From NOAA Chart 12233. Enlarged to 108%.

NOT FOR USE IN NAVIGATION

121

Saint Clements Island

Piney Point Lighthouse

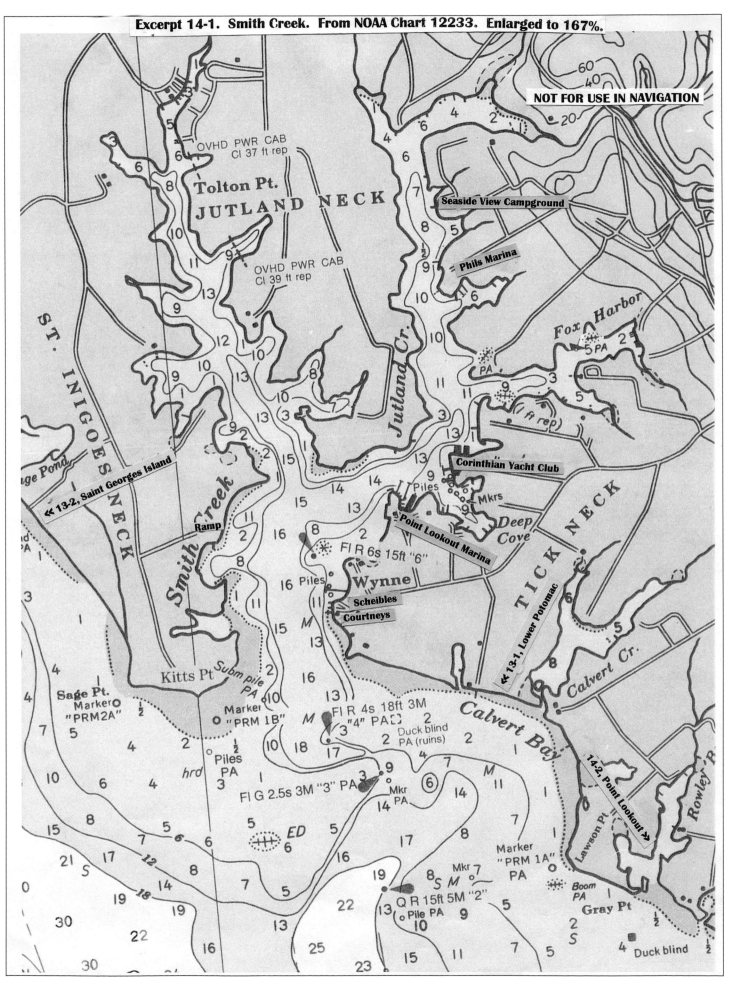

Excerpt 14-1. Smith Creek. From NOAA Chart 12233. Enlarged to 167%.

NOT FOR USE IN NAVIGATION

Tolton Pt.
JUTLAND NECK

OVHD PWR CAB
Cl 37 ft rep

OVHD PWR CAB
Cl 39 ft rep

Seaside View Campground

Phils Marina

Fox Harbor

5 PA

PA

(ft rep)

ST. INIGOES NECK

Jutland Cr.

Corinthian Yacht Club

Piles

Mkrs

Deep Cove

TICK NECK

13-2, Saint Georges Island

Ramp

Smith Creek

Point Lookout Marina

Fl R 6s 15ft "6"

Wynne

Piles

Scheibles

Courtneys

M

13-1, Lower Potomac

Calvert Cr.

Kitts Pt.

Subm pile
PA

Sage Pt.
Marker
"PRM2A"

Marker
"PRM 1B"

Fl R 4s 18ft 3M
"4" PA

Duck blind
PA (ruins)

Calvert Bay

14-2, Point Lookout

Piles
PA

hrd

Fl G 2.5s 3M "3" PA

Mkr
PA

Lawson Pt.

Marker
"PRM 1A"
PA

ED

Mkr

Boom
PA

Gray Pt

Q R 15ft 5M "2"

Pile PA

Duck blind

Rowley R.

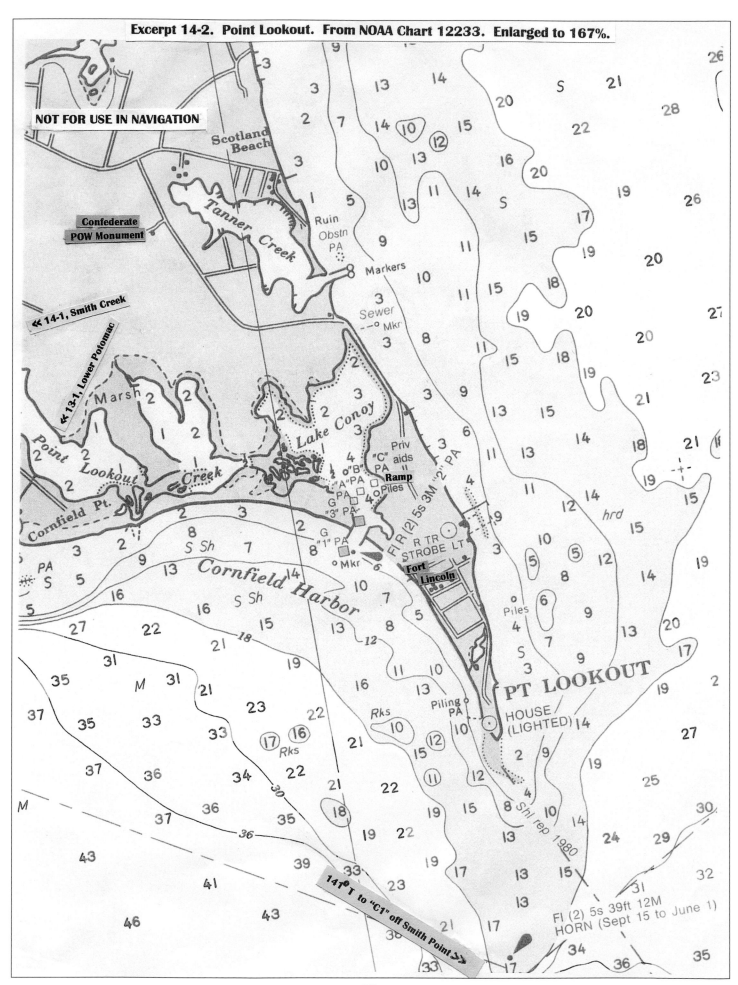

Excerpt 14-2. Point Lookout. From NOAA Chart 12233. Enlarged to 167%.

NOT FOR USE IN NAVIGATION

Scotland Beach

Tanner Creek

Confederate POW Monument

Ruin Obstn PA

Markers

Sewer Mkr

≪ 14-1, Smith Creek

≪ 13-1, Lower Potomac

Marsh

Point Lookout Creek

Lake Conoy

Priv aids

"C" PA

Ramp

Piles

o"B" PA

"A" PA

G PA

"3" PA

Cornfield Pt.

G "1" PA

Mkr

Fl R (2) 5s 3M "2" PA

R TR STROBE LT

Fort Lincoln

Cornfield Harbor

S Sh

S Sh

Piles

Rks

Rks

Piling PA

PT LOOKOUT

hrd

HOUSE (LIGHTED)

Shl rep 1980

Fl (2) 5s 39ft 12M
HORN (Sept 15 to June 1)

141°T to "C1" off Smith Point ≫

124

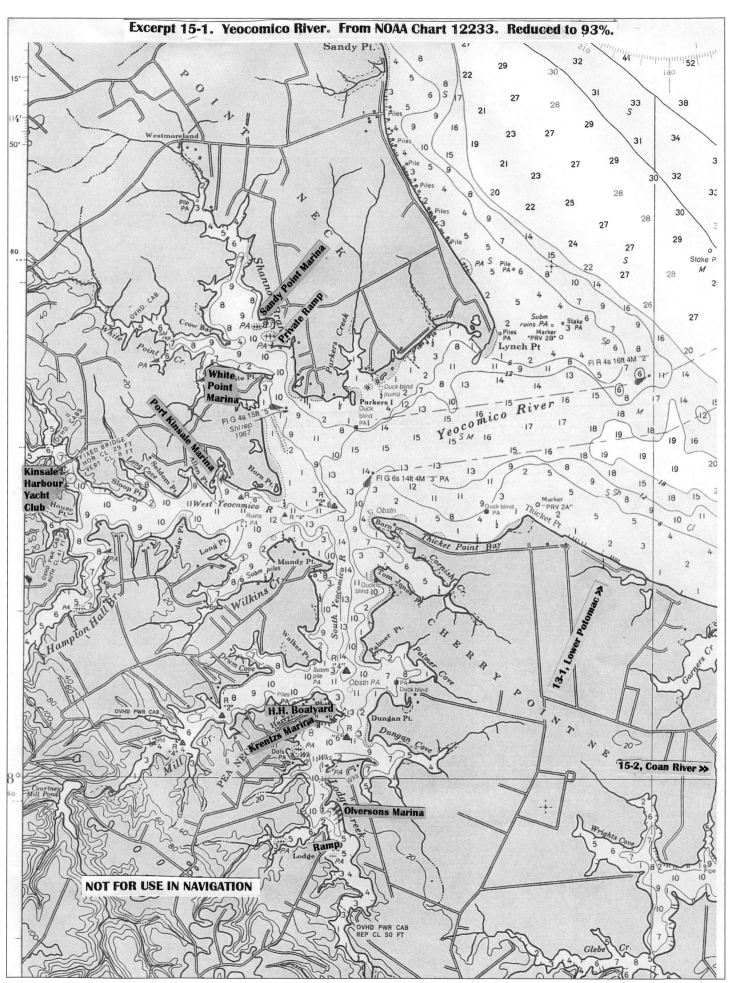

Excerpt 15-1. Yeocomico River. From NOAA Chart 12233. Reduced to 93%.

NOT FOR USE IN NAVIGATION

125

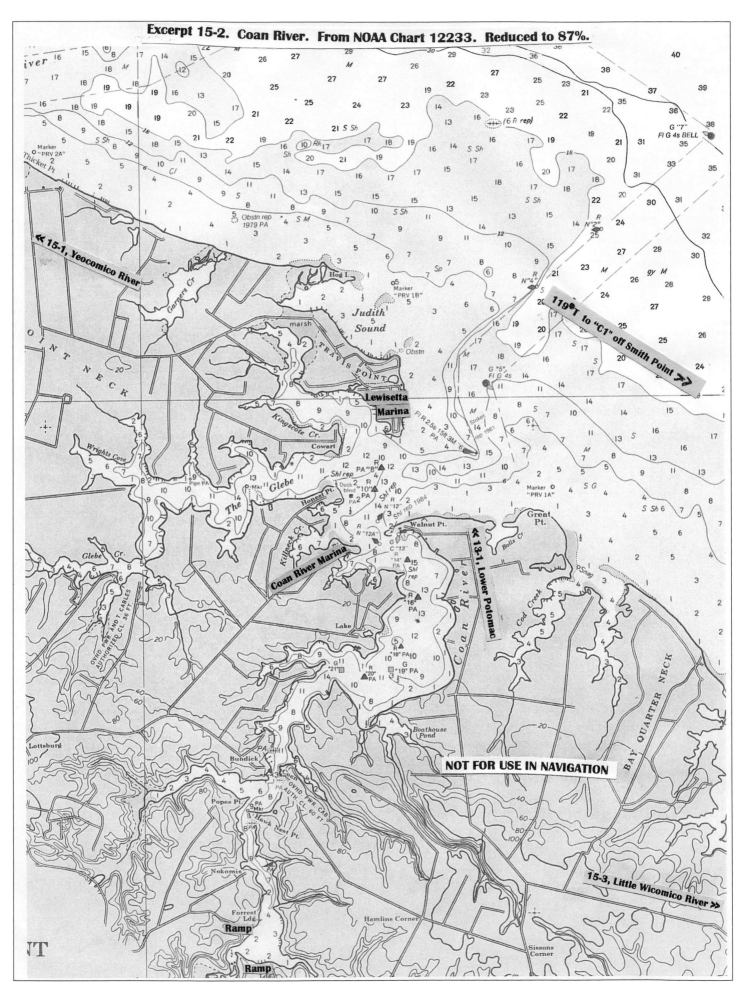

Excerpt 15-2. Coan River. From NOAA Chart 12233. Reduced to 87%.

<< 15-1, Yeocomico River

119°T to "C1" off Smith Point >>

Lewisetta Marina

Coan River Marina

<< 13-1, Lower Potomac

NOT FOR USE IN NAVIGATION

15-3, Little Wicomico River >>

Ramp

Ramp

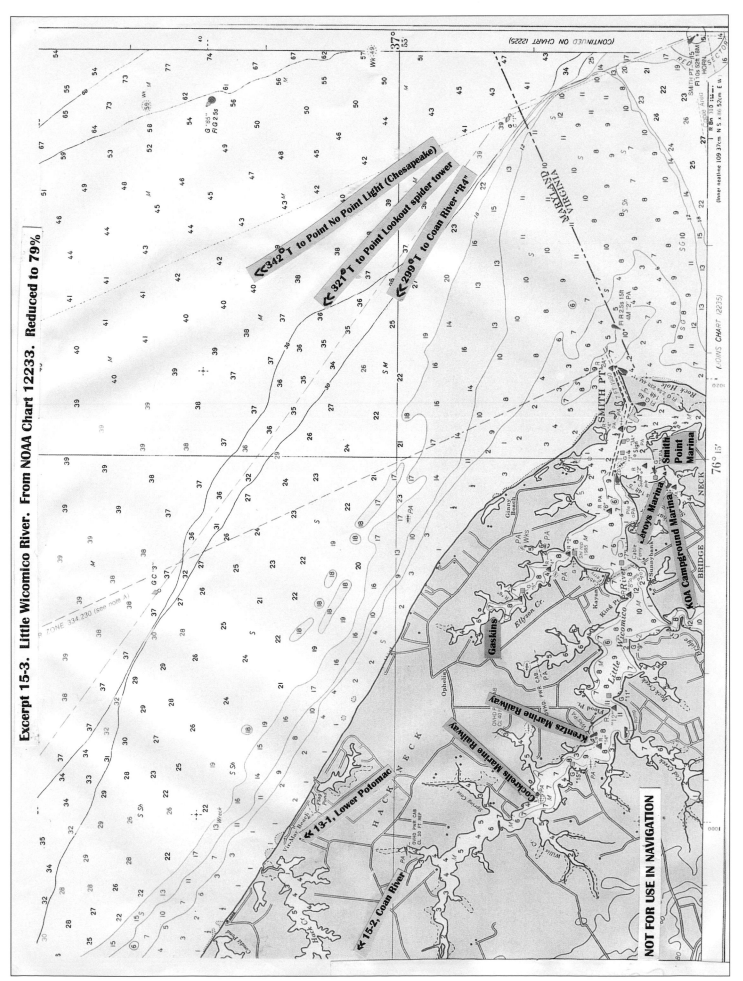

Excerpt 15-3. Little Wicomico River. From NOAA Chart 12233. Reduced to 79%

342° T to Point No Point Light (Chesapeake)

321° T to Point Lookout spider tower

299° T to Coan River "R4"

13-1, Lower Potomac

15-2, Coan River

Cockrells Marine Railway

Krentzs Marine Railway

Gaskins

Jerboys Marina

Smith Point Marina

KOA Campground Marina

NOT FOR USE IN NAVIGATION

127

Currioman Landing near Nomini Bay

Watermen Working a Pound Net

Dennis Point Marina (☏ 301 994-2288) is the primary facility here. Dennis Point has 115 slips serviced mostly by 30-amp electric. They can accommodate up to a 110-footer. They sell gas and diesel, block and bag ice, a good assortment of boating supplies, and limited bait and fishing supplies. The marine police also harbor two boats here. A pool, a campground, a picnic ground, a laundry room, a bathhouse, a sewage pump-out, and a boat ramp are also on the grounds. See appendix B for a dock layout sketch. When the owners, the Gardiner family, are not tending boats, some help out in the Still Anchors Restaurant. Dennis Point also sells and services Tiger Shark jet skis. They have a 25-ton open-end travel lift and a forklift. Dennis Point has a good dry storage capability with forklift storage and a fair-size yard. They recently built a 40-foot tall work shed. The marina has a sizeable maintenance staff for various kinds of boat repairs.

Feldman's Marine Railway (☏ 301 994-2629) is less than a half mile up Carthagena Creek from Dennis Point Marina, on the opposite side of the creek. Bill Feldman has two piers, a ramp, and two railways. Feldman's is a professional low-key operation specializing in wooden workboats, and doesn't have many facilities for transient boaters.

SAINT INIGOES CREEK

A military compound, once known as "NESEA," is across the Saint Marys River from Carthagena Creek. Today that compound is called Naval Air Station, Patuxent River, Webster Field Annex. The northern confines of the base extend into Saint Inigoes Creek. Civilian visitors are restricted because it's a closed military post. The compound also houses the US Coast Guard Station, Saint Inigoes (☏ 301 872 4344), the only Coast Guard station on the Potomac. USCG Saint Inigoes generally patrols the lower Potomac and nearby Chesapeake with two boats.

Saint Inigoes Creek extends more than a mile northeast beyond the military compound. See NOAA chart excerpt 13-3. There are no commercial facilities in Saint Inigoes Creek. However, many private docks and nice homes are nestled along the steep shore of the creek and its several coves. There are shallows off the south shore of the creek. Give this shore plenty of room after entering the creek.

SAINT MARYS CITY

Saint Marys City is east of Church Point. The spire of the stately *Trinity Episcopal Church* lies on the bluff east of Church Point. *Saint Marys College* spreads out north and east behind Church Point. See appendix C for a map of the area. Saint Marys City is a national historic landmark, consisting primarily of a college, colonial remnants, and an outdoor museum. The college has its own marina and a fleet of small sailboats. If there's side-tie space at their main dock, it's usually on a first-come, first-served basis, and free. Sailing is an active pastime year around. In chilly December, there's an alumni race. During hot August, the Governor's Cup Race, Maryland's premier sailboat race, ends here. Besides its sailing heritage, Saint Marys College is known to have good liberal arts programs.

The *Governors Cup Race* starts in the afternoon, in the Chesapeake off Annapolis, usually on the first Friday in August. After a night of racing, the fastest sailboats usually arrive here close to, and sometimes before, daybreak. The first boats tie-up to the college docks. Then a couple hundred more boats, as they arrive, build an immense floating raft off the docks. Many boats will anchor out too -- there's plenty of room. Even the sailors in the last boats arriving have plenty of merriment left on the schedule. It is quite a festive affair. Many years ago, northbound in the middle of the Chesapeake at night, and before I was aware of the Governor's Cup, I ran head-on into the race. I then learned never to sail northbound in the mid-Chesapeake, during the first Friday night in August! Sailing into that spread-out race and dodging red and green running lights all night long was unforgettable.

The first Lord Baltimore, George Calvert, converted, or as some say uncovered his hidden beliefs, to Catholicism in 1625. In 17th century England, he paid a price for this unpopular conversion. George Calvert was also a man of determination and means. After a lot of finagling and a failed attempt in Newfoundland, Calvert convinced King Charles I to let him establish a "religious tolerant" colony in what was to become the state of Maryland. George died in 1632, on the eve of the fulfillment of his dreams, but his three sons carried the ball. The oldest son, Cecil, as the second Lord Baltimore, persevered long and hard with English authorities and saw the expedition off in October, 1633. Cecil never visited America, but he politicked on behalf of this new colony in England for 40 years.

George Calvert's second-oldest son, Leonard, lead the expedition of about 200 brave souls aboard the *Ark* and the *Dove*. The *Ark* was 125 feet and carried all the passengers. The *Dove*, much smaller at 49 feet, carried most of the new colony's provisions. During the Atlantic crossing, the ships separated during a storm. After more than a month apart, the *Ark* feared the *Dove* was lost. To everyone's delight, the ships happily reunited in Barbados. Together they sailed up the eastern seaboard, into the Chesapeake and into the Potomac. In March 1634, they landed on Saint Clements Island. As mentioned earlier, father Andrew White offered a mass of "Thanks," the first English Catholic mass in the new world, on Saint Clements Island. On a later return trip to England in 1635, the *Dove*, loaded with beaver pelts and timber, was lost at sea.

After first landing at Saint Clements Island, the colonists learned from the Native Americans that a good homesite could be found back downriver at Saint Marys City. These colonists were even classy enough to pay the Indians for the land where they placed the settlement. The colonists and Native Americans got along well. The native Yaocomico Indians supplied corn and fish and taught the colonists how to make cornbread and hominy.

From 1634 to 1695, life was hard, but Saint Marys City prospered. Tobacco, or "sotte weed," emerged as the staple for the economy. Cecil Calvert's son, Charles, the third Lord Baltimore, was the first Lord Baltimore to visit the new colony. Charles became governor of the colony after Philip Calvert, the third son of George Calvert. In 1689, more dogmatic Protestants wrested control of Saint Marys City from Charles Calvert. A new capital for the Catholic colony had to be established elsewhere. In 1695, Annapolis became the capital, and Saint Marys City was all but forgotten. In 1839, a seminary for women was established near Church Point. In the 1960s that seminary evolved into the present-day Saint Marys College. The college now has about 1,500 undergraduates, and about 70 percent of the students live on campus. The college is proud of a 14-to-1 student-to-faculty ratio.

There are many events throughout the year in Saint Marys City. In late March, there's Maryland Days. In the summer, besides the Governor's Cup Race, there are Militia Days, Archaeology Dig Days, Tobacco Culture Days, Working Hands Days, and Planting Days. In the fall and winter, there are Indian Culture Days, Militia Muster Days, and Thanksgiving and Christmas events. You can telephone the Saint Marys City Visitor Center (T) 301 862-0990 or (T) 800 SMC-1634, for more information and an annual schedule.

UPPER SAINT MARYS RIVER

Beyond and northwest of Saint Marys City, the river goes for more than two miles. It is comfortably deep almost all the way to the end. See NOAA chart excerpt 13-3. The last navigation aid, "R4" is southwest of Horseshoe Point. Don't even think of cheating "R4" as a shallow sandy spit goes almost right to this daymark. However, I registered more than 12 feet of water only a few feet south of "R4". Unlike Saint

Inigoes Creek, the river here is not congested with docks and has a much more open feeling. There are well-spaced nice residences and a few docks scattered along the river. Beyond Long Point, there is no development along the southwestern shore. The river looks like it would have when the first colonists were here more than 360 years ago.

Tippity Wichity Island is about as far as you can go before the river shallows. One account of how the name came to be is a corruption of "Tippling and Witchery Island." Supposedly, for a short period after the Civil War, a house of ill-reputed activities lured mariners to the island. Unlike other Potomac islands, Tippity Wichity is high and wooded with mostly pines. There is a building nestled in the wooded hills. A small dock sits on the southeastern side of the island. A canoe landing area and some powerlines to the "mainland" are located on the northeastern side of the island. It's hard to see those powerlines in a the background of trees. The water is much shallower on the northeastern side of the island. If you're thinking of trying to get behind the island in your (shallow-draft) boat, approach the back of the island from the southwestern side.

Chapter 14
SAINT MARYS RIVER TO POINT LOOKOUT, MARYLAND

Smith Creek
Point Lookout and Cornfield Harbor
Rounding Point Lookout

SMITH CREEK

Smith Creek is about a mile and a half east of the wide Saint Marys River. See NOAA chart excerpt 13-1. Smith Creek houses the closest marina to the Chesapeake Bay, Point Lookout Marina, as well as a few other small facilities. If you position yourself at 38°05.5'N/76°24.3'W, you'll be right on top of "R2". The channel to Smith Creek makes some turns. See NOAA chart excerpt 14-1. If you require a reasonable amount of water under your keel, don't cheat any of the navigational aids. As you enter the creek, Courtney's will be on your starboard side and Kitt's Point will be on your port side. A narrow, sandy county-maintained boat ramp is about a half mile north of Kitt's Point.

Courtney's has a trailer park, a restaurant, three docks, and a few buildings. **Scheible's Fishing Center** (☏ 301 872-5185) is just north of Courtney's. Scheible's has a nice restaurant, a motel, a lounge, and a 500-foot pier, and is a center for headboat operations. Scheible's also has gas and diesel at their 6-foot MLW dock. They sell ice and fishing supplies, and have showers. If you eat at Scheible's restaurant and there's room at the dock, you can likely tie-up overnight. Many knowledgeable folks have claimed that the best fishing in the entire Chesapeake is right in this area -- where the Potomac River and Chesapeake Bay start to combine.

If you're a college basketball fan, it might be interesting to note that the first African-American head basketball coach of the University of Kentucky was raised a couple miles east of Scheible's. Growing up on the small family farm, Tubby Smith grasped many of the values that would later propel him as well as guide his team to a national championship. But Tubby was not the first from Saint Marys County to find his way to Kentucky. About a couple of hundred years prior, a large contingent of settlers departed Saint Marys County for that Kentucky "frontier."

Smith Creek forks after the last navigation aid, "R6". Jutland Creek heads to the east (i.e., to the right), while Smith Creek continues north (i.e., straight ahead). Neither creek has much development, but Jutland Creek has more, including a few commercial operations. Both creeks are comfortably deep, but there are shoal patches off several of the points, especially in Smith Creek. A brownish water coloration may often give these shallow patches away. The eastern shore of Jutland Neck (i.e., on Jutland Creek) has some tall stands of pine trees. The shoreline in upper Smith Creek seems more uncovered.

Point Lookout Marina (☏ 301 872-5000) is the premier facility in the area and located about a half mile northeast of Scheible's, inside Jutland Creek. The marina has 162 slips (52 covered), 3 gas, and 3 diesel pumps. Spinnaker's Restaurant, a pool, a bathhouse, a laundry room, and a sewage pump-out, are on the very nice grounds. See appendix B for a dock layout. Point Lookout Marina primarily caters to bigger boats (e.g., the MLW is not less than nine feet), and they don't have a launch ramp. The marina sells block and bag ice and some boating supplies. They have a 35-ton open-end lift and an 85-ton marine railway for hauling big boats (see picture). The marina has a large maintenance staff for all kinds of boat repairs. For transient boaters, bicycles and a courtesy car may be available. Point Lookout Marina also has a discount arrangement with a rental car company in Lexington Park. Bob Knight's two towboats, a 42-footer and a 25-footer, are based out of Point Lookout Marina.

The **Corinthian Yacht Club** is on the next peninsula northeast in Jutland Creek. This is a private club with a pool and about 40 covered slips. The Corinthian Yacht Club was founded in Washington DC and moved here many years ago. There is no less than eight feet of water off of their docks. The Corinthian Yacht Club doesn't have a fuel dock.

Fox Harbor is after the next point on Jutland Creek. You might see some nice workboats tied-up at private docks in Fox Harbor. At the head of Fox Harbor, you'll find Clark's and Courtney's docks. Both have shallow water slips, and old, perhaps inoperable, marine railways. These docks at the head of Fox Harbor don't have much else to offer.

Phil's Marina (☏ 301 872-5838) is back on Jutland Creek, in the next cove north. There's barely five feet of water off Phil's docks. Phil's Marina has three piers (one covered), about 40 slips, and a launch ramp, but not much else. Continuing north on Jutland Creek, you'll come to the **Seaside View Campground** (☏ 301 872-4141). They have a fixed pier (about 5 feet MLW), a sandy boat ramp, a campground, and a trailer park. Seaside View also has a camp store that is open year around, where you can buy block and bag ice and more. There's also a restaurant and lounge on the premises.

POINT LOOKOUT AND CORNFIELD HARBOR

Point Lookout was originally called Saint Michael's. Father Andrew White so named it because he thought the resplendent scene ought to be named in honor of the foremost angel in heaven.

During the Civil War, Hammond Army Hospital was located on Point Lookout. After the battle of Gettysburg, 4,000 soldiers were treated here. Also after Gettysburg, the area north of the hospital was developed into a prisoner-of-war camp for Confederate soldiers. By the end of the Civil War, 52,000 Confederate soldiers passed through Camp Hoffman. More than 3,500 died at the prisoner-of-war camp. Today, a monument to those Confederate soldiers stands less than two miles northwest of the actual tip of Point Lookout.

A nonworking lighthouse building and a geodesic dome, part of a tracking station, sit near the very tip of Point Lookout. This area is closed to the public. The 1,046-acre **Point Lookout State Park** sits behind the restricted area. The park has a solid concrete fishing pier on the Chesapeake Bay side and a nice beach and protected inlet on the Potomac side. Point Lookout State Park also has a boat ramp, a boating facility, a visitor center, a campground, and a Civil War fort.

The protected inlet is called **Lake Conoy**. Lake Conoy houses four paved boat ramps, boat docks, a pump-out station, and a boating facility. The boating facility is not a marina for transient boaters. Furthermore, the entire park is designated "trash free." There are no trash receptacles anywhere. For park visitors, all refuse brought into the park must be carried back out. I'll bet the first couple of dumpsters outside the park get thoroughly abused. The boating facility does sell ice, bait, tackle, gas, sandwiches, and fishing permits. They also rent motorboats, rowboats, and canoes.

Cornfield Harbor is an indentation in the Potomac shoreline, northwest of Point Lookout. See NOAA chart excerpt 14-2. Once in Cornfield Harbor, position yourself at 38°02.96'N/76°19.82'W, and you should be nearly atop the jetty entrance to Lake Conoy. Unlighted "G1" and lighted "R2" sit at the end of the jetties to Lake Conoy. "G3" sits further in the entrance. Almost completely in the entry and near the shoreline, are rock piles on each side of the entry. These rock piles have wooden fences safeguarding the unwary boater. No doubt, the rock piles have an erosion-control purpose.

The *Captain Tyler* tour ship (T 410 425-2771) is docked in Lake Conoy. The *Captain Tyler* makes a one-hour, 40-minute trip across the Chesapeake Bay to Smith Island MD. The 65-foot boat can take 150 passengers. If you're interested, you need to call for more information on departure days and times.

Smith Island MD and Tangier Island (in Virginia) are two isolated islands on the eastern side of the Chesapeake Bay. Most of their inhabitants earn their living directly from the water. There are a few restaurants catering to tourist boats, but not much else on either island. There is no tour boat service to Tangier Island from the Potomac. To visit Tangier Island, you must depart from Reedville VA on the Wicomico River. Also in Crisfield MD, on the Eastern Shore and across the Chesapeake Bay, there are tour boats that travel to both Smith and Tangier Islands (T 410-968-2338).

There is a nice beach from the tip of Point Lookout to the Lake Conoy jetty for sunbathing and swimming. *Fort Lincoln*, a Civil War fort, is about 20 yards in from the beach and river, and fairly close to Lake Conoy. You can still see the well-defined rectangular earthen berms of this 1864 fort, along with four restored buildings inside the bermwork.

Like Saint Marys City, Point Lookout has a wide array of events scheduled throughout the year. There are Easter events, Halloween events, and a couple of Civil War events in the park. For more information telephone (T) 301 872-5688.

ROUNDING POINT LOOKOUT

The Chesapeake Bay lies east of Point Lookout. Hampton Roads and the Atlantic Ocean are about a hundred miles south.

The Chesapeake and Delaware Bay Shipping Canal is about hundred miles north near the northern end of the Chesapeake. Many ocean-going cargo ships traveling to and from Baltimore and points north, navigate through this sea-level canal. The eastern end of the short canal is on Delaware Bay. Delaware Bay mixes with the Atlantic south of Cape May, New Jersey. If you ever use the Chesapeake and Delaware Canal in a "small" boat, you need to be aware of that you'll be sharing the narrow canal with ocean-size traffic. If you catch an adverse tidal flow through the canal, you will also be unduly tormented.

A tall strobe light tower stands about three-quarters of a mile north of the tip of Point Lookout. You could miss this strobe light during the day. However, at night it is unmistakable. The strobe is primarily an airplane navigational aid, but we boaters can use it too.

There is a shoal about three quarters of a mile south of the tip of Point Lookout and a 39-foot steel tower stands in the water marking it. This tower also sounds a horn signal from September 15 to June 1. When rounding the point from either direction, I usually aim for this tower. As I get close to the tower, I give it a safe berth to one side or the other but I would not cut well inside of the tower and too close to the shore. See NOAA chart excerpt 14-2. I have occasionally seen other small floating buoys and spars in the water northeast of the tower on the Chesapeake side. Back in the Potomac, the first Potomac mid-channel buoy, Mo(A)"A" is about a mile southeast of the tower.

Often, one side of Point Lookout, (e.g., the bay) will be calm and the other side (e.g., the river) will be extremely rough. A modest northwest wind will greatly help with a southbound passage down the bay. After more than one pleasant broad reach down the bay, I've been slammed with short and steep six-foot waves on my nose after entering the Potomac and heading northwest. A modest northeast wind will have the opposite effect. A nice beam reach out the Potomac will turn into a slog against the wind and waves after entering the Chesapeake. Listen to the NOAA radio weather forecast for wind DIRECTION and strength predictions, and plan your trip accordingly. In a strong northwest wind, if you get badly pasted after you depart the Chesapeake for the Potomac, it may behoove you to take the weather less on your nose and aim for a protected anchorage inside the Coan River. Likewise, if you can't make any northbound headway once in the bay after rounding Point Lookout, it make behoove you to retreat to Lake Conoy and wait for favorable winds on the Chesapeake.

Northbound in the Chesapeake, you should soon see the 52-foot high Point-No-Point Light, about five miles north of Point Lookout. The Point-No-Point Light is a good northbound aiming target. Tanner Creek is slightly less than a mile north of the Point Lookout fishing pier. Tanner Creek has two jetties protruding into the bay. The entrance is about 30 yards wide between the jetties. Tanner Creek is uncharted and presumed to be very shallow. Saint Jeromes Creek is about three and a half miles north of Tanner Creek and about two and a half miles east-southeast of the Point-No-Point Light. Saint Jeromes Creek has a charted entry but is also pretty shallow. I've been in this protected creek, but not too far in, with a four-foot draft vessel. Solomons, on the Patuxent River, is the first really deep harbor with many kinds of amenities north of Point Lookout. As you leave the Potomac and round Point Lookout, vibrant Solomons is about 20 miles to the north.

Chapter 15
THE LOWER NORTHERN NECK OF VIRGINIA

Yeocomico River
Coan River
Little Wicomico River

The Northern Neck of Virginia is sometimes referred to as the cradle of our nation. It is the birthplace of three of our first five presidents --Washington, Madison, and Monroe. Today, many affluent folks from Washington buy second homes or retire in this part of our country. The lower Northern Neck is a refreshing change of pace from urban Washington. But with this charm and rural lifestyle, you might find that the main motel or restaurant in a particular town might not accept your (or anybody's) credit card. Arguably, the most enchanting anchorages along the entire Potomac River can be found in the Yeocomico, Coan, and Little Wicomico Rivers.

YEOCOMICO RIVER

The Indian tribe name "Yeocomico" roughly means "tossed about by the waters." More than a half-dozen boating facilities are nestled in the Yeocomico River. The river divides in three sections a ways past the mouth. See NOAA chart excerpt 15-1. The Northwest Yeocomico, or Shannon Branch, harbors White Point Marina and Sandy Point Marina. The West Yeocomico harbors Port Kinsale Marina and Kinsale Harbor Yacht Club. Near Harryhogan Point, the South Yeocomico divides into Mill Creek, Lodge Creek, and two smaller coves. Lodge Creek harbors Olverson's Marina (home of the Lodge Creek Yacht Club) and Krentz's Marina.

An unusual navigation aid, popularly called the "birthday cake," marks the Yeocomico entrance. If you position yourself at 38°02.45'N/76°29.97'W, you will be just off the concrete and steel birthday cake with it's "one candle," in about 12 feet of water. From the "R2" birthday cake, it's almost two and a half miles in a west-southwesterly direction to the next mark, "G3". If you're going into the center branch, or the West Yeocomico, be careful. Very shallow water extends a half mile out from Horn Point. You should head south for a while and leave the West Yeocomico "R2" to your starboard, before turning west into the West Yeocomico. The West Yeocomico starts the border between Westmoreland and Northumberland county, the easternmost county on Virginia's Northern Neck.

Mundy Point separates the West Yeocomico and **SOUTH YEOCOMICO**. You'll see O'Biers & Sons Packing House on the east side of Mundy Point and in the South Yeocomico. Harryhogan Point is almost a mile into this branch. There was never a Harry Hogan around here. The name of the point is a corruption of an Indian name that sounded somewhat similar, Arehokin.

The **Boatyard at Harryhogan** (☏ 804 529-5826) is right on Harryhogan Point. This facility has no transient wet slips, but it is a place where good and inexpensive major yard work can be done. Prices are likely to be half what you'd pay in the Annapolis area. The boatyard has a 50-ton railway and a 15-ton closed-end lift. Modest-size sailboats can be lifted with the closed-end lift. On my last visit, a 50-foot by 100-foot enclosed shed housed nine hauled-out boats and a large ketch was getting new planking while in the water. The Boatyard at Harryhogan does wood, fiberglass, mechanical work, and more. Their specialty is major jobs like replanking and rekeeling boats. Owner Doug Daiss has been on the Potomac a while and has been devoted to boats since the 1960s. The Fishing Center is the small pier north of the Boatyard at Harryhogan.

Krentz's Marine Railway (☏ 804 529-6800) is west of Harryhogan Point and technically in Lodge Creek. Krentz's has a large 50-ton open-end travel lift, a hydraulic trailer, a marine railway, and a large boat shed. This facility also does a wide assortment of boat repairs. Krentz's has 40 slips (35 covered) serviced by 30-amp, 50-amp, and 15-amp electric. The facility sells bag ice and has showers.

Olverson's Marina (☏ 804 529-6868) is the largest wet-slip facility on Lodge Creek, as well as on the entire Yeocomico. They have no boatyard capability except for a small place to store a few trailerable boats. Olverson's has five piers, 100 covered slips, and 70 open slips. Electrical service is 30-amp and 50-amp. Olverson's sells gas and diesel, and block and bag ice. They have a sewage pump-out station and a launch ramp. On the grounds, there's a bathhouse, a heated-swimming pool, and a laundry room. See appendix B for a dock layout. Olverson's welcomes transient boaters and will have a courtesy car available should you want to visit Callao or other nearby places.

A wide paved boat ramp with two piers is less than a half mile further up Lodge Creek and on the opposite side from Olverson's. The ramp area has a nice, wide turning area on a small peninsula.

After entering the **WEST YEOCOMICO**, be mindful of the shoal off of Long Point. About a half mile after Horn Point and on the north shore of the West Yeocomico is **Port Kinsale Marina** (☏ 804 472-2044). The Moorings Restaurant, with waterfront dining, faces the lovely West Yeocomico. Port Kinsale has 73 slips (8 covered) with 30-amp and 50-amp service. This facility sells gas and diesel, and block and bag ice, and has a sewage pump-out. Bob Gebeaux also runs a small ship store offering limited fishing supplies and a decent selection of boating supplies. The grounds are nestled in a pine stand with a pool, a trailer park, a launch ramp, and a campground. You will find a bathhouse, a laundry room, and a small beach. The marina operates a 30-ton open-end travel lift on a roomy, spread-out boatyard.

Kinsale Harbour Yacht Club (☏ 804 472-2514) is about a mile past Port Kinsale Marina, on the north side of the West Yeocomico. You can't miss the tall grain elevator next to the marina. The marina is adjacent to a low road bridge. The facility has 91 open slips serviced by 30-amp electric, a pump-out station, and a paved launch ramp. They also sell gas and diesel at the end of the first dock. There is a small swimming pool, a tennis court, and a picnic and camping area nearby.

There's not much to do in the nearby town of Kinsale, besides visiting the museum. But the town has quite a past! It is the oldest town on the Virginia side of the Potomac and it is named after an Irish seaport town, which in Gaelic means "head of the saltwater." Throughout the early 18th century, Kinsale was an active seaport and a ship-building center. The town was burned by the British during the War of 1812. During the Civil War, the area was a base for Southern blockade runners, and Union ships regularly bombarded the town. During the latter half of the 19th and early part of the 20th century, Kinsale thrived with steamships. Timber, tobacco, pulpwood, and tomatoes were shipped out of Kinsale. In the early 20th century, highway bridges began to knit the Northern Neck, and the days of steamships were numbered. Boating activity in Kinsale receded.

A packing house juts out on White Point. The point is stabilized with a lot of riprap. There are two quite different marinas in the **NORTHWEST YEOCOMICO (OR SHANNON BRANCH)**. Less than a half mile west of White Point is **White Point Marina** (☏ 804 472-2977) which has 50 modern slips (45 covered) serviced by 30-amp and 50-amp electric. This facility sells gas and diesel, and block and bag ice, and has a sewage pump-out. A pool, tennis courts, and nice bathrooms are on the grounds. There is no launch ramp, but there is a 50-ton marine railway and a large covered shed. There were only a few vacant slips during the winter and there might be little room for transient boaters in the summer. With no boatyard and that one large marine railway, their specialty is major hull repairs on bigger powerboats.

Sandy Point Marina (T 804 472-3237) is about a half mile north of White Point Marina on the opposite side of the Northwest Yeocomico. The venerable Earl W. Jenkins still runs the place. Mr. Jenkins has a storied past on these waters. He has hauled lumber to Baltimore aboard steamships and spent the better part of one cold winter frozen-in on a boat near Pocomoke City MD. In addition to his rich history, Mr. Jenkins is well versed on current world events. He can hold his own with anyone from Washington, and his assessment will probably be proven more accurate! Sandy Point Marina has 40 slips (35 covered) serviced by 15-amp and 30-amp electric. The marina sells gas and diesel and has a sewage pump-out. There is a marine railway and a launch ramp as well as a fair-size yard for storing trailerable boats. Some trailerable boats could be stored under cover.

Bevan's Oyster Packing House is about a half mile north of Sandy Point Marina. You'll see workboats on the docks out front and high piles of discarded oyster shells all around this large modern packing house. Another marine railway with three docks is about a quarter mile south of Sandy Point Marina. A sandy boat ramp is next to this railway; however, a faded sign nearby indicated that this ramp is for exclusive use of Shannon Park Land Owners.

COAN RIVER

The Coan River has fewer amenities than its nearby neighbor, the Yeocomico. Like the Yeocomico, there are dozens of spectacular anchorages here. One of my favorites is right behind Walnut Point. There's a nice sandy beach at the tip of Walnut Point. Like the Yeocomico, the Coan River has three initial branches. See NOAA chart excerpt 15-2. Kingscote Creek veers off to the northwest with the placid riverfront town of Lewisetta south of Travis Point. The Glebe is a long and fairly deep arm extending due west and loaded with picturesque pastoral anchorages. The main branch of the Coan River, the only branch with official navigation aids, snakes its way past Walnut Point in a southerly direction for about four miles. This branch is also loaded with tranquil places to anchor.

When I aim for the Coan River from the Potomac, coming from either the north or south, I usually head for "R4" instead of "R2". If you want to head for "R4," aim for 38°00.77'N/76°26.59'W. You'll be in about 20 feet of water a couple of miles from the mouth. There is a caution to using "R4" as your first entry mark. In the summer months, the bottom is especially fertile with crabs, west and northwest of "R4". Hence, if you're approaching "R4" from the northwest, be mindful that you may have to dodge hundreds of crab pots north of Judith Sound. If you're entering at night or you don't want to dodge those crab pots, you're better off heading for "R2" which is about a mile further out than "R4". For "R2" head for 38°01.16'N/76°25.98'W. You'll be in about 30 feet of water at "R2".

If you turn northwest into Kingscote Creek, you'd find **Lewisetta Marina** (T 804 529-7299). The marina has a sturdy gas and diesel dock, a sewage pump-out, a bathhouse, and a launch ramp. The launch ramp doubles as the travel lift bay. Lewisetta Marina sells block and bag ice and some fishing supplies. They only have about 25 wet slips (17 covered), and some are serviced by 15-amp electric. However, their forte is hauling out boats for the winter. They have a 25-ton open-end travel lift and a 20-ton closed-end lift and seven and a half acres of yard. They've had more than 85 boats (many sail) hauled here some winters. Mark Scerbo and his yard crew have the capability for many types of yard work and repairs (fiberglass, mechanical, painting, etc.).

Lake Francis is about a half mile northwest of Lewisetta Marina. This small pond with rickety docks harbors about a dozen shallow-draft workboats. The entry to the pond is marked by four PVC poles. The channel in Kingscote Creek narrows significantly in a few places. Follow NOAA chart 12233 carefully.

South of the entrance to the Glebe, in the little cove south of Honest Point, you'll see a packing house with some small docks. Afterward, you'll see another packing house, Headley Seafood, across the main Coan channel south of Walnut Point. Between these two packing houses, and south of Stevens Point is the largest wet-slip marina on the Coan, the **Coan River Marina** (☏ 804 529-6767). John and Linda Hornby have 48 slips and some are up to 45-feet. Most of the modern well-maintained slips are serviced by 30-amp electric; some even have 50-amp. The marina has gas, diesel, a sewage pump-out, a boat ramp, clean bathhouses, a laundry room, and plans for a restaurant. They also sell some boating supplies as well as block and bag ice. The Coan River Marina has a 25-ton open-end travel lift and an electrified boat storage yard. See appendix B for a dock layout. Trailered boats can be stored under a roofed area.

The sprawled-out Cohart Seafood and Packing facility is further in the Coan River and around the point nearest "R20". This is the largest seafood packing house on the Coan. The Forrest Landing boat ramp is two miles past Cohart's. This ramp is gravel and the trailer turnaround space is good. The Coan River stays eight feet deep until almost the Forrest Landing ramp. Another boat ramp, Rowe's Landing, is across the cove from Forest Landing. The Rowe's Landing ramp is "bumpy" concrete with a short pier to the west.

LITTLE WICOMICO RIVER

The manmade entrance jetty for the Little Wicomico River is at Smith Point, and this river arguably dumps into the Chesapeake Bay. But before the jetty was built, the Little Wicomico dumped into the Potomac. As a matter of fact, a nor'easter in early 1998 blasted a hole northwest of the jetty and the Little Wicomico was once again flowing into the Potomac! If the Corps of Engineers haven't closed this hole when you arrive, don't try it. Go to the jetty entrance. Study NOAA chart excerpt 15-3.

The **Smith Point Lighthouse** is in a squat white building about three miles offshore east-southeast of Smith Point. From out in the Chesapeake, it flashes a 10-second white light. That 10-second light also has a red sector, like the lights off of Maryland Point and Cobb Point Bar. If you're coming down the Potomac and staying close to Hack Neck, you'll probably see Smith Point Light flashing a red signal. On Hack Neck, there's a public beach, Vir-Mar Beach, about five miles before reaching Smith Point. Hull Neck, east of Vir-Mar Beach, is where the seven-and-a-half-mile Potomac River Swim to Point Lookout starts. The last charity race was in June 1995.

If you have any kind of draft to your vessel, you need to enter the jetty area from a southeast direction. Shallow water is north and east of Smith Point. If you are coming from the Potomac, round Smith Point about halfway between the land and the Smith Point Light. Once in the Chesapeake, stay at least a mile away from "R2" until you can approach it on a northwest heading. Getting to "R2" may be the trickiest part of the Little Wicomico entry. See NOAA chart excerpt 15-3. After arriving at "R2" head for the center of the jetty entrance. Reportedly, there's a sunken barge in *deep water* near the jetty entrance and the green floating buoy marks it. Locals pass close to, and on either side of, this green buoy. Sometimes boating traffic can be heavy here. Once in the jetty, like in all jetties, unless you know something different, navigating near the center is best. Andy Cockrell, a knowledgeable local, relayed that the north side of the jetty is more apt to shoal than the south side. The Corps of Engineers dredges the channel regularly, but, even if they didn't, this channel would find its equilibrium maintaining a five-foot depth. At maximum ebb or flood tide, the current in between the jetties can be quite measurable.

The Little Wicomico or "Little River" has a nice flavor. There are many great places to anchor. You'll find packing houses, workboats, grain silos, farm houses, a few new big waterfront homes, and a car ferry guided by a cable. You're definitely in "southern pine" country. Five marinas are also in the Little Wicomico. **Smith Point Marina** (T 804 453-4077) has the most amenities and is in the second creek to your south, Slough Creek. Don't take any shortcuts in Slough Creek. Follow the well-marked channel. Smith Point Marina has gas, diesel, a sewage pump-out, a bathhouse, and a launch ramp. They have 80 slips (43 covered) serviced mostly by 30-amp electric. They sell bag ice and some boating supplies. The yard is of reasonable size and well is maintained. They have a 12-ton closed-end travel lift, but they are still able to haul fair-size mast-unstepped sailboats. See appendix B for a dock layout of Smith Point Marina.

The marine police and **Smith Point to the Rescue** harbor boats at Smith Point Marina. Smith Point to the Rescue (T 804 453-4551), on VHF 16, is an admirable volunteer organization dedicated to helping distressed boaters in the area. The volunteers, mostly retired individuals, use a 30-foot Bertram and a 42-foot Tiffany. Smith Point to the Rescue operates a second boat near Reedville VA.

The Little River campground, is adjacent to and just south of, Smith Point Marina. **Leroy's Marina** is on the opposite side of Slough Creek, past Smith Point Marina. Leroy's has about two dozen covered docks and a trailer park. **The Chesapeake Bay/Smith Island KOA Campground and Marina** (T 804 453-4051) is next to and just past Leroy's sharing the same cove. This nice campground has a launch ramp, ice, a pool, and about 20 covered slips. A seasonal daily ferryboat departs from the KOA Marina to Smith Island MD. This 65-foot vessel can also accommodate group trips to other locales on the bay and Potomac. If you want to take a ferryboat to Tangier Island, you can go to Reedville, four miles south.

Northwest of Slough Creek and across the Little Wicomico River, is a small creek marked by three green and two red daymarks. Ellyson Creek is the next creek west on this north shore and is well marked and deep. My favorite anchorage is southwest of the entrance to Ellyson Creek. Near the head of Ellyson Creek, you'll find a couple of docks belonging to Gaskin's Seafood Packing House, a wholesaler. The cable ferry is just past "G7" back on the Little Wicomico. This ferry is the main artery between Ophelia and Sunnybank VA.

Krentz's Marine Railway is beyond the cable ferry and Flood Point and near "R14". Krentz's has about 35 covered slips and four open slips with some electrical service. Their marine railway is southwest of the covered dock. There is another marine railway on the east side of Bridge Creek.

Cockrell's Marine Railway (T 804 453-3560) is about a mile past Krentz's and also on the north side of the Little Wicomico. Andy Cockrell has about 16 covered slips, a sewage pump-out, a launch ramp, and a 30-ton railway. He carries some marine supplies and does hull and engine repairs. He also has a yard for storing trailerable boats.

Reedville VA, the nearest "sizeable" town, is on the Great Wicomico River, one river south. Reedville was established in 1874, and the town soon became the home port of the entire Atlantic menhaden fishing fleet. Many New Englanders settled here and built Victorian mansions. This "menhaden capital" had the highest per capita income in the United States for a time during the early 20th century. The *Reedville Fishermans Museum* on Main Street, relives some of this past. Today, a large fleet of menhaden ships contracting with Zapata-Haynie [fish] Protein is harbored in Reedville. Some people, mostly outsiders, consider the "aroma" wafting from the menhaden processing plant offensive. Most locals don't. Jett's Hardware Store, on the road to Reedville, sells some marine hardware and related supplies. From Reedville, you can catch the *Chesapeake Breeze*, a tour boat, to Tangier Island if you don't want to take your own boat there.

ACKNOWLEDGMENTS

I am indebted to many. In my early boating years on the Potomac, Greg Hoover, Lewis Lederer, Bill Wilson, and Karl Edler taught me many ropes. Greg and Mary Hoover connected me to sailing the Potomac on bigger boats. Lewis Lederer introduced me to many aspects of living aboard. Bill Wilson help me with some technical skills. Karl Edler, who mostly singlehanded a 31-footer from Cobb Island to Australia, started me dreaming of an extended cruise beyond the Chesapeake. Furthermore, Barbara and Karl Edler reviewed this guide and helped me present it more effectively.

After two sailing trips to Central America and my first cruising guide completed, I owed many more. Hank Ulrich, Louis Kouvaris, Ralph Fischer and Jack Sante help me forge south from the Potomac. Hank reviewed this guide and helpfully elucidated many navigational nuances. Louis provided some input on the lower portions of the river. My brother, Keith, also provided some helpful powerboating and fishing insights.

Once in foreign waters, I encountered many fine adventurers, but two young men especially stand out. Brent Davis, now operating his own salmon boat out of Cordova, Alaska, help me cover 2,000 miles in the Northwest Caribbean over the course of two Central American trips. Whenever the challenge was most intense, Brent welcomed to meet it. Captain Townsend Goddard, with a fresh graduate degree in Marine Affairs from the University of Rhode Island, and I also covered about 2,000 miles. We did this in six weeks, while bucking seven late winter and early spring cold fronts from Central America to the Potomac. Townsend also contributed some professional insight to this guide.

I needed help from several corners arranging the color material -- the NOAA chart excerpts and photograph selection. Vince Ferrari and Lou Kouvaris scanned most of the NOAA chart excerpts, and Bruce Lai (Photos Plus) scanned the pictures. Automated Graphics Systems, Inc. was also more than helpful when it came to adding the final touches to the color work. Lou Kouvaris, Bill Hoffmeier, Stacey Linn, and especially Bill Lipovsky, contributed to the final selection of pictures.

Rolland Duncan provided the artistry for the locale and marina layout sketches. Julie Wright deserves special credit. On short notice, Julie was able to edit the entire text and grasp many facets beyond the breadth of even a good editor.

Impatience is among my many foibles. After a detainment on my first guide, I fell into a state of extended angst. The encouragement of four sets of special folks through that ordeal, unknowingly gave me the momentum to tackle this second guide on the Potomac River. For their encouragement, I especially thank Townsend Goddard, the Ridenours, the Durhams, and my father. My father reviewed and improved the early manuscript and encouraged me when most in need. There is no way I can adequately thank my dear father.

DEDICATION

And so this book is dedicated to Mr. E. Richard Rhodes -- a poor Polack who grew up in Chicago, a Marine Corps veteran from World War II, a retired executive, a community volunteer, a sound philosopher, a devoted husband, and my father. Thanks, Dad.

APPENDIX A

LIST OF NOAA CHART EXCERPTS

EXCERPT NUMBER	AREA OF COVERAGE	SHORT TITLE	NOAA CHART	NOAA SCALE	PERCENT REDUCED/ENLARGED	APPROX LENGTH OF 1 NM	TOP ORIENTATION
6-1	Washington Channel and Vicinity	Wash. Channel	12289	1:20,000	69%	2.5"	NW
6-2	Potomac and Anacostia Rivers Near Washington	Wash. Rivers	12289	1:40,000	85%	1.5"	NW
7-1	Hains Point, Washington to Wilson Bridge	Hains Pt--South	12289	1:40,000	119%	2.2"	N
8-1	Alexandria, Virginia to Broad Creek, Maryland	Alexandria--South	12289	1:40,000	113%	2.1"	N
8-2	Broad Creek, Maryland to Mount Vernon, Virginia	Fort Washington	12289	1:40,000	108%	2.0"	NE
8-3	Mount Vernon, Virginia to Indian Head, Maryland	Mt Vernon--South	12289	1:40,000	77%	1.4"	NE
9-1	Occoquan Bay, Virginia and Vicinity	Occoquan Bay	12289	1:40,000	86%	1.6"	N
9-2	Freestone, Possum Points, Va to Mattawoman Cr, Md	Mattawoman Cr	12288	1:40,000	79%	1.4"	N
9-3	Possum Point, Virginia to Smith Point, Maryland	Quantico--South	12288	1:40,000	71%	1.3"	N
9-4	Smith Point, Maryland to Metomkin Point, Virginia	Big Bend	12288	1:40,000	56%	1.0	N
9-5	Aquia Creek, Virginia	Aquia Creek	12288	1:40,000	129%	2.4"	NW
10-1	Nanjemoy Creek, Maryland and Vicinity	Nanjemoy Creek	12288	1:40,000	92%	1.7"	N
10-2	Upper Cedar Point, Md to Persimmon Point, Va	Port Tobacco	12288	1:40,000	68%	1.2"	NNW
10-3	Persimmon Point, Va to Lower Cedar Point, Md	301 Bridge	12287	1:20,000	76%	2.8"	N
11-1	Lower Cedar Point, Md to Popes Creek, Va	Kettle Bottom Sh	12286	1:40,000	55%	1.0"	NE
11-2	Dahlgren, Virginia and Vicinity	Dahlgren	12287	1:20,000	71%	2.6"	NW
11-3	Rosier Creek to Mattox Creek, Virginia	Colonial Beach	12286	1:40,000	91%	1.7"	NNW
11-4	Monroe Bay, Virginia and Vicinity	Monroe Bay	12286	1:40,000	290%	5.3"	NNW
11-5	Popes Creek, Virginia to Huggins Point, Maryland	St Clements Is	12286	1:40,000	56%	1.0"	NNE
11-6	Nomini Bay, Virginia and Vicinity	Nomini Bay	12286	1:40,000	100%	1.8"	N
11-7	Huggins Point, Maryland to Bonum Creek, Virginia	Ragged Point	12286	1:40,000	55%	1.0"	NE
11-8	Lower Machodoc Creek and Coles Neck, Virginia	Coles Neck	12286	1:40,000	90%	1.6"	N
12-1	Wicomico River, Maryland and Vicinity	Wicomico River	12286	1:40,000	56%	1.0"	NNW
12-2	Cobb Island, Maryland and Vicinity	Cobb Island	12286	1:40,000	167%	3.0"	NNW
12-3	Saint Margaret Island to Heron Island Bar, Maryland	Dukeharts Ch	12286	1:40,000	108%	2.0"	NW
12-4	Saint Clements Bay and Breton Bay, Maryland	Newtown Neck	12286	1:40,000	78%	1.4"	NW
12-5	Herring Creek to Piney Point, Maryland and Vicinity	Piney Point	12333	1:40,000	137%	2.5"	NNW
13-1	Bonum Creek, Virginia to Point Lookout, Maryland	Lower Potomac	12233	1:40,000	46%	0.8"	NE
13-2	St George Island and Lower St Marys River, Md	St George Is	12233	1:40,000	95%	1.7"	NNW
13-3	Upper Saint Marys River, Maryland	St Marys City	12333	1:40,000	108%	2.0"	NNW
14-1	Smith Creek, Maryland	Smith Creek	12233	1:40,000	167%	3.0"	NNE
14-2	Point Lookout, Maryland and Vicinity	Point Lookout	12233	1:40,000	167%	3.0"	NNE
15-1	Yeocomico River, Virginia	Yeocomico River	12233	1:40,000	93%	1.7"	N
15-2	Coan River, Virginia	Coan River	12233	1:40,000	87%	1.6"	N
15-3	Little Wicomico River and Smith Pt, Va and Vicinity	Little Wicomico	12233	1:40,000	79%	1.4"	N

APPENDIX B

SKETCHES OF MARINA LAYOUTS

KEY:

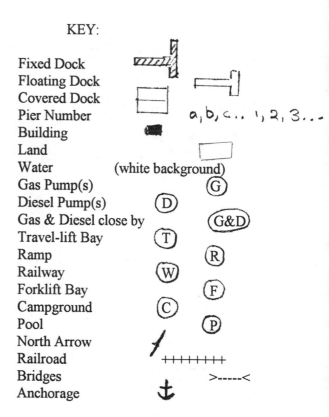

Fixed Dock
Floating Dock
Covered Dock
Pier Number   a, b, c.. 1, 2, 3...
Building
Land
Water   (white background)
Gas Pump(s)
Diesel Pump(s)
Gas & Diesel close by
Travel-lift Bay
Ramp
Railway
Forklift Bay
Campground
Pool
North Arrow
Railroad
Bridges
Anchorage

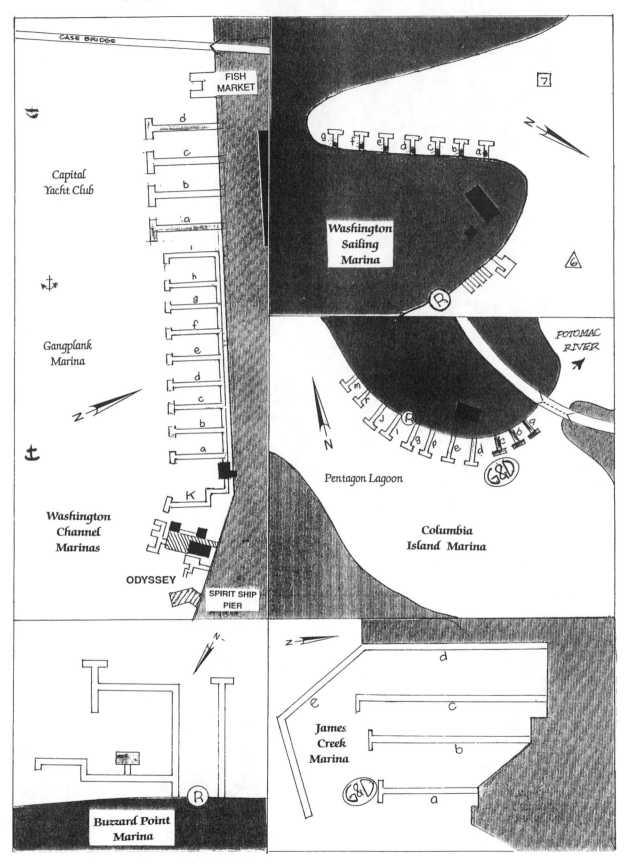

VARYING AND IRREGULAR SCALES

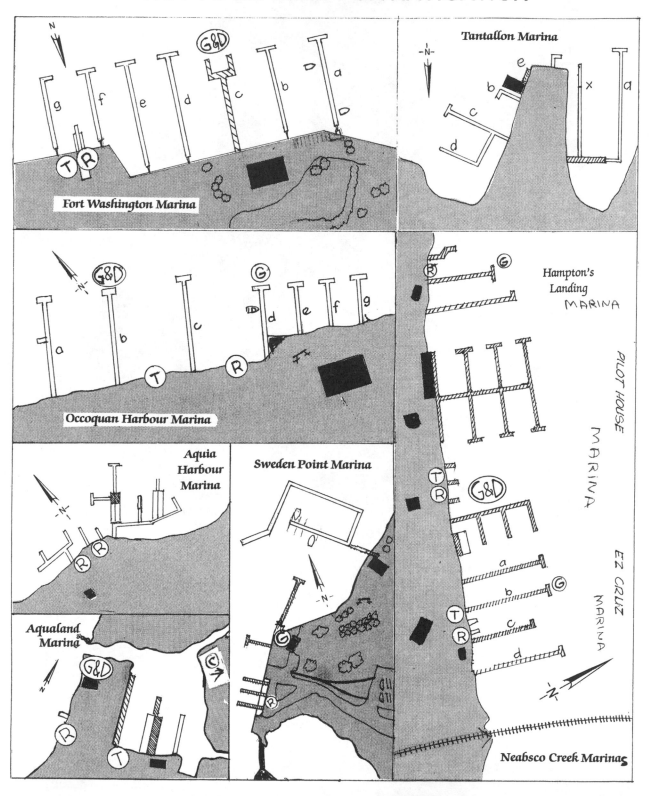

Fort Washington Marina

Tantallon Marina

Occoquan Harbour Marina

Hampton's Landing MARINA

PILOT HOUSE MARINA

EZ CRUZ MARINA

Aquia Harbour Marina

Sweden Point Marina

Aqualand Marina

Neabsco Creek Marinas

VARYING AND IRREGULAR SCALES

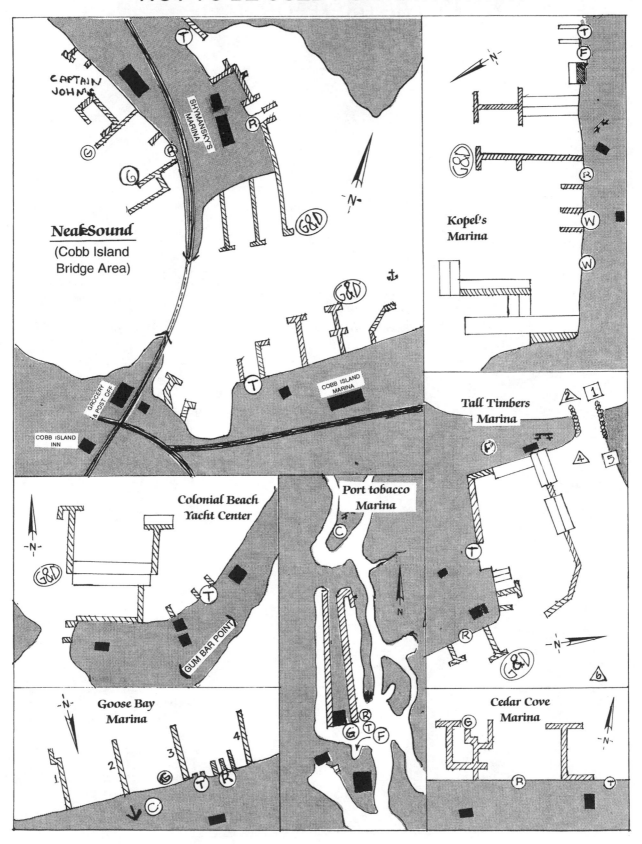

VARYING AND IRREGULAR SCALES

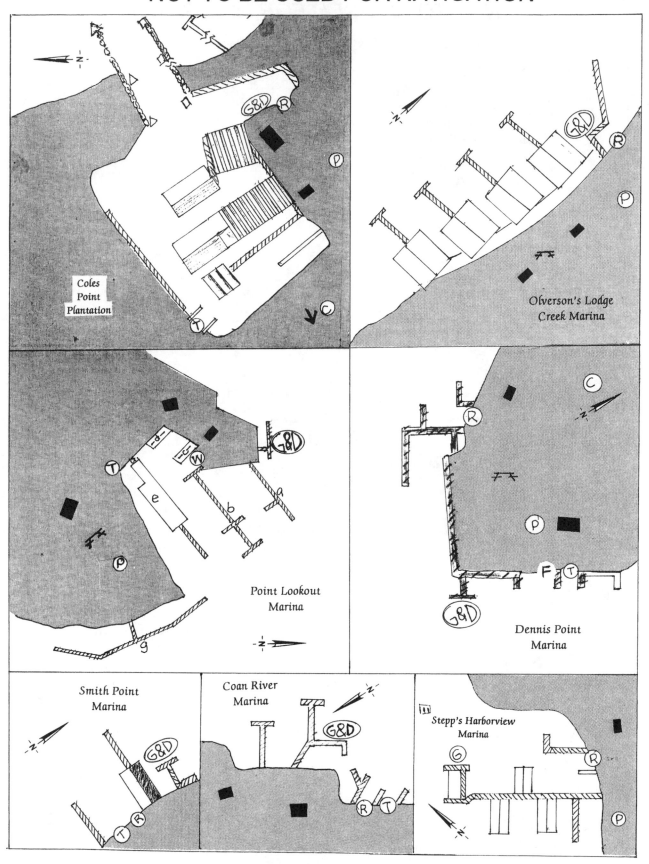

Coles
Point
Plantation

Olverson's Lodge
Creek Marina

Point Lookout
Marina

Dennis Point
Marina

Smith Point
Marina

Coan River
Marina

Stepp's Harborview
Marina

VARYING AND IRREGULAR SCALES

APPENDIX C

LOCALITY SKETCHES

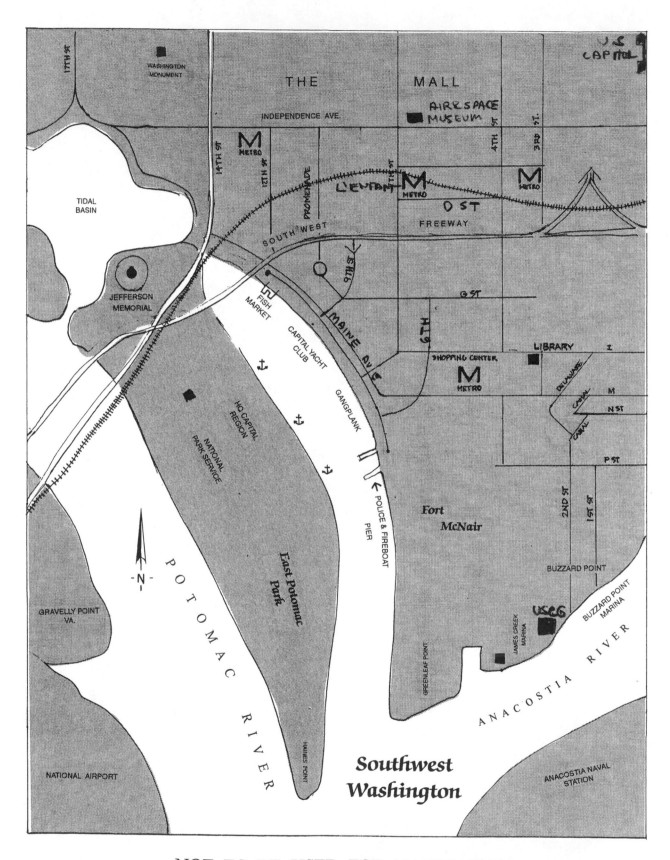

NOT TO BE USED FOR NAVIGATION

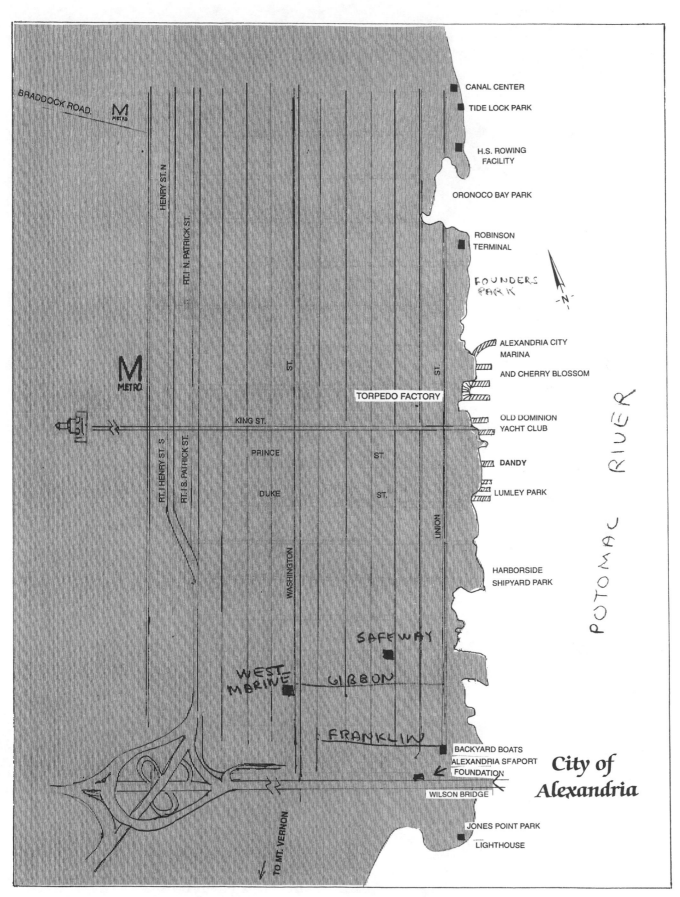

NOT TO BE USED FOR NAVIGATION

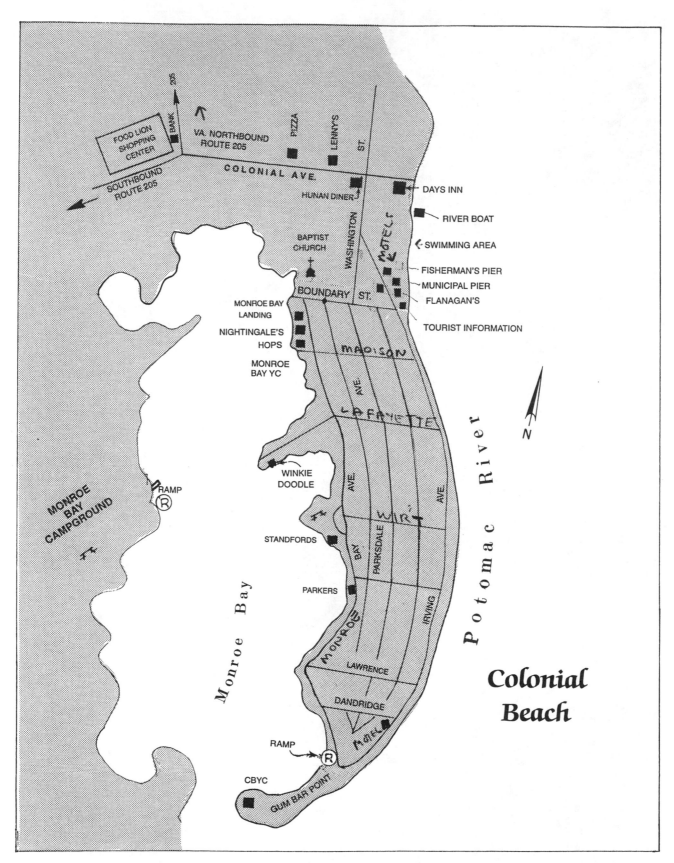

NOT TO BE USED FOR NAVIGATION

152

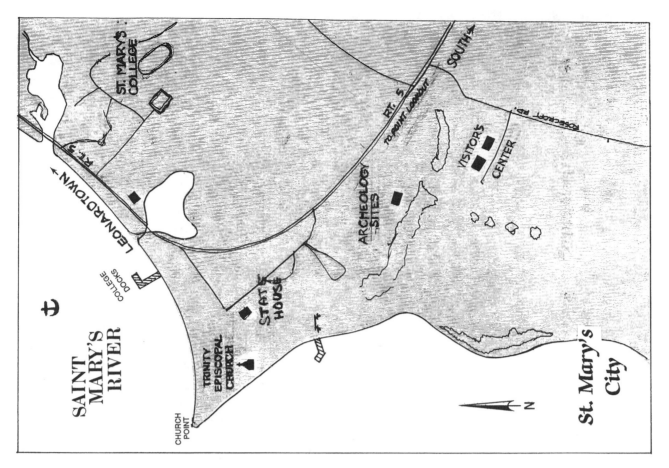

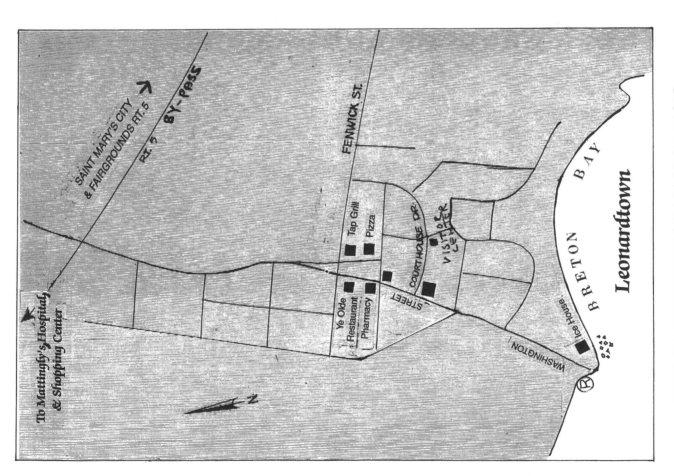

APPENDIX D

GPS WAYPOINTS

APPENDIX D
GPS WAYPOINTS

Location	Waypoint Coordinates
Washington Channel and Anacostia River	38°51.49'N/77°01.18'W
Washington Channel and Potomac River	38°51.06'N/77°01.30'W
Wilson Bridge, Center Span	38°47.60'N/77°02.25'W
Swan Creek, MD	38°43.16'N/77°01.99'W
Piscataway Creek, MD	38°42.52'N/77°02.45'W
Mount Vernon, VA	38°41.81'N/77°05.24'W
Craney Island:	
North Cut Point	38°37.75'N/77°08.00'W
South Cut Point	38°37.35'N/77°09.25'W
Occoquan Bay, VA	38°36.44'N/77°12.44'W
Mattawoman Creek, MD	38°33.60'N/77°13.50'W
Quantico Marina, VA	38°31.12'N/77°17.09'W
Wadcs Bay, MD	38°25.54'N/77°15.63'W
Aquia Creek, VA	38°22.91'N/77°18.15'W
Potomac Creek, VA	38°20.65'N/77°16.63'W
Fairview Beach, West (near Crabhouse), VA	38°19.99'N/77°14.83'W
Fairview Beach, East (near Marina), VA	38°20.03'N/77°14.12'W
Nanjemoy Creek, MD	38°24.12'N/77°06.73'W
Port Tobacco, MD	38°26.54'N/77°01.85'W
Goose Bay, Port Tobacco Creek, MD	38°27.15'N/77°02.62'W
Captain Billy's, Popes Creek, MD	38°23.87'N/76°59.60'W
Aqualand Marina, MD	38°21.98'N/76°59.10'W
US Route 301 Bridge, Center Span	38°21.77'N/76°59.44'W
Lower Cedar Point Cut, Northern Waypoint	38°20.34'N/76°59.03'W
Cuckold Creek, MD	38°18.77'N/76°55.87'W
Neale Sound, West (Cobb Island), MD	38°15.98'N/76°52.02'W
Potomac Beach, VA	38°16.56'N/76°59.76'W
Municipal Pier, Colonial Beach, VA	38°15.08'N/76°57.50'W
"R4" Monroe Bay, Colonial Beach, VA	38°13.62'N/76°57.72'W
Mattox Creek, VA	38°13.35'N/76°57.40'W
Wicomico River, MD	38°14.39'N/76°49.34'W
Neale Sound, East (Cobb Island), MD	38°15.95'N/76°50.38'W
Cliffs, VA:	
Horsehead	38°10.38'N/76°51.80'W
Stratford	38°10.10'N/76°50.95'W
Nomini Cliffs, near center of cliffs	38°10.16'N/76°48.09'W
Nomini Creek, VA	38°08.50'N/76°43.52'W
Lower Machodoc Creek, VA	38°08.65'N/76°39.25'W
Ragged Point Harbour, VA	38°08.60'N/76°36.70'W
Herring Creek, MD	38°10.56'N/76°33.01'W
Smith Creek, MD	38°05.5'N/76°24.3'W
Cornfield Harbor, MD	38°02.96'N/76°19.82'W
Yeocomico River, VA	38°02.45'N/76°29.97'W
"R4" Coan River, VA	38°00.77'N/76°26.59'W
"R2" Coan River, VA	38°01.16'N/76°25.98'W

APPENDIX E

OTHER PUBLICATIONS

Guide to Cruising Chesapeake Bay: Annapolis, MD: Chesapeake Bay Magazine, updated annually. 368 pages but only 24 pages on the Potomac. Colorful but loaded with advertisements.

Gutheim, Frederick: *The Potomac*: Baltimore MD: Johns Hopkins University Press, 1949, 1977, 1986. 436 pages. A very good account of much history of the Potomac and beyond the tidal Potomac.

Maloney, Elbert: *Chapman Piloting: Seamanship and Small Boat Handling*: New York, NY: Hearst Marine Books, 62nd ed., 1996. More than 600 pages. Arguably the bible on this subject.

Michener, James: *Chesapeake*: New York, NY: Random House, 1978. 865 pages. Action packed. Nobody captures the historical flavor of an area better than Michener. Maybe one of Michener's best books.

Neale, Tom: *Chesapeake Bay Cruising Guide -- Volume I, Upper Bay*: Stamford, CT: Wescott Cove Publishing, 1996. 384 pages but none on the Potomac.

Reed's Nautical Almanac: Boston, MA: Thomas Reed Publications, updated annually. More than 900 pages. Loaded with Almanac-type information. Many aspects are very interesting and helpful.

Shellenberger, William H: *Cruising the Chesapeake: A Gunkholers's Guide*: Camden, ME: International Marine, 1993. 432 pages but only 36 pages on the Potomac. Well done, with many interesting insights.

INDEX

LIST OF PHOTOGRAPHS

FRONT COVER:

Nomini Bay Fishing Shack, Nomini Creek, Virginia (upper left corner)
Work Boats on Island Creek, Saint George Island , Maryland, (lower left corner)
Washington Monument across Tidal Basin at Cherry Blossom Time (middle right side)

BACK COVER

Heron and Docks on Neale Sound, Cobb Island, Maryland

PAGE 28

Entry to Quantico Marina, Quantico, Virginia

PAGE 32

Locals near Nanjemoy Creek, Maryland
Marine Railway at Point Lookout Marina, Ridge, Maryland

PAGE 118

Nanjemoy Creek, near Friendship Landing, Maryland

PAGE 122

Saint Clements Island, Maryland
Piney Point Lighthouse and Museum, Piney Point, Maryland

PAGE 128

Currioman Landing Ramp, Currioman Bay near Nomini Bay, Virginia
Watermen Working a Pound Net near Dukeharts Channel